THE BETTER
MUSETRAP

To Fabian, Kit and Imogen.
The three most amazing people I know.

SIMON PONT

THE BETTER MOUSETRAP

BRAND INVENTION IN A MEDIA DEMOCRACY

KoganPage

LONDON PHILADELPHIA NEW DELHI

First published in Great Britain and the United States in 2013 by Kogan Page Limited

120 Pentonville Road	1518 Walnut Street, Suite 1100	4737/23 Ansari Road
London N1 9JN	Philadelphia PA 19102	Daryaganj
United Kingdom	USA	New Delhi 110002
www.koganpage.com		India

© Simon Pont, 2013

The right of Simon Pont to be identified as the author of this work has been asserted by him in accordance with the Copyright, Designs and Patents Act 1988.

ISBN   978 0 7494 6621 3
E-ISBN   978 0 7494 6622 0

British Library Cataloguing-in-Publication Data

A CIP record for this book is available from the British Library.

Library of Congress Cataloging-in-Publication Data

Pont, Simon.
  The better mousetrap : brand invention in a media democracy / Simon Pont.
    p. cm.
  ISBN 978-0-7494-6621-3 – ISBN 978-0-7494-6622-0   1. Branding (Marketing)   2. Brand name products.   3. Internet marketing.   I. Title.
  HF5415.1255.P66 2012
  658.8'27–dc23
                                                                2012031191

Typeset by Graphicraft Limited, Hong Kong
Print production managed by Jellyfish
Printed and bound in the UK by CPI Group (UK) Ltd, Croydon, CR0 4YY

CONTENTS

PART III DAWN OF A MEDIA DEMOCRACY 189

EPILOGUE – TAKE COMFORT, 'NOBODY KNOWS NOTHING' 272

ACKNOWLEDGEMENTS 275

THE LISTS 276

PROLOGUE

I shop therefore I am

> *Build a better mousetrap, and the*
> *world will beat a path to your door.*

So said Ralph Waldo Emerson in toast of the innovative spirit and the rewards that (should) follow. I guess 'Build it and they will come' is an abridged riff on the same. That is, assuming 'it' is any good. And that's always the trick.

I take 'the better mousetrap' to be a compact metaphor for consumerism and the 'creation of want', that bad-wrap discipline called 'advertising'.

Unlike Emerson who comes over rather chipper, ES Turner was clearly having an off day when he uncharitably penned:

> *Advertising is the whip which hustles humanity up*
> *the road to the Better Mousetrap. It is the vision which*
> *reproaches man for the paucity of his desires.*
>
> THE SHOCKING HISTORY OF ADVERTISING! (1952)

ES Turner wasn't an ad fan. Well okay, you can't please all the people...

I've worked in advertising for a decade and a half. What I know of advertising is this: it keeps the capitalist world turning; it pays my bills and allows me to buy stuff. I know, it kinda sounds like I'm responsible for my own hamster wheel, so let me also add this.

Advertising is the inevitable output of a world we choose to live in. Maybe we don't even have a choice. Our world is a reflection and statement on our *nature*, our need to be individuals, our need to belong, our need for comfort, our need for *things*, our need to *want*. I don't see this as ugly or small. Paucity doesn't apply. It is as it is, but it's also bundled up in our very Big & Ambitious need to progress, to hunger and drive for More & Better.

Advertising is a lot about Emerson's mousetrap, and only 'bad advertising' applies to Turner's proposal of punishment. But the punishment isn't born of small desires, it's deserving of limited imagination and invention.

I think advertising can be great. Great advertising, that is. That's my goal. I love brands, and I delight in some of the work I've played a part in and some of the very smart people I've worked with. My role? I try to build better mousetraps.

SP.
London, 2012

EVERYTHING CHANGES, EVERYTHING STAYS THE SAME

> Technology,
> Society,
> Media,
> these are
> mutable
> forms, forever
> re-purposing
> themselves.
>
> They sit within
> the wild, weird
> and wonderful
> frame of change.
> But there is
> a frame — certain
> Fundamental
> Truths remain
> rock-solid.

I've heard it said, 'The only constant is change'. I don't quite believe that.

The Greek philosopher Heraclitus (535–475 BC) was big on the idea that 'nothing endures but change', but like I said, I'm not so sure. Some variables are constant. Others can't keep still. What's fascinating to me is the interplay.

I do acknowledge that change, progress – and its pace, ever quicker – has become the backbone of 21st-century living. I think life has become one of acceleration, instant access and expected immediacy.

Technology, society, media: these are mutable forms, shape-shifting, forever repurposing themselves. They sit within the wild, weird and wonderful frame of change.

But there is a frame.

I don't believe change is the only constant, but that certain fundamental truths remain rock-solid. Up remains up, down down, gravity prevents us falling into a big blue sky... and people don't fundamentally change.

This is the frame.

I believe human nature is a constant. Needs, hopes, ambitions, the motivations behind why people do what they do, behave in the ways they do – I believe these are constants.

Vance Packard's seminal (and it really was seminal) text *The Hidden Persuaders* was first published in 1957. Against a backdrop of 'conspicuous consumption', Packard discussed how advertising was deft manipulation, hidden in plain view. The Ad Men had turned psychologists. Straplines were motivational hooks. Brands were being billed as the salve to our discontented souls. And the Ad Men were making sure we stayed discontented and forever buying.

More than half a century down the road, understanding human motivation, unlocking 'the why', finding all those keys, encouraging people to buy: these remain the fundamentals of advertising and branding.

'Know your audience' remains the imperative, just as it was in Vance's day. Only the 'field of play' – the ring in which brands now get to slug it out – has become unrecognizable. 'Shifting sands' doesn't even come close to describing today's media landscape. Everything is all 0s and 1s. Everything's gone or going digital. It's a bold and bright new dawn that has got every brand reaching for its shades and every marketeer asking, *'Just what does this all mean?'*

PART ONE

IN SEARCH OF BRAND CHARISMA

INTRODUCTION

> Brands have not
> suddenly become
> fish with feet.
>
> As ever,
> they look to seduce
> and captivate
> and intoxicate us,
> to draw us in,
> draw us close,
> never let us go.
>
> But like Alice's
> adventures in
> Wonderland,
> the world of brands
> is one of riddles
> and contradictions.
>
> Welcome to the
> rabbit hole.

spent a good deal of time mulling the words that went into the subtitle 'In search of brand charisma'. You might (very fairly) wonder why. On reflection, I might too, but that would just notch-up more time mulling.

Instead of 'search', I started with 'birth'.

'The birth of brand charisma' implies something truly new has arrived, in a very recent sense, implying let's all stop what we're doing, grab a pen, start taking down some notes. But I decided that 'birth' was a misrepresentation, a maybe convenient kind of thing to imply if you happen to be writing a new book, but not exactly true. 'Birth' was over-egging it. Let's be clear. Brands have *not* suddenly become fish with feet. Brands have not suddenly become charismatic, where previously they were dullards.

The digital age presents ever new and very major opportunities for brands, for how they may behave, and how they may strike new rapports and relationships with consumers, and in this regard we are living through an impossible to over-egg epochal shift. But this is all about brands *carpe*-ing the *diem* provided by a new context. The watershed moment is one of *extrinsic* factors, in media, born of technological change.

Brands *intrinsically* continue to do the same thing today that all brands have attempted since they first rose from the primordial soup of product stuff. They look to seduce, captivate and intoxicate consumers, to draw them in, draw them close, never let them go. It's a never easy, never-ending task, requiring a near-mystical blend of quixotic charm and ruthlessly insightful manipulation. Most brands fall clearly short, and some never make it out the gate.

What I've always found and continue to find so fascinating is how almost all of us love certain brands, yet feel anything from lukewarm to casually indifferent about others. Some brands get it so right, while others don't even register. Never mind drawing them close to our hearts, some brands are *nothing* to us, their existence a non-event. So the brands that get it right are, in my opinion, an elite minority – and by this thinking, it's about *searching out*, praising and explaining the notable few. So it's 'search', not 'birth'.

The other word that took up some real head-time was charisma. Why charisma? The brands that make their mark on the world are the ones that *create want*, that stir us – those that we want in our world, in our company. They have *something*. Charisma is an awesome word, elusive and *by exception*, both as a quality and its ability to be truly described. You know it when you see it, you know it when you don't, and you might be at a loss to pinpoint just what that certain something is, but it is a *something*. That you *feel*.

'Brand' and 'charisma' are both such slippery critters, both deftly able to swerve and elude descriptive capture. And yet...

While charisma isn't a clear formula that's easily bottled, most behaviours are learned things, units that build into one kind of social (stereo)type or another. Most of us know our type; we know our foibles, quirks, talents and shortcomings, and their consequences.

> *My strong point is not rhetoric, it isn't showmanship,*
> *it isn't big promises – those things that create the glamour*
> *and the excitement that people call charisma and warmth.*
>
> RICHARD MILHOUS NIXON,
> 37TH PRESIDENT OF THE UNITED STATES

Watergate aside, there's a very good reason why Richard Nixon remains the least-loved president in the history of American politics.

All the things Nixon knew he *wasn't* are all the things a truly successful brand must be. And where brands adopt certain manners designed to captivate and lure us, it is first a decision that has to be made by the custodians of those brands, the marketing and agency folk sitting on the budgets and forming a plan. Where the majority of social interactions follow stimulus-response patterns you could build into a flow chart, so does the brand builder have to chart a winning course for a brand. Brands have to ensure that 'winning people over' is their strong-point.

Today's really loved brands are strong flavours, big personalities, are wholly *desirable*, and they are truly charismatic because they have a capacity to make people feel good about themselves.

> *How can you have charisma? Be more concerned about*
> *making others feel good about themselves than*
> *about making them feel good about you.*
>
> DAN REILAND, AUTHOR & EXECUTIVE PASTOR
> OF 12 STONE CHURCH, LAWRENCEVILLE, GEORGIA

For those who like a bottom line, try this one. Brands are all about making people *feel good*. Charismatic brands do this best of all, because their focus is less on what they say about themselves, and more how they allow us to express ourselves through them.

The dispatches that follow navigate a path down the rabbit hole. But they only take us so far. Like Alice's adventures, the curious world of brands is one of riddles and contradictions.

Consider a brand's name and logo. Both play a huge part in what a brand is all about, but they're also only a signifier for the deeper stuff. Looked at another way, the brand name and logo is an irrelevance.

Consider the dynamic between masterbrand and sub-brand. It almost parallels a master-servant relationship, but one in which the sub-brand may liberate its master from the heavy shackles of so many time-honoured and uptight conventions.

Consider how a brand should be 'on-brand' – consistent in how it behaves but also able to channel its Dark Knight alter ego, subvert expectations and keep consumers guessing.

Almost every brand 'rule' has an exception. Almost every successful campaign evidences an equal and opposing point of view. Defining and unlocking brands is not a locked-room murder that can be solved in a final act, by gathering all the suspects.

I think brands are very human things that we make in our own image, contradictions included. They reflect back who we are, and our ideas of who we want to be. Brands mirror. They are a journey through wonderlands and looking glasses.

The screenwriter and director Cameron Crowe, in contrast to his pre-viously speedy form, took two years writing and rewriting the film script for *Jerry Maguire* (1996). It was two years well justified, according to Crowe, who simply said, 'I wanted to get it right.'

I wanted to get it right.

The same applies to subtitles. The degree to which I got it right can remain a point of conjecture: that I can live with, just like I can live with this subtitle, *In search of brand charisma*.

Welcome to the rabbit hole. Like Alice, we'll know it when we see it.

SP.

BRANDS: THORNY, GNARLY, EVER-SO-TWISTY

 Just what the hell is
a 'brand'?

It's such a lovely,
thorny,
gnarly,
ever-so-twisty,
I-double-dare-you-to-
try-and-answer
kind of question.

Just what the hell is a 'brand'? It's such a lovely, thorny, gnarly, ever-so-twisty, I-double-dare-you-to-try-and-answer kind of question. Jeremy Bullmore, that living legend of Adland, offers the following quite brilliantly delicious description:

> Brands are fiendishly complicated, elusive, slippery,
> half-real/half-virtual things. When CEOs try to think
> about brands, their brains hurt.

Slippery, elusive, real... and unreal, it's the kind of description upon which myths, heroes and super villains are born. Brands, they dodge like mercury.... and as for getting them to do what you want... hell, you'd have more luck trying to snare lightning! Branding – clearly not for the faint-hearted.

Mystique-building aside, Bullmore also offers up a number of defining parameters:

> Products are made and owned by companies. Brands, on the other
> hand, are made and owned by people... by the public... by consumers.
> A brand image belongs not to a brand – but to those who have
> knowledge of that brand.
> The image of a brand is a subjective thing. No two people,
> however similar, hold precisely the same view of the same brand.

I think the above is hugely helpful, but what remains clearly tricky is that even 'in their telling', brands remain elusive, because it's not about what a brand says or does but how it is *perceived*. Brands are, therefore, quite rightly 'elusive' because to most intents and purposes they are... *illusory*. Jeremy again:

> No two people, however similar, hold precisely the same view.

So, how to de-stick the wicket when a brand (and the message it conveys) operates within a 'theatre of the mind', where all minds are different, where the Grand Jedi Bullmore's descriptors wholly apply: owned by people, the sum total of personal knowledge, wholly subjective? Blimey.

The idea that everything is everyone else's subjective solipsistic reality can... quite simply... turn you crazy. *Where does that leave your brand strategy?*

There is, of course, always some kind of common-ground collective, (nearly) objective truth we can shoot for. And in an effort to hold up the roof before the floor gives beneath our feet (so to speak), let's try this:

> *A brand is a bundle of meanings and values, but as seen and perceived in the eye and the mind of a consumer.*

I've been using this line for a while. For me, it holds up, keeps me away from the edge and out of trouble. Partly because it also provides clear 'Pass-Go-&-Collect-£200' direction.

Out of perceived (read: personal and subjective) meaning, a brand-builder looks to create *want*, to create emotional connection and deep-seated affinity.

Very simply, brand-building is about *want creation*.

A brand's success is therefore through effectively communicating a *perceived* point of difference, whereby it evokes some clear and winning sense of *distinction*. Where I believe it is easy for us all to agree and not go for our semantic guns is in the fundamental role of all brands: to realize their use, value and potential.

Any brand's ultimate potential lies in its power to persuade and prompt *action*, to trigger behavioural change and personal preference versus any set of alternative purchases. Put neatly, any brand's success rests in its ability to strike a chord, to convince in practical and emotional terms, to resonate on rational and irrational levels.

The singular task of the marketeer is simply this: to build brands of *greatest appeal*.

FIGURE 1.1 Brands of greatest appeal

WE ARE ALL WITNESSES.

NIKEBASKETBALL.COM

THE BRAND ORGANIC

> " Brands are organisms of huge growth potential, that require the right tending, watering, light, and yes, love.
>
> Because the converse holds equally true.
>
> You can kill a brand. "

Organic – adjective
Developing in a manner analogous to the natural growth and
evolution characteristic of living organisms.

DICTIONARY.COM

'm very taken with the much-held idea of brands being organic, as in they are *living*. Organisms of huge growth potential, but that require the right kind of tending, watering, light and, yes, love. Because the converse equally holds true, perilously true: you can kill a brand.

It only requires the wrong kind of external stimulus, the right blend of opposing external forces, some kind of PR tsunami, a lashing culture-quake, and blink... the light goes out. When marketeers talk abstractly of 'brand health' scores, they're closer to the supermarket-shelf realities than they necessarily realize.

ORANGE KIDS: A PRE-CURSOR

Remember Procter & Gamble's Sunny Delight? Marketed with the implication of sunburst goodness and a hearty orange juice content (actually only 5 per cent), when Britain's tabloids started running headlines to the effect, 'Sunny Delight will turn your child orange', there was little scope for comeback from P&G, little way of spinning something that had spun out of control.

The tangerine-hued kids in question were drinking more than 1.5 litres a day, over twice the recommended adult intake, and by consequence the (albeit harmless) carotene contained in Sunny Delight was altering their skin pigment. Of course, the scientific whys and wherefores were largely academic. Here was a big American conglomerate peddling syrupy sweet soft drinks to which innocent children were becoming sufficiently addicted as to start looking like Umpa Lumpas.

The ad agency ran a TV ad showing a snowman turning orange, though not in some daring, ironic response but *before* the fact, which just added to the PR disaster. And nothing the ad agency could then magic-up in riposte to the media blows offered any hopeful comebacks. (And rest assured, we tried.)

Parents who had blindly allowed their children to drink so much Sunny Delight didn't enjoy feeling complicit in the negligence of it all, but sidestepped responsibility by claiming that they'd been sold a wrong-un by an ad campaign that misled through suggestions of 'natural goodness'.

To cut a long story short, Sunny Delight was dead in the water. Drop six letters and rename it Sunny D, change the packaging... try and spin it all you want, over was over.

So yes, you can kill a brand. No question. Public indignation, moral high-grounding, media bandwagon-ing: syringe it all up and you've got a shot of something instant and evil, with or without any air in the chamber.

Sunny Delight was a mid-1990s cautionary brand tale, with all the right kind of high drama: unprecedented success followed by unfixable failure. But more interesting is how the story of Sunny Delight is prescient of the way that today's brands, more than a decade on, so actively and reactively bob on the pixelated wave of consumer-posted opinion.

Sunny Delight is, I think, an analogue precursor to a 'blog-post-submit world reorder' where brands (and much of their fate) now rests in the hands of a digitally mobilized, comfortably vocal and powerfully influencing public.

I have examples, cheerful ones, because fortunes run in both directions; spontaneous public uprising can also revive the fortunes of a brand. In fact, more than a brand's fortunes: with the right swell of public enthusiasm, a brand can quite literally return from the dead. And be no less pretty for it.

PANDA SUITS, GEORGE CLOONEY AND SIENNA MILLER

I did some work with Cadbury in 2008, not long before they were bought out by Kraft Foods. I don't believe one was the consequence of the other, and at the time, with the circling buzzards of takeover too high in the sky to see, Cadbury faced a different problem. A good problem, in truth: the problem of how to relaunch one of their chocolate bars, Wispa.

Why this was such a good problem was that Wispa was returning by popular demand. There had been a fleeting return in 2007, a limited run, due to 14,000 people joining a 'Bring Back Wispa' group across Facebook, Bebo and MySpace. The (yes it really is) interesting part in all this was that the 'Bring Back Wispa' movement had absolutely nothing to do with Cadbury. An unsolicited 14,000 individuals got behind a cause, specifically to reinstate a chocolate bar available in the 1980s and 1990s (and discontinued in 2003).

Some people take up arms against the arms race, others take umbrage at university fees or gas-guzzling motor cars chocking the planet, and some still rally for the return of a chocolate bar that nostalgically reminds them of their youth.

The total Wispa marketing budget was sub-one million sterling, which is not such a lot if you want a high-profile campaign working across mass media, reaching lots of people, and not when that sub-million figure also includes the production budget.

The advertising solution to Wispa's dilemma was a nifty one. A tease campaign invited people to pledge absolutely anything, then took those pledges of people, pets, places *et al* and threw everything inclusive of kitchen sinks into the pot, out of which came a two-minute brand film that could also work as a cut-down TV execution 'to celebrate Wispa's return'. Notable pledged 'props' included choir groups, a rugby team, mini hovercraft and a panda suit. The resulting *For the love of Wispa* is unquestionably creative, uplifting and celebratory, and walks an attractively gentle line in surrealism.

Now the cynic might say that free public pledges are a helpful way to subsidize a marketing budget. Certainly that was a fringe benefit, but the central idea was more sincere than that. Make an ad campaign that *imitates* life. That's the beating heart of it. For the love of retro (see also 'Back in the day', page 39), a group of people wanted the return of a chocolate bar, and they used social media to ask for it. An ad campaign celebrating Wispa's return then called upon the same heartfelt participation, inviting people to be part of the ad, an ad about a chocolate bar that people already thought of as *theirs*. One spot aired on UK terrestrial channel ITV during the X-Factor season finale. It was supported by a 'Thank You' execution in the national press.

In the 13 weeks that followed, the Wispa ad (a campaign launched by ad agency Fallon) was watched more than 500,000 times online, with Wispa's Facebook fans growing to 400,000. In the UK 36.4 million bars were sold, netting value sales to the tune of £18.4 million. Wispa is a happy brand tale, and it's ultimately one about *participation*.

Participation is the filthy-big signpost pointing at the direction in which much smart advertising is going. Audiences once passive and silent are giving way to a new breed, active and vocal, and it's this audience that is defining the very organic direction in which many brands are heading. Nespresso shoots multiple TV ads, then contacts its customers online and asks them to vote for the George Clooney version they most like, and that they think best represents the Nespresso brand. The ad most liked by the Nespresso-loyal few then becomes the ad everyone else sees. Nespresso believes that Nespresso drinkers are best placed to judge and discern the advertising most befitting the brand.

When Hugo Boss launched their first women's fragrance, Boss Orange, they produced a TV ad that paired brand ambassador Sienna Miller with The Beatles' track 'Baby you can drive my car'. The target audience: '20-something women who are naturally expressive and happy in their own skin'.

It's not that the resulting ad was a piece of creative genius. It's not high art, but it wasn't trying to be. High art was never the intention. The ad's borderline brilliance lies in its vibe and simplicity, so simple that it inspires imitation. You see, YouTube is full of uploaded copycat versions of the Boss Orange TVC, girls who've filmed themselves imitating Sienna, making the same moves and throwing the same shapes they've seen Sienna make and throw in the ad.

Advertising is a 'war on passivity', waged against audience apathy and indifference. Boss Orange produced a campaign that incited people not just to buy the product but actually to remake their ad, where they jived front-and-centre in their own reimagining. For any brand, this has to be the ultimate flattery.

PEOPLE WANT TO HAVE A GO

We can learn a lot from these tales of artificial orange juice, retro chocolate bars, luxury coffee capsules and women's Orange perfume.

What is plain for all to see is that people want to lend a hand, play their part, have a role. It's our hard-wired participatory nature, our wanting to be included and involved, which is reshaping what today's brands are all about. Brands are in the hands of consumers, no longer in simple terms of them being taken off the shelf, but in terms of a brand's *form* and *fate*. Consumers are becoming the new brand-builders, the sculptors and shapers of *their* brands. And brands must be open-minded and flexible enough to let them.

BRANDS MUST BEHAVE, MUST WOO

> " The Magic Bullet
> theory has
> little-to-no magic
> left in it.
> It's a dud.
>
> 'Straight
> advertising' is
> the equivalent of
> ignoring your
> girlfriend over
> dinner. Branded
> content, and CRM,
> and co-creation
> is the opposite.
> It's telling her
> she's hot. "

Brands can no longer get by through simply 'advertising' themselves. Brands peddling their wares on page and screen to an at best semi-interested audience are doing little more than touting.

The Magic Bullet Theory (identify the target, aim, fire... sit back and watch) has little-to-no magic left in it. It's a dud; an old model piece of thinking, archaic if the gloves are off and the truth be told, like putting leeches on the skin to clean the blood.

While audiences are at best semi-inclined to the commercial message, they're no longer semi-literate. In these 'time famished' times they're *all-the-way media literate, brand multi-linguists...* and they're busy filtering and editing and plain ignoring the vast deluge of commercial noise streaming at them 24/7.

It's a 'new consumer' and a 'new tech' order, with little wiggle room left for old world marketing models where the 30' TVC is the marketeers all and everything.

All meaning, very simply... yes, you got it... everything and everyone has to work harder. Brands have to work harder. Brand planners have to work harder. Advertising has to work harder... because invariably the 'advertising' has to pretend it's something else. It's *not* a TV ad, it's a *brand film*. It's not a 'commercial message', it's *content*, almost *entertainment*, that's just for you Dear Consumer, to have fun with... and maybe tell your friends?

FIGURE 3.1 'Time famished' times

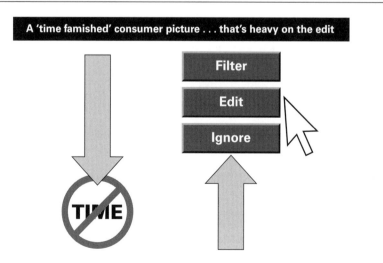

For consumers to *love* their brands, see them as *their* brands, there has to be dialogue and interaction. There has to be *interplay*. There's a social dynamic at work. 'Brand' and 'consumer' is a courtship, and 'brand-mance' (that, I know, won't catch on) is a relationship like any other, which needs to be continually kindled and stoked. Brand *loyalty*, brand *promiscuity*: we use these words rightly enough.

'Straight advertising' has become the equivalent of ignoring your girlfriend over dinner. Branded content and CRM (customer relationship management) and 'co-creation' is the opposite: it's telling her she's hot. And there's nothing wrong with telling someone they're hot. (Doubly so if they are really hot.)

And while it's a fine line between cliché and truism, I'd courteously label this a truism we all know and should lovingly apply: *behaviours breed behaviours*.

FIGURE 3.2 Consider your brand's body language

Behaviours breed behaviours

By building the right set of
BRAND BEHAVIOURS,
we may trigger desired
CONSUMER BEHAVIOURS

More so, behaviours *attract* behaviours. And they *trigger* behaviours. And we're in a game where we want people to *preference* and *buy*.

Brands influence, persuade and succeed through how they behave. If we, in designing campaigns, want to win over consumers, we need to *mirror* consumers and *pre-emptively* mirror them, to get in there first and implicitly encourage them to mirror us.

Brands must flirt.

Brands can't sit back and expect consumers to skip over to them, for Cupid's arrow to serendipitously do all the work. Brands need to reject those not-so-magic bullets and be their own Cupid, fire their own arrows, practise their own conversation starters and opening gambits. Brands need to make all the effort, do all the chasing.

In the grand seduction to win market share, it's not possible to be too keen. Consumers are worth it. Shakespeare may have been thinking more about the fairer sex than communication planning when he wrote:

> *She's beautiful, and therefore to be wooed;*
> *She is a woman, therefore to be won.*
>
> WILLIAM SHAKESPEARE, *KING HENRY THE SIXTH (PART I)*

But parallels can be drawn. Consumers are to be won; they're made for wooing.

'SAME DIFFERENCE':
THE COUNTERPOINT BRAND

" To be a Category
Hero, a brand needs
to contrive a
worthy villain,
a suitable
counterpoint,
irrespective of how
same or different
they truly are.

Every brand needs
its Moriarty, its
Joker, its Blofeld. "

NEKHORVICH
Every search for a hero must begin with something
that every hero requires, a villain. Therefore,
in our search for a hero, Bellerophon, we created
the monster, Chimera.

Mission Impossible II (2000)

Without evil, good cannot exist. Let's not get too weighty here, only make the point that things become knowable and understood in relation to another, to some point of contrast. It doesn't have to be as literal as establishing opposites – good-evil, black-white – but points of comparison do serve to identify difference.

Some time ago, I started playing around with the idea of the 'counter-point brand', and this still holds up for me. The counterpoint brand is often the second-to-market or Number 2 brand in a category. Over time, it asserts that it is absolutely and positively *not* 'the second best option' but the viable, maybe radical, perhaps sexier, *even better* alternative. And a lot of it, naturally, is perceptual rather than substance-based.

Take BMW and Audi. I'm sure diehard BMW and Audi fans will swear these brands – 'their brands' – are poles apart, and there is maybe a little Cain and Abel going on... but really... c'mon... Audi and BMW are cut from the same cloth. BMW, more 'the Establishment'; Audi, 'edgier' and arguably younger and sexier. All in all, though, they're both the embodiment of German engineering excellence from pioneering design houses. Two sides, *same* coin.

The chassis, under the bonnet, the cabin-build quality, 'the drive': the choice between Audi and BMW is born of emotional brand appeal, because the physical qualities are inherently similar. Take a blind test drive and it would be a 50:50 call identifying which marque you'd been driving. That is, of course, assuming you were still in good shape and had walked away from a blind test drive... but you take my point.

What becomes compelling, which is where advertising and image creation comes in, is how BMW and Audi drivers, with their eyes wide open, strongly differentiate themselves from each other.

'Audi? Oh no. For me, it's BMW all the way.'
'I'd never drive BMW, I'm very much an Audi kinda guy.'

The reality is that Audi's existence helps *define* BMW; BMW gives comparative *meaning* to the Audi brand. Each establishes a bearing in relation to the other, like a ship offshore fixing on the beam from a lighthouse.

It's a curious thought that the efforts of Audi's marketing department is, in part, defining what BMW stands for. And, of course, the vice-versa applies, as it applies to a good many other brands and their companion counterpoints. For example:

- Häagen-Dazs and Ben & Jerry's;
- McDonald's and Burger King;
- Google and Bing;
- Facebook and Twitter;
- Apple and Microsoft.

'I'M A...'

Apple's '*I'm a Mac...*' campaign has been nothing short of a PR nightmare for Microsoft, building such an eloquent and seemingly unassuming case that there's no chic in geek, only unloved, spreadsheet-loving geek. And nobody, including Microsoft, wants to be seen as one of those.

Microsoft's '*I'm a PC*' campaign, launched in 2008, was a forced counter-lunge to Apple's '*Get a Mac*' cry. The fact that Microsoft had to so pointedly respond to Apple betrayed, I think, just how much Microsoft were hurting. I also believe that going blow-for-blow on a theme that was Apple's home-advantage was misguided. The NLP (neuro-linguistic programming) enthusiasts use 'redefining' and 'pattern interrupts' to redirect conversations and assert advantages, but '*I'm a PC*' only ever ensured that Microsoft stayed on the back foot, helping to remind people that a PC is not a Mac. Microsoft didn't try to steer the debate, they just continued it, driving home their disadvantage.

I'm not suggesting that '*name the counterpoint brand*' is a fun and fail-safe game that can kill an eight-hour car journey, but it's a potentially instructive vantage point when trying to get to the bottom of the 'where and why' behind a brand's meaning and appeal.

Search engines, computer software and hardware, premium ice creams and hamburgers – the counterpoint principle can apply to most categories, where brands may derive perceived meaning (and tribal allegiance) from their juxtaposition. Audi, Apple, Bing, Burger King – all are clear, and clearly vocal, counterpoint brands.

And what is more, vocal is good. Vocal brands that stand up for themselves are what people need – because it's hard to make decisions in isolation, within a void empty of 'compare and contrast'.

'Is this toaster cheap or expensive, well-made or shoddy?' Without comparison, people's heads spin. They feel in the dark, ill-informed, even a little brain-queasy. We all 'go compare' on instinct, which is why the internet is awash with price-comparison sites, all claiming to be these demystifying 'make-easy' agents in a world of too much choice. (See also 'The age of the accelerated consumer', page 97.)

A NEED FOR VILLAINY

All product categories are battlegrounds, where brands bare teeth and knuckle in their attempts to come out on top. Their distinction (pseudo or real) is a function of comparison. For all brands, the assertion of 'different and better' is an eternal pursuit, and it means that branding is all about relativity. To me, it's a vis-à-vis kind of dynamic.

In the film *Unbreakable* (2000), a wheelchair-bound Samuel L Jackson had to blow up a plane, burn down a hotel and derail a train, killing a whole heap of people, before a wreck-proof and unaware superhero emerged from the ashes. As Bruce Willis mugged end-scene horror, Samuel spelt it out with, *'Now that we know who you are... I know who I am.'* Samuel was just a crazy guy trying to define himself and only able to do so once he'd found his opposite. His means are, of course, more than a little radical.

The fact is that our competition – our equals and our opposites – define us. We can't be winners if we have no one to compete with. Milestones require context. Definition is a matter of relativity.

To be a category hero, a brand needs to contrive a worthy villain, a suitable counterpoint, irrespective of how same or different they truly are. Every brand needs an opposite number, ideally a nemesis – a Moriarty, a Joker, a Blofeld. It's how brands know who they are and, by turn, how we may know them, too.

REFRAMING: ORIGINALITY AND BUSTING IT UP

> **"** Apple's originality didn't just reframe the personal computing category.
>
> Steve Jobs took a sledgehammer to a set of doctrinally-held conventions, busted 'em up real good. **"**

No one said being original was easy. Coming up with something new, fresh and dazzling? This is seldom the consequence of a walk in the park, proverbial or green.

In answering the call to originate, create and conceive, how do you pick up the gauntlet, put it on and come out swinging?

James Dyson argues that the inventor's endeavour is NOT born of trying to meet an existing need. I heard him speak a few years back, where he happily admitted that no one was crying out for 'cyclonic suction'. His invention was the equalizer to a personal frustration. He hated his vacuum bag filling with lots of lint, hair and suckable household crap. Dyson figured he could do better – *'Why bother with the bag?'*, he thought – and there's no question that he has.

Invention is born of frustration – a frustration at the way the world is, and an endeavour to try to fix it. Invention is a positive, out of a negative. Dyson's start-point is the negative.

The same is often said of great comedy. Comedy is born of anger. Most comedians are angry people; they're angry and truly miffed at the way things are. They need to 'call it', to mock and usurp it. Comedy and invention are the consequence of every *'Don't you just hate it when...?'*

Have you ever watched Denis Leary performing stand-up? Denis doesn't hold back, he is only too happy calling it out. Seldom does he appear to have sipped from a cup of 'happy', and I don't think it's just his shtick. Denis is simply one loquaciously angry Mo-Fo.

REFRAMING

I think 'originality' may be curiously interpreted as a simple shift in the frame of reference. A matter of reframing. Originality doesn't have to be about wholesale genesis. More so, it's simply a 'build': an added layer on that which 'already is'.

Dyson is still all about vacuuming. They just debunked the age-old conventions that surround it. Vacuuming was previously framed within the housewife's problem-solution. The contextual frame was one of domesticity, of chore and utility. From the recent past, you can follow a taught thread back to the most brazen chauvinisms of mid-century advertising – so many smiley, skipping, apron-wearing domestic goddesses, stay-at-home contentment as conceived in the Ad Man's eye.

FIGURE 5.1 Suction on wheels: enough to make you skip

FIGURE 5.2 Dyson – vacuum cleaning products to covet and desire

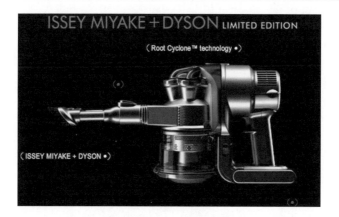

But Dyson came along and made suction sexy!

Dyson inverted the convention and flipped the energies. Dyson turned negative into positive, 'reframed' the consumer-brand debate. A design you WANT to own, AND functionality that's superior. 'Dyson' – vacuum cleaning products to covet and desire! It was nothing short of inventive genius.

And yet, at a brand communication level, Dyson really just 'did an Apple'. (In 'Colour me happy!', page 129, I toast Apple's invention of 'tech-sex desirability'.)

Apple reframed what computers and computing was all about. The category conventions generated advertising eulogizing 'the spec', detailing the technology *on the inside,* as sexy to MIT and IT types, all geek with no chic.

FIGURE 5.3 Back in the day: all geek with no chic

Apple's originality didn't just reframe the computing category. It took a sledgehammer to a set of conventions that were doctrinally held and busted 'em up real good.

And Apple marketing genius continues in its ability to be a product range that reconciles (the fundamental contradiction of) tribal belonging and brand badge individualism. In this achievement, of course, they're not alone.

To a degree, Apple 'just did a Nike'.

Rewind to the mid-to-late 1980s, where commercially Nike was being slammed by Reebok and the aerobics craze, where Nike products were a bit too much for hard-core athletes; a dry brand that took itself too seriously. Then, 1988 and 'Just do it' cried out from TV ads with end-lines such as, 'And it wouldn't hurt to stop eating like a pig.'

And have that! Provocative, daring, in-your-face creative executions, literally shaming people into working out. Detractors at the time called the ads (of which there were 12) 'sociopathic', possessing a 'poverty of warmth'. But in a big way the detractors were in the minority.

> *With its 'Just Do It' campaign, Nike was able to increase its share of the domestic sport-shoe business from 18 per cent to 43 per cent, from $877 million in worldwide sales to $9.2 billion in the ten years between 1988 and 1998.*
>
> SOURCE: CFAR – CENTRE FOR APPLIED RESEARCH

'Cha-ching!', as they say. What's the power of branding? What's the ROI (return on investment) on creativity? For Nike, US$9 billion plus over 10 years.

> *Nike rose about as high and fast in the '90s as any company can. It took on a new religion of brand consciousness and broke advertising sound barriers with its indelible Swoosh, 'Just Do It' slogan and deified sports figures. Nike managed the deftest of marketing tricks: to be both anti-establishment and mass market.*
>
> JOLIE SOLOMAN, 'WHEN NIKE GOES COLD', *NEWSWEEK*, MARCH 30, 1998

Nike, Apple, Dyson – these are 'original' brands and business success stories, born of reframing the categories in which they operate.

We're on the home straight now, but please indulge me; I want to take one more swing at this.

MASHING AND THE MOVIE BUSINESS

'Originality', through breaking norms goes by another name: genre-busting. To which I offer three exhibits: *The Matrix* (1999), Quentin Tarantino and Shakespeare.

Exhibit A: *The Matrix* (1999)

I defy anyone to say this is not one seriously cool film. Seriously. Doesn't matter what you think of Keanu Reeves. With box office takings of $171 million in the US, and $460 million worldwide, *The Matrix* is maybe the archetypal genre-buster. A Japanese anime-inspired, kung-fu superhero sci-fi action romance, set against a cyber-punk dystopian backdrop. Now that's some heavy-duty reframing.

Exhibit B: Quentin Tarantino

For pastiche, homage, blatant rip-off, and an all-round postmodern melting-pot celebration of pop culture... Quentin Tarantino, the referential reframing grand master. It would almost be easier to list the genres and influences that *haven't* made it into Tarantino's oeuvre.

Tarantino even pays homage to himself, which pretty much takes reframing to a place where postmodernism folds in, over and around itself... and where pop culture implodes... or explodes... or at least goes pop... or maybe nothing happens at all? Whatever.

Exhibit C: William Shakespeare

Shakespeare's canon is 400 years old and will always be alive, kicking and doing the rounds in one form of reimagining or rebooting or another.

Consider Prospero as *Prospera*: part Mad Max, part Gandalf, part Yoda, all Helen Mirren (*The Tempest*, 2010), or Ralph Fiennes's version of *Coriolanus* (2012), which plays out like a bad day in the Balkans.

When it comes to originality, there's no such thing as sacrilege or iconoclasm. It's open season. It's what keeps the movie industry alive and hustling.

Because before the fact, no one knows with absolute and anything like divine authority whether or not *any* movie is going to succeed commercially. Any movie can tank, any director can have an off-day or year. If you're a studio executive, you know you're not Nostradamus, and you want to stack the odds. By consequence, green-lighting genre mash-ups makes solid career sense.

> *PIRATES are cool; so are NINJAS. So pirates fighting ninjas must be frickin' AWESOME! And why not make them all beat up some ROBOTS while we're at it? Oh – and don't forget ZOMBIES!*
>
> 'COOL VERSUS AWESOME', TV TROPES.COM

Consider the very bankable franchises like *Underworld* and *Resident Evil*. They total seven movies between them, and have amassed a worldwide box office revenue of around US$975 million. This kind of figure makes movie studios and studio executives very happy. Consider *Blade Runner* (1982), where the birth of 'Future Noir' created an undisputed modern classic. It's the kind of originality that makes pretty much all film-lovers happy.

There are, of course, stubborn exceptions to remind us that genre-mashing is no *de facto* success-formula. *Outlander* (2008) proved itself no *Highlander* (1986), making back little more than 12 per cent of its production costs. Honest Abe, giving it some Buffy-style vampire slaying in 2012's *Abraham Lincoln: Vampire Hunter* sounded on paper like potential celluloid gold, but it underwhelmed audiences. After a tidy opening weekend, a high-altitude drop-off followed, posting eventual figures of US$37.5m (US domestic) and US$53.2 (international) respectively. That's not even close to earning a cigar, never mind a bigger office on 'The Lot'. But instead of having pirates fighting ninjas, if you happened to be the guy who assembled the Avengers (a kind of *within*-genre mashing), then you might be entitled to start signing your autographs '*Mr Hollywood*'. Costing US$220m to make, *The Avengers* (2012) became the twelfth film ever to reach the US$1 billion milestone, which it managed in just 19 days.

THE *OTHER* MOORE'S LAW

So I say this: originality can never die, which is a reassuring thought for us all. Originality is a new take on whatever currently exists; is simply an 'add-on', which may sound rather small, but an add-on can be epoch-shifting in effect.

Dyson, Apple, Nike, *The Matrix*, Quentin Tarantino, *The Tempest*. Final word on this can go to comic-book writing legend, Alan Moore...

> Life isn't divided into genres. It's a horrifying, romantic, tragic, comical, science-fiction cowboy detective novel. You know, with a bit of pornography if you're lucky.

Maybe this is the *other* Moore's Law? And if so I rather like the balance; one for computer science, another for 'the essence of originality'.

We divide life into genres – just pigeonholes so that we can make some sense of it all, but that's not how we *live* life. An alternative sense comes through living it and looking upon it differently, through which we may mash and bust it up.

To one and all, happy mashing.

BRAND DUALITY: CONSIDER YOUR BRAND'S BATMAN

" We reject characters
in books and movies
that are painfully
two-dimensional.

I think the same
holds true for
brands.

We are all composites
of part-opposites;
Lover-Cage Fighter;
Poet-Artisan;
Jekyll-Hyde.

By extension,
consider
The Duality of Brand. "

When someone challenges that an idea is 'off-brand'... or argues that an idea is unfalteringly right because it feels so 'on-brand'... I'd respectfully suggest that it's worth taking a pause to really consider the genuine 'iron-cladness' of either perspective.

Here's why.

Who's to say what 'the brand' is actually all about? For starters, you've got the subjective perception card to play (see 'Brands: thorny, gnarly, ever-so-twisty', page 7). All brands live in the minds of others, and that's as foreign as a place can be, with no two landscapes looking much the same.

But perhaps what's even more interesting is the idea that brands are wildly subjective and idiosyncratic personalities *in their own right*, and that campaigns can be developed that pursue and amplify the many gloriously contradictory dimensions upon which a brand's personality is built.

It's a thought. Stay with me here, please, I'd like the company.

Brands are not only organic, they're permanently work-in-progress personalities, spilling over with quirks, anomalies, contradictions, drivers and all. We typically reject characters in books and movies that are painfully two-dimensional. We flinch at their lack of depth or imagination. I think the same is true of brands. Who's going to fall in love with a poorly drawn two-dimensional brand? Surely we want our brands to run a whole lot deeper than that, to keep us interested, keen, still guessing after however long it's been?

One favoured approach to personality profiling, the Myers-Briggs Type Indicator, is based on Jung, who was keen on the idea that people are all composites of inherent contradiction. Our scales are never static. We are at differing times and to differing degrees lover and cage fighter, poet and artisan, introvert and extrovert, Jekyll and Hyde, Batman and Bruce Wayne. You get the idea.

So, by extension of the duality of man, consider the duality of brand: that every brand, if you like, has a Dark Knight that compliments its charming billionaire alter ego.

A couple of years ago a friend of mine, Faris (truly one of the sharpest advertising minds around), posted the notion of brands having a dark side, a brooding yin to complete the white and fluffy yang that brands more customarily project to the outside world:

> *Brands need to embrace their shadows. To create stronger, robust, believable brands, we must turn to the dark side.*
> FARIS YAKOB, *TALENT IMITATES, GENIUS STEALS*

Then, as now, I love this thought and the message behind it, that marketeers should not be afraid to explore their brand's dark side.

I think that today that call to explore is even less of an appeal, and more of an imperative. 'Brand stretch' is more elastic than most folk think, more like superhero spandex. I'm not suggesting being kamikaze or cavalier with pushing where a brand can go and what it can do, but I am saying there's scope to go 'a little schizoid', so long as it's, y'know, 'in a good way', a crusading way – because brands need to stimulate and surprise their audiences, to misdirect and challenge preconceived expectations. Otherwise, brands, like people, just go stale.

Brands can never afford to be bores, but they really should consider their inner Batman.

'LOSE THE NIPPLES': WHAT'S IN A LOGO?

 In the finest
semiotic
tradition, a
brand's logo is
a signifier,
a Stargate
through which
we may pass into
the emotional,
rational,
Philosophical
Universe
of that brand. "

W hat's in a logo? The shortest answer is 'lots'.
You can potentially cram a logo full of all sorts of meanings and feelings; make a logo stand for pretty much anything. It's one of those small, yet great wonders of advertising.

A brand's logo can be an incredibly elegant visual shorthand for any amount of opinions, ideas and associations. In observing the finest semiotic traditions, a brand's logo is a signifier and, when done well, it can signify so much.

An ironic reference point, but as Naomi Klein puts it in *No Logo* (1999):

> *Brands have become cultural accessories and personal philosophies.*

A brand's logo therefore becomes a gateway, a portal through which we pass into the emotional, rational, philosophical universe of that brand. Yes, kind of like a Stargate if you want to take the analogy in that direction.

Take Nike:

FIGURE 7.1 Nike logo

You see the swoosh and it's so identifiably Nike. And that swoosh immediately signposts 'Just do it', and that takes you into a busy and buzzing universe of feelings, many you don't even have to put into words or apply labels to. You just feel it.

FIGURE 7.2 'Just do it', Nike's global tagline (and belief system)

I cited the Nike swoosh as part of a global brand strategy I once pitched to Deutsche Bank. Deutsche Bank were (and remain) very proud of their logo: a square encasing a rising diagonal line.

FIGURE 7.3 Deutsche Bank logo

The logo was designed in 1974 by 'the pioneer of Constructive Graphic Art', a German called Anton Stankowski. Probably his most famous design, it was intended to signify 'controlled growth', and it doesn't require a semiotic mastermind to derive this clear meaning.

Deutsche Bank's issue was that their logo wasn't universally recognized for 'controlled growth' or otherwise. They had any amount of brand tracking, which scored high on awareness (in the latent sense) and low on affinity (in the 'brand I dig, brand for me' sense). The world over, Deutsche Bank's logo was little more than as it appeared to people: a diagonal line inside a square. An added dimension was that Deutsche Bank wanted their brand (and their logo) to stand for 'Passion to Perform', a tagline in their advertising and literature but also a tagline that they stressed was so much more than just a tagline, rather an entire value system and differentiating way of doing business and making money. 'Passion to Perform' was the proposition that drove and defined them.

FIGURE 7.4 'Passion to Perform', Deutsche Bank's global tagline (and belief system)

Passion to Perform

The long-short of Deutsche Bank's brand dilemma was that a logo that meant one thing had inherited another less obvious meaning, and few audiences around the world were feeling it.

Reassuringly, making one thing synonymous with another, even if they initially appear incongruous, is very doable. It's where Nike's swoosh provides a handy example. The Nike swoosh was created in 1971 by Carolyn Davidson, a graphic design student. She was briefed to conceive a design that could fit on a soccer shoe, as produced by Blue Ribbon Sports, the company that became Nike (as named after the Greek goddess of victory) in 1978, a whole 10 years before Dan Wieden (of agency Wieden+Kennedy) infamously told his client, *'You Nike guys, you just do it.'*

FIGURE 7.5 Nike swoosh: from 1971 to global superbrand

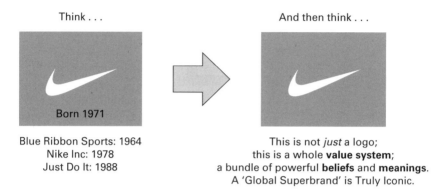

Think . . .   And then think . . .

Blue Ribbon Sports: 1964
Nike Inc: 1978
Just Do It: 1988

This is not *just* a logo;
this is a whole **value system**;
a bundle of powerful **beliefs** and **meanings**.
A 'Global Superbrand' is Truly Iconic.

Heavy investment and unswerving commitment behind a big powerful ideal – a *philosophy* as Naomi Klein might call it – and the swoosh has become Nike's semiotic Stargate, a 'white hole' of associations: inheriting, expanding and inculcating.

My pitch to Deutsche Bank was simply this. Your logo is an icon... but not an icon in the sense of a Marilyn Monroe or a James Dean. More like an icon you double-click on. Consequently it packs modest meaning and little emotional punch. Your icon needs to realize its potential, to be all it can be – a deep well of emotion and meanings, through a consistent set of brand behaviours and activities. It needs scale and stature. It needs to become timeless. It needs to be more than an icon, it needs to be ICONIC. Because being truly iconic evokes awe.

The snappy platform idea for this was 'from icon to iconic'. We then dramatized a five-year roll-out of this iconography strategy, proposing that Deutsche Bank work with a number of global media partners (*The Economist*, CNN and CNBC) to produce the kind of on-message short- and long-form content that appeals to CEO, entrepreneurial and high-net-worth mindsets.

Our thinking really resonated with Deutsche Bank; that symbols are felt, not just understood – but that first symbols have to be taught. And once taught 'brand icons' may become powerful emotional signifiers (and not just 'message carriers').

Four months after we pitched the overarching platform – two months after successfully being appointed to work with Deutsche Bank – the Bank announced their intentions to the world. The following article appeared in *Marketing Week* with the headline 'Deutsche Bank makes bold move with visual identity':

> *Deutsche Bank is to separate its name from its logo as part of its new brand identity in a bid to demonstrate it has the confidence to be part of a 'very select set of global superbrands.' The company's visual identity will display its logo with the bank's 'Passion to Perform' claim, which is now hand written. The bank says it wants to emulate superbrands such as Nike, which is known by its swoosh logo and 'Just do it' strapline.*
>
> RUSSELL PARSONS, *MARKETING WEEK*, WED, 10 FEB 2010

LUST AND NIPPLE LOSS

Starbucks, too, have set themselves on a semiotic path to wannabee 'super-brandom'. To mark their 40th anniversary, they announced on 5 January 2011 that 'Starbucks Coffee' was being dropped from their logo. After 40 years of devoted service, CEO Howard Schultz declared that 'The Siren' was long overdue her promotion. More so, she just didn't need the signposting (any more than the nipples she once sported).

> *We've given her a small but meaningful update to ensure that the Starbucks brand continues to embrace our heritage in ways that are true to our core values and that also ensure we remain relevant and poised for future growth.*
>
> HOWARD SCHULTZ, CEO, STARBUCKS

FIGURE 7.6 Starbucks drops 'Starbucks Coffee' (and nipples) from logo

1971   1987   1992   2011

The move by Schultz was shrewdly calculated, emphasizing *and* de-emphasizing of Starbucks' visual identity; a 'pairing back', a *de-branding* gesture, which may also underline the brand's strength and stature. The removal of lettering arguably 'softens'; it also may offer a soothing retort to the anti-corporate brigade and *No Logo* trumpeters, while at the same time inferring a confidence that Starbucks is now a brand so big that it no longer needs to spell it out.

Is it possible to take away, but also add? To maximize two meanings, even when they're inherently contradictory? To turn up the dials on *bold and global* and *cuddly and local* at the same time?

Only time, brand tracking and coffee sales will tell.

As a toast of all things logo, a final word on this should go to the former Apple executive Jean-Louis Gassée, who had this to say of the company's bite-afflicted fruit motif:

> One of the deep mysteries to me is our logo, the symbol of lust and knowledge, bitten into, all crossed with the colors of the rainbow in the wrong order. You couldn't dream of a more appropriate logo: lust, knowledge, hope and anarchy.

Lust, knowledge, hope, anarchy.

A logo is never *just* a logo.

'BACK IN THE DAY': NOSTALGIA BRANDS AND THE RETRO SELL

> " 'The Past' conjures all the magic and mystique of a travel brochure destination, without a handy Time Machine to disprove the allure and expose the truth.
>
> For brands, 'nostalgia' can be one helluva compatible and curvy bedfellow. "

> *The past is a foreign country: they do things differently there.*
>
> LESLIE POLES HARTLEY, *THE GO-BETWEEN* (1953)

I'm told that women very quickly forget the extreme pain of childbirth. To ensure further procreation, the brain pulls a sniper-accurate insomnia trigger. Because total recall would mean a lot of one-child families. I suspect nostalgia is the same kind of operator.

I'm pretty convinced that nostalgia never paints an accurate picture. There's hyperbole in the paint-mix (maybe that's the 'red'?). Even a little allegory; one's past 'made myth' (that could be the 'purple'?). And voila, we've got ourselves 'rose'.

So the past is a myth, a sleight-of-hand deception, truly a foreign land, as Hartley suggests, because it *never actually existed*. Not the way we remember it. The past conjures all the magic and mystique of a travel brochure destination, without a handy time-machine to disprove the allure and expose the truth.

Where I'm going with this is: if brand-building is an exercise in the creation of appeal through association and evocation, then nostalgia can be one helluva compatible and curvy bedfellow. Of course nostalgia isn't a gambit that can be played by every brand, or even every brand old enough to be credibly able to play it. But at the right moment, given the right context, nostalgia can be a great brand-building device.

NOSTALGIA PAYS ITS WAY

Nostalgia is all about context. *Then...* as compared to *now*. When 'now' represents tough times, we hark back all the more to times that were happier. Lego is one of the few brands that has shown itself to be 'recession proof'. In fact, Lego has become a beneficiary of a recessionary climate:

> *UK profits soar for Lego*
> *Lego's latest financials show a storming 12 months, with significant double digit growth for UK sales for the fifth consecutive year. Lego also increased its global market share to 4.8%.*
>
> SOURCE: *TOY NEWS*, MARCH 4, 2010

Nostalgia has provided a kind of Kevlar for Lego's bottom line, because purchase provides a kind of comfort blanket for consumers. When times are uncertain, folks revert to brands they feel certain of. Buying Lego for your child is buying something you know, that you understand and remember. It's the happy glow of a warm, safe place at a time when, financially speaking, so many feel like they're sleeping on a ledge.

> The public demand for nostalgic toys and brands they know and trust has meant we've fared well.
>
> MARKO ILINCIC, MD, LEGO UK & IRELAND

PAST MYTHS MADE REAL

Lego, Hovis, Heinz Baked Beans, Fairy Liquid: these are brands that 'channel' nostalgia. They vibrate with a set of values – homespun, more innocent, pure, of simpler times – that 'time-worm', that golden age of never-was right into the hand of the consumer every time they pull a loaf or can or bar from the shelf.

> Hovis: as good today as it's always been.

That's a little slug of feel-good right there with every buy. Agency CDP knew this back in 1974 when they asked Ridley Scott to direct a TVC that proclaimed, 'As good for you today as it's always been'.

Here was Dvořák's *New World Symphony* setting the tone for sepia-infused, uncurbed nostalgic enthusiasm, a bread delivery boy taking on steep cobbled inclines and free-wheeling home to the ultimate reward of a Hovis loaf containing 'many times more wheatgerm than ordinary bread'.

Twenty-four years later, in 2008, agency Miles Calcraft Briginshaw Duffy simply reinforced the message. A nicely ambitious and sweeping piece of film-making, *Go on lad*, chronicled the last 122 years of British history in 122 seconds, tracking the movement of a young boy through time and space from a start point of 1886. It's claimed that the execution was subsequently responsible for a 13 per cent increase in annual sales of Hovis.

Virgin Atlantic doesn't go back 122 years, but it doesn't have to. A quarter-century is more than enough equity to get in on the act. Their *25 years, Still Red Hot* TVC is a gloriously knowing nod to a decade that possessed close-to-zero self-awareness. Strutting through Heathrow airport for the first time on '22 June 1984', we witness a red-costumed coterie of air stewardesses paying leg-service to Robert Palmer, accompanying a square-jawed Virgin pilot who may once have been the Marlborough Man. The 90-second swaggering set-piece is set to the soundtrack *Relax*, courtesy of Frankie

Goes To Hollywood. The whole experience is like hoovering a pure, uncut line of absolute 1980s direct from Tony Montana's personal supply.

But what if you're a marketeer who doesn't have the production or media budget to commission new TV ads that affectionately parody the past?

The resurrection and re-airing of classic TV ads from yesteryear has also been a trend of recent years. The Milky Bar Kid, the Bisto Family, the Cadbury Caramel Bunny: ads and images you last saw 25 years ago are being re-beamed into people's living rooms. With every intention, the brand builders are mining deep, using the living room as the entry point, but hoping to travel much further into the murky memories of childhood, dredging up sugar-and-gravy associations that live in our 'I remember when's'. There is an opposing professional school of thought amongst some of my peers that this is no more than 'lazy marketing', but I think it runs considerably deeper than that.

THE RIGHT KIND OF OLD

Lego, Hovis, Heinz Baked Beans, Fairy Liquid: these are exemplar brands of the nostalgic tradition, genuine household names with masses of latent goodwill and implicit feelgood factor. New ad campaigns with re-enforced or updated messaging can top them up, add a few fresh litres to the image tank, reinvigorate them and perhaps cause some reappraisal (as we see with Hovis)... but fundamentally these brands don't need to have something new to say. They stand for all they've become.

Nostalgia brands have stood the test of time, are proven, made credible by the fact they're still in the game *without* becoming outmoded, outdated, superseded.

But here's the 'but'.

Working on a nostalgia brand doesn't mean you can always break early for lunch, kick back, sit on your hands and rest on your laurels, hold on to your market share. You can still negligently kill a nostalgia brand by turning it into the 'wrong kind of old'.

I once worked on a household cleaning brand whose longevity as a business is triple-digit. As a company you'd never really appreciate their roll-call of achievements unless you looked it up, or happened to work for them. What stood out when I dug into this company's achievements is how this manufacturer had, in their own way, made their mark, decade after decade, helping in some small way to move us on in the game of progress.

Here was a 100-year-old manufacturer of power tools who also happened to be inducted into the Space Foundations Hall of Fame for its contributions to NASA's Gemini and Apollo missions. Its contribution to wonky DIY shelves the world over remains unsung.

I was working on an assignment to launch a new product line. New product lines are all about having something new to say. At least, you hope they have something new to say. You hope there's credible scope for the product's truth in articulating the benefit to people, spelling out the 'why they should believe'.

Boiling it right down, the product line's 'at its heart' proposition (I'm abridging here) was: 'Smart, quick-cleaning products that make your life easier.' They may have used a few more words, but (short or long) this proposition is water-tight in a boulder dam kind of way. Because the consumer need, for 'quick-cleaning products that make life easier' is *timeless*. Because housework is boring; it's right up there with death and taxes in its disagreeable inevitability, so any piece of product-smarts that takes some pain away and does the job in less time is always going to be a better mousetrap for people.

The tightrope balance of heritage and innovation was the crux of it: how to ensure we could play to 'origin story and provenance', and *still* really dial-up newness. It was a case of new born of old, where old is also a really good thing.

The watch-out for every nostalgia brand is how you guard against becoming a *yesterday brand*, how you stay relevant and fend off someone else banging a drum that they've just hit town with the next best thing since sliced bread.

It's a balancing act, but possible to get it right and have it both ways, to play both ends of the see-saw.

FIGURE 8.1 The nostalgia brand balancing act

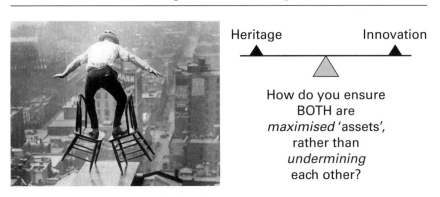

Heritage   Innovation

How do you ensure
BOTH are
maximised 'assets',
rather than
undermining
each other?

For Nivea, 2011 marked '100 years of skincare'. A hundred years is an achievement in anyone's brand book, and rightly a very real reason to celebrate and slap on some self-congratulations. But these kinds of announcements are never without hazards.

Every time you remind people you've been around for 100 years, you remind them how old you are. Upside: stood the test of time. Downside: surely superseded by something new and improved?

Nivea's solution was to partner with Barbadian R&B recording artist Rihanna (b. 1988).

FIGURE 8.2   Nivea & Rihanna (77 years younger) celebrating 100 years of skincare

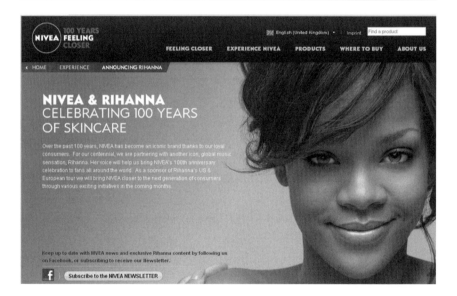

Understandably, Nivea doesn't want to be a brand that ages with its ageing users – because the ultimate outcome is a dwindling-to-zero one. Rihanna represents a whole other, younger fan base, and that could spell new Nivea users for generations to come. But how congruous and compatible is this partnership? Nivea also doesn't want to alienate its biggest fan base, its core loyal users, who are over 40 and unlikely to be all that impressed with a 23-year-old's maverick musicality, overt sexuality or chequered private life. Where's the identification for them? How does a 43-year-old relate to the new face of a brand that has been 'her brand' for the last 15 years?

With hope, Nivea's core users are sufficiently loyal, and the association will help contemporize the brand's image, which is obviously the intention.

RETRO ORIGINALS, FOR THOSE WHO WEREN'T ORIGINALLY THERE

In *Ogilvy on Advertising* (1983), the man himself defines 'a brand' as:

> *The intangible sum of a product's attributes: its name, packaging, and price, **its history**, its reputation, and the way it's advertised.*

A very fair-enough roll-call of attributes from David O, and they all surely make a contribution to the intangible sum. The hope is that, in the finest Gestaltian tradition, they all weigh-in and add to a greater whole, with each attribute being something you can dial up or down, depending on the weather.

Of Ogilvy's roll-call of attributes, for me, 'its history' is a standout point. (Of course, it was for you too, because I put it in bold.) 'Its history' is a gentle nod to this subject of nostalgia, and furthermore to the 'retro' sell. Nostalgia and retro are part of the same bag of tricks; they stem from the same bundle of meanings, from this desire we have for 'things past'.

> *Nostalgia – noun*
> *A wistful desire to return in thought or in fact to a former time in one's life, to one's home or homeland, or to one's family and friends; a sentimental yearning for the happiness of a former place or time.*
>
> SOURCE: DICTIONARY.COM

So, by definition, 'nostalgia' is something you CANNOT sell to the kids, because they weren't there first time round.

Nostalgia is a luxury and indulgence of the old *enough*; a consequence of being old enough to have accumulated some rose-tinted memories; to have built a sufficient bank of good times as to feel the pang of melancholic loss, a realization that not all times are good times.

'Retro', on the other hand, is a two-gambit sell. It lets the 'old enough' relive it and, for everyone else, it breathes new life into an old idea.

FIGURE 8.3 Fredperry.com: I've had a love affair with the Fred Perry label since I was 14

A brand's 'history attribute' may be a point of 'feel-good' (nostalgia) or, very simply, by alternative 'feel cool' (retro). This latter example very commonly pays rent in the heartland of the fashion world.

Consider Vans, Converse, Nike, adidas: all are brands where 'retro' is either a facet of their identities, or a core component. Converse, founded in 1908, is a brand sum comprising of a 100+-year-history, and collaborations with 1920s basketball player Chuck Taylor and 1930s Canadian badminton champion Jack Purcell. British fashion label Fred Perry lives on precisely the same street as Converse; a place of vintage style, tradition and authenticity born of personal sporting accomplishment.

Adidas's 'Originals' collection sits neatly under the adidas masterbrand as a stand-alone vertical, pitching themselves as 'vintage clothing, retro shoes and urban wear that blend timeless 70s and 80s designs with sports styles.' Those consumers targeted by adidas Originals will certainly not be old enough to have purchased these ranges when they originally hit the shelves.

THE KINGDOM

Everything can be killed except nostalgia for the kingdom, we carry it in the colour of our eyes, in every love affair, in everything that deeply torments and unties and tricks.

JULIO CORTAZAR, WRITER

I don't know for sure, because I never met him to ask, but I take Cortazar's reference to 'the kingdom' to mean one's past, the memories we have and hold dear – good and bad – that we carry with us. We are the sum of our experiences, but specifically the sum of how we remember those experiences. From memory, we make the past real, even if it's not actually how the facts originally played out. Why let the facts get in the way of a good memory? Imagination. Reinvention. Re-imagining. It's what we human beings do. And quite often, created in our image, it's what our brands do too.

'YOURS DIGITALLY': BRAND CHARISMA'S SECOND COMING

> " Digital brands exist
> in the ether,
> in that abstract
> frontier called
> cyberspace, through
> the looking glass of a
> computer screen, a
> screen that may be big
> or small, portable or
> desk-bound, a computer
> that may also be
> a phone.
>
> The Digital Age is
> redefining branding.
> Some of the old themes
> still apply,
> but new truths
> have entered the game. "

'**B**rand-in-hand', that was the phrase, that was *the* ultimate marketing goal. Trial, purchase, a first-hand experience – a tactile one: getting 'brand-in-hand' was what all the advertising in the world was pointing everyone at, beyond which it was then down to 'the experience'.

The advertising that worked had taken the horse to water. Once 'in hand', it was crunch time, down to product truth – no smoke, no mirrors, no more straplines. The soap had to lather, the shoe fit, the dishes clean shiny and bright. Product experience *had* to deliver, to re-enforce the ad promise, and if it did align then all was very well and you were on to a winner, a repeat purchase, maybe even a first-person recommendation.

That was 'then', of course, back in the day when brands assumed a phys-ically tangible form, had a three-dimensional shape to them. In these very different days, occupying three dimensions isn't what it used to be, is no longer a prerequisite in the brand game. That thinking is all rather old hat, back when the hat was analogue.

The digital age is *redefining* branding. While some of the old themes cer-tainly still apply, new truths have entered the game.

New truth 1: time, in memoriam, doesn't help, isn't necessary

Physical (analogue) brands were typically forged over time. They had his-tory – ideally retuned into some kind of mythology – to help build their mystique, back when 'standing the test of time' really stood for something.

By contrast, digital brands have permission to 'come out of nowhere', because it is quite literally what they appear to do, as are the accepted and governing norms of the digital universe. Yesterday, they were simply not there. Then someone somewhere uploaded a file and it's: *'Welcome to the party! Come join my group! Tell me what you like!'*

Digital brands don't need a back-story and don't need to convert back-story into consumer trust. For digital brands, their 'instant mystique' may lie in their origins, maybe their founder or the company ethos behind their pixelated form, whether a Mark Zuckerberg or a Jack Dorsey or a procla-mation like, *'Don't be evil'*. However, a sense of origin is far from essential. Meeting a new need, one you never even knew you had, is more than compelling enough to build a near-exponential tribal following.

Before cell phones (BCP), people had to 'prearrange' where and when they met. A phone box could help, but only if you were calling someone at a fixed location, where *they* were near a landline. It all sounds positively archaic, and it was. A phone in everyone's pocket changed all that, created a whole new need and presented a whole new level of ease and convenience. (See also 'Mobile: the new dependency', page 221.)

Back to the present, and we have Foursquare (**www.foursquare.com**), a 'social network-cell-phone-GPS' mash-up. Now we can have a sense of 'community' and social connectivity, *with satellite support*. Digital brand Foursquare is redefining how we *feel* about our physical space.

> *Foursquare started out in 2009 with limited availability in only 100 worldwide metro areas. In January 2010, Foursquare changed their location model to allow check-ins from any location worldwide. As of January 2011, the service had 6 million registered users internationally.*
>
> SOURCE: WIKIPEDIA

Which all takes me to...

New truth 2: 'useful and relevant' has been usurped by 'indispensable and immediately satisfying'

Useful and relevant remain the cornerstones of any healthy brand, digital or otherwise... but digital brands are becoming indispensable. Successful digital brands are needs-based and, more specifically, 'immediate need' based.

The need to find information, accurately and right away.

The need to learn.

The need 'to buy'.

The need to 'connect' with others, to 'be in the know and in touch', to acknowledge our compulsions as social creatures.

The need to pass comment, criticism, judgement, approval.

The need to have a voice.

The need to not feel alone.

I believe 'brand-in-hand' is taking a back seat to 'brand-at-fingertip'. Digital brands, as accessed through keyboard or touch-screen are becoming more powerful than their 3-D occupying forefathers, more powerful than anyone could have conceived 10, even 5 years ago.

Facebook could be worth as much as US$50 billion; Twitter worth $3.7 billion. The Google *brand* is said to clock in at a staggering $114 billion, according to Millward Brown Optimor's 'BrandZ Top 100' (2010 survey).

On BrandZ, Google takes the Number 1 brand spot, followed by IBM ($86 billion), Apple ($83 billion) and then Microsoft ($76 billion). Coca-Cola

($68 billion) and McDonald's ($66 billion) stand next in line. As illustrations go, I think this is stark.

Bottles of Coca-Cola were first sold in 1886. (How's that for a brand backstory?) McDonald's has been open for business since 1940 and currently serves 58 million burger lovers a day. Google, founded in 1998, will celebrate its 14th birthday in September 2012.

Coca-Cola's advertising investment runs to the tune of $2.5 billion per annum (source: Advertising Age), and it's been making some kind of per annum investment every year for the last 125 years. By modest comparison, Google's annual global ad spend is speculated to be around $188 million.

To me, the really rather remarkable thing is that you can go out and 'buy' a Big Mac or an iPod or a can of Coke, but Google, Facebook and Twitter are *only* accessible through screen-based interaction. Digital brands exist in the ether, in that abstract frontier called cyberspace, through the looking glass of a computer screen, a screen that may be big or small, portable or desk-bound, a computer that may also be a phone.

And yet...

New truth 3: hearts and minds can be won in cyberspace

While you can never wear or taste a digital brand, that doesn't make them any less real. A digital brand is as alive as any physical brand. It exists not on physical but *emotional* dimensions. It is 'made real' through its usage, through the experiences it facilitates, the utility it provides, in how it meets people's fundamental needs, in how it fulfils and gratifies.

In 'Brands: thorny, gnarly, ever-so-twisty', page 7, I talk about how brands are '*real... and unreal.*' How they exist '*in the eye and the mind of a consumer*'. By this logic, it is utterly reasonable for digital brands to be as perceptually 'concrete' as those that also take a physical form.

New truth 4: digital brands don't peddle desire, they peddle dependency; they are narcotic

Desirable physical brands are brands you want to 'have', to possess, to go out and buy. By glorious contrast, social media brands, for example, are digital brands you want to *spend time with*, be in the company of.

Once you 'possess', the fix can quickly wane, the thrill-of-the-want now over... but with digital brands, the thrill lies in the (ongoing) experience, a fix that doesn't diminish, never tarnishes, stays ever sparkly and buff.

The Spanish social hub Tuenti (**www.tuenti.com**) now boasts 90 per cent domestic penetration amongst 14 to 35 year olds, and an average daily use of 82 minutes per person (2011). And these are not 82 passive, lean-back minutes. These are 82 minutes of highly engaged 'me' time.

WILDLY CHARISMATIC

> *Charisma – noun*
> *A spiritual power or personal quality that gives an individual*
> *influence or authority over large numbers of people.*
>
> SOURCE: DICTIONARY.COM

Digital brands wield the power of dangerous addiction. They are like wildly charismatic heart-and-soul-of-the-party types: the John Belushi, Dennis Hopper, Ollie Reed, Fun Bobby of our (increasingly digital) brand orbit.

As we are fast appreciating, digital brands simply have the ability to be *more* charismatic than their physical counterparts. They appear to build consumer trust almost overnight, and can create drug-like dependency and borderline zealotry amongst their tribe of users. They can go from underground to seemingly everywhere in the stroke of a return key, and there's rarely a TV ad urging anyone to visit a 'w-w-w-dot'. *This* is charisma.

And the 'how' of it is increasingly evident. We cannot get enough of our digital brands *because* they are truly *ours*, because they can make life easier and allow us to be who we are and live the way we prefer.

We wear our physical brands like badges, to help define us – but we *use* our digital brands to help express who we are, to *update* and *redefine* us. They allow us to vividly *be*, to hold a mirror up to ourselves, and it is clear. We like what we see.

Maybe Mark Zuckerberg is worth all those billions after all?

SUB-BRAND SPLENDOUR

"
A sub-brand is
like a wayward
child, an accepted
black sheep, an
indulged teen
allowed to live
a few wild years,
and even toasted
for it.

Sexy, cheeky,
playful, Diet
Coke got to be
everything
Coca-Cola wasn't.
"

There's something so very splendid about 'sub-brands'. Not literally all of them, that is, but some in particular, and all in terms of their latent potential.

I suspect it has a lot to do with language: because they're called 'sub', people don't get so stressed, wound up, or in a panic over how they behave. This goes for the marketeers, the particular custodians of said 'sub-brand', and also consumers.

Sub-brands can be such a splendid thing because they're allowed to break a few rules; they're cut more slack, very simply, allowed to be 'more'. That 'more' can be any number of things. More experimental, more cheeky and irreverent, more light-hearted.

The parent brand, the masterbrand from which the sub-brand originates, can often seem to be so much more stuffy and earnest by comparison. Human nature is hierarchical, and so too is the world of brands. It's one example of how we conceive brands in our image. And because any master-brand is the overarching brand, it sits across the top of any and all product verticals, a bit like a crown – ascendant in its kingdom. This royal status is probably why the masterbrand is revered, seldom questioned, more likely to lead to practices that uphold the status quo and honour established conventions. Challenging the crown can be a dangerous business. '*Off with their head*' customs are typically best avoided.

But a sub-brand on the other hand...

A sub-brand is like a wayward child, a permissible black sheep, an indulged teen allowed to live a few wild years and even toasted by others for it. For those involved in encouraging these kinds of brand behaviours, head-loss never really feels like a possibility.

Take two remarkable sub-brands: Diet Coke and iPod. Both are 'remarkable' because from humble but roguish outlier beginnings they helped reignite (Coca-Cola) and reframe (Apple) the fortunes of their masterbrands.

DIET COKE

Diet Coke got to be everything, for a time, that Coca-Cola wasn't. Sexy, cheeky, playful, *Diet Coke Break* and *Diet Coke Guy* were inspired interpretations of a simple strategy: to create a consumption moment. Feel good about drinking a Diet Coke at 11.30 in the morning. By extension, define the drinking moment so as not to potentially cannibalize other Coca-Cola drinking occasions.

In creative execution, Diet Coke tapped into something, a kind of yummy-mummy Mrs Robinson, female empowerment theme. Diet Coke was a slice of *Sex and the City* sass that actually predated Sarah Jessica Parker and her NYC gal pals. *Sex and the City* slinked on to our screens for the first time in 1998. For a good couple of years prior, first generation Diet Coke hunk, Lucky Vanous, had been baring his torso in the name of Cola sales.

There was nothing 'sub' about Diet Coke's mid-1990s success. Indeed, 'sub' in this case started to feel kind of superior: Diet Coke was more in touch with and reflective of its time, while it felt like Classic Coke was growing cobwebs in its ears. By virtue, however, the sub-brand halo started to play back on to the masterbrand, giving full fat a healthy dust-off.

I think Diet Coke was able to be all it could be because it didn't feel stifled by the weighty burden of being the masterbrand, *Coca-Cola* (you can almost hear the hallowed angelic chorus); all that heritage, all those past achievements, the start-point in any marketing conversation on Coke most likely being, *'Is this consistent with our brand past?'*

THE SUM OF ALL SUB-BRANDS

How can we make our computers more popular?

That was pretty much the posing question inside Apple Inc in the days before iPod and the mainstream Mac religion that followed. It is, of course, quite hard to fully believe, Apple being all that it now is, a brand adored by so many. Yet there was a time when they were simply a manufacturer of computers, and little more.

And the answer to that question, of how to increase their popularity?

The answer was 'music'. Because everyone loves music.

iPod became iTunes, and later expanded the Apple universe further by taking it sideways into phones, tablets and clouds, all carrying an i. 'Music' was the start of Apple becoming something bigger.

Arguably, Apple's brand worth lies in it being the sum of all its sub-brands. Each 'i' feeds the masterbrand – builds it bottom-up – so much so that Apple almost isn't a masterbrand at all, not anymore, but an *idea*, a philosophy built on the three i's of innovation, intuition and individualism. (Originally, the 'i' in Apple sub-brands stood for 'internet', denoting the ease with which you could internet-connect their iMac. *'There's no step 3. Say hello to iMac'*, ran the ad.)

Apple's many sub-brands are a portfolio that – crucially, for this to work as well as it does – becomes a lifestyle orbit for people, allowing them to enter the Apple world through their own preferred gateway. Buy an iPhone, use iCloud, walk into a store: the *Apple-ness* is in everything, every point of entry, meaning that there's no longer an actual hierarchy to the brand system – which could well account for why Apple has become such a phenomenal consumer-centric success. (See also 'Through a glass clearly', page 122.)

There is no question that iPod became some kind of sub-brand Hercules, a kind of demigod in its own right, seemingly less mortal and more important than the masterbrand that bore it. Apple's genius lies in the fact that they didn't flinch from the happy monster they'd created. They embraced it, rode the beast rather than trying to slay it. Apple's ultimate appeal stems from a bold willingness to make their sub-brands limitless.

SONY COULD HAVE BEEN APPLE

Instead, they remain Sony.

Sony seem to have some kind of gift for creating sub-brands that capture the imagination... only then to let them wither. Walkman has got to be the most glowing example of a 'sub' that arguably became more attractive than its masterbrand prefix. *Sony* – the Japanese electronics giant; *Walkman* – portable audio that suddenly allowed everyone to apply a soundtrack to their daily lives.

Walkman was liberation for people; it was always going to be a winner. In the 1980s, when Walkman was big, it was huge. It was a sub-brand that transcended into becoming the product category descriptor. A portable audio device *was* a 'walkman', whether you bought it from Sony or not, and more likely than not you wanted it to say Walkman on the side.

Jump a good few time tracks forward and... if Sony had embraced MP3 technology, they could have capitalized on their Walkman heritage and made old Walkman the new iPod. Apple had nothing like the credibility that Sony had, but Apple saw a future while Sony busied hanging on to their past. Maybe in a parallel universe it plays out differently, where we're all listening to our iMans or WalkPods?

FIGURE 10.1 That was then... and this is now

With less consequence, but consistent form, Sony's return to the global computer market in 1996 achieved a level of sub-brand success that has subsequently thinned to product brochure obscurity. Vaio was a smart concept. The Vaio laptops particularly so. Vaio was high-on-style hardware for the design enthusiasts who were PC-users at heart, or through working-world nurture. Vaio became a cool alternative to iBook, aesthetically satisfying to the aesthete who didn't feel all that great about an intuitive operating system, and who had to spend company time in the company of .xls and .ppt.

Like Walkman, Vaio had its 15-minute fame window, but it didn't convert.

FIGURE 10.2 Sony Vaio laptops – taking on Apple at their own 'desirability game'

BBC IPLAYER, BECAUSE SUB-BRANDS CAN BE DIGITAL TOO

The BBC's launch of iPlayer has only done good things for the broadcaster's brand overall. BBC iPlayer first launched on 25 December 2007. It was one of the first on-demand web TV players in the UK; a pioneering gesture from 'The Beeb', and a statement that they were a broadcaster who felt good about grasping a digital nettle.

> *Before the launch in December 2007, the BBC had hoped the service would reach half a million users in its first six months. This turned out to be a gross underestimate, as 3.5 million programmes were streamed or downloaded in the first three weeks alone. By May 2010, the site was getting 123 million monthly play requests.*
>
> SOURCE: WIKIPEDIA

The site's original strapline, '*Catch up on the last 7 days of BBC TV & Radio*', was pretty Ronseal and underlined the point that it was BBC-content only that you were watching on iPlayer. The later, more catchy and copywritten strap, '*Making the unmissable, unmissable*', played into the benefit-based reason for launching iPlayer in the first place. People don't like missing their favourite shows, and they can now catch up through the internet.

'Dues' to Auntie Beeb for being an early riser and leaning into the digital day.

WE SHOULD ALL BE MORE SUB

So 'sub' suggests inferior, but the way we react and respond to language allows us to feel and be more liberated with our sub-brands. We might not even know that our new favourite Cola or MP3 player is a 'sub' anything, and in fact, the truth is, it's not.

Consider what *Sonic the Hedgehog* did for Sega, and what *Mario* has done for Nintendo. Mario games have sold over 200 million copies.

Sonic, Mario, GoldenEye, Gears of War: these games are sub-brands of a kind but, in effect, strongly branded product lines that have hugely influenced people's choice of 'masterbrand' console.

Sub-brands can achieve greatness, without so much before-the-fact weight of expectation around them. I think we set them up to succeed when, as brand-builders, we approach them with a certain lightness. We're willing to take more chances, throw the dice, bluff our hand, because it simply feels like the percentages are more in our favour. There's a bigger upside, and no one's neck is on the line. By accidental design, therefore, sub-brands can be the rookie, wild-card draft who wins it in the dying seconds; an underdog with the potential to become an overlord.

Sub-brands, inferior? Think different.

DROP THE 'THE': WHAT'S IN A NAME?

> Nike, is *Nike*, irrespective of whether you know she's also the Greek Goddess of Victory… or not.
>
> Google's become an action, a verb.
>
> Brands are the opposite of *Newspeak*. They are run-deep One-Word bundles of all kinds of meanings.

> SEAN PARKER
> Drop the 'The'. Just 'Facebook.' It's cleaner.
> *The Social Network* (2010)

aming something, now there's an undertaking. The responsibility of naming a child often feels enormous at first. You're going to give them 'a name', and any name will trigger associations of some kind or another, will *define* them in some way.

You'll have observed how any first name triggers instant reaction, transparent like or dislike on the face of every audience. *How pretty! Come again? That's lovely! You're seriously considering calling them that?*

What if the name doesn't fit the child, their looks, their temperament, their wardrobe, their anything? What if they grow up to hate their name, think one of your first true acts of parenthood was to make a singularly crumby decision? When you realize that it'll only be one poor decision in a long road of many, then the weight starts to lift. And it lifts some more when you accept that *they* will define what their name means to people, and not you.

But names are important. They *do* define. For new brands, the name helps assert their meaning and reason to an audience, to explain to an open-eared (or not so open) world why they indeed are in it, the role they have to play. New brands are looking for understanding, for early acceptance, and the choice of name can help.

For established brands, the brand name is the accumulated sum of deeds: the advertising; the behaviour of the company; the opinion of consumers; the opinion of the collective; all that's gone before, good and bad. To a large degree, it doesn't matter what the brand name originally meant, but what it has come to mean. Ultimate meaning comes with time, through associations with an audience and through the connections an audience makes.

By this thinking, a name can derive from absolute gibberish, and over the *longue durée*, meaning is grafted on to it, any kind of meaning. You can create a consumer understanding of something from pretty much anything.

Nike *is Nike*, irrespective of whether you know she's also the Greek goddess of victory... or not.

I think names derived from an actual brand's intention is a shrewd start-point, even if not downright essential. It's never a bad thing to have an athletics brand that is associated with winning. But anything can become a *sememe*, a signifier of meaning, a stand-alone unit that gets its intended message across.

If you google '*What does Google mean?*', you get this top of the list:

> *Google – verb*
> *Use an Internet search engine, particularly Google.com:*
> *'she spent the afternoon googling aimlessly'.*
> *Search for the name of (someone) on the Internet to*
> *find out information about them.*

Google's become a *doing word*: 'to google'. It's become a verb, the category generic for internet searching, in the way Hoover, Tipp-Ex and Xerox first defined their categories.

Google founders Larry Page and Sergey Brin initially referred to their search engine as 'BackRub', '*because the system checked backlinks to estimate the importance of a site*' (Source: Wikipedia). 'BackRub' then became Google, a mindful misspelling of the word 'googol', the name given to a number – in this case, a one followed by a hundred zeros. Other than Pi, who knew that numbers had names?

And while I think Google was always going to become a verb, because of the type of company it's become and because of the utility it offers people, I also think the double-O helped its mnemonic cause.

'OO'

For the bygone comedian Frankie Howerd, 'oo' was pretty much his catch-phrase, oft followed by an '*I say!*' Likewise Kenneth Willams (another comic of the same era) 'oo-ing' into an exclamation of '*matron!*', or some similar end-of-pier British-seaside naughtiness. Camp stuff, and of its time, but it helped build comedy careers.

There's something so very satisfying about saying 'oo'. Typhoo tea pivoted their entire advertising on it once upon a long ago. '*You only get an "OO" with Typhoo.*' Although the fact is, you don't, because you also get an 'OO' with Google. And you don't get one but two, with instant messaging product ooVoo, who've taken the 'oo' principle to the next level.

There's a lot to be said for how things sound, things that sound as they mean. Like dynamic, which sounds very, well, dynamic. Like squelch. Alka-Seltzer used to jingle, '*Plop, plop, fizz*'. Kellogg's Rice Krispies still run with '*snap, crackle and pop*'.

Onomatopoeias are great, even if onomatopoeia doesn't follow its own example, and sounds nothing like its meaning.

Roald Dahl, a word-inventing genius, was also partial to 'oo'. His oompah-lumpa's were, I'd guess, inspired by a brass band's oom-pah-pa. Of little surprise, Dahl had a word for his extensive vocabulary of words that weren't *officially* words. That word: *gobblefunk*, for Dahl inventions such as... *duper, hoggish, gollop, mushious, grumptious, squizzled, swash boggling and phizz whizzing*.

Can you imagine what Dahl could have done for brand names?

WORD-MERGE PROCREATION

Originality is often defined as taking two existing entities and, for the first time, putting them together. You have one thing, you take another, join them – and you get a third, *new thing*. One plus one can sometimes make three; the procreation equation.

Many brands enter the world as word-merges: the birth of a third (original) word from a compatible and inspired coupling. Following Andersen Consulting came Accenture, a word-merge, a non-word-new-word, symbolic of the company's new beginning. 'Accent on the future.' *Accenture*. Good stall-setting stuff, with the right-pointing accent on the 't' in Accenture's logotype providing added typographic emphasis. There's no question what direction these guys are looking in, just look at that font!

And dues go to Danish employee Kim Peterson, who submitted the name 'Accenture' in response to an internal company competition, much to the chagrin of the marketing consultants who were cannon-balling to be first to the finish line.

Lego is similar, a creation of pairings, of *leg* and *godt*. Both are Danish words, *leg* for 'play', *godt* meaning 'well'. 'Play well', a very charming name for a toy company, as conceived by Lego's founder, Ole Kirk Christiansen.

The list happily rolls on.

Samsonite. Samson, one of the original tough guys, with God-granted supernatural strength... and 'ite', making Samsonite, which sounds like it belongs in the periodic table or Mohs' scale of hardness.

Durex. Durable and Rex, as in erect or upright, like a... T-Rex.

Brands aren't beyond the three-word-merge either: Vodafone (voice, data, telefone); Smart (Swatch, Mercedes, art).

THE LEFT BRAIN ALTERNATIVE

Ronseal: *Does exactly what it says on the tin.* A strapline that's taken its place in the lexicon of popular culture. And it's a good strap. It gives serious blue-collar attitude, defines the brand in all its no-nonsense left brain glory.

Ronseal elegantly articulates the entire alternative route that brand names can take. No fuss, keep it simple, play it straight.

FIGURE 11.1 The brain: does what it says on the side

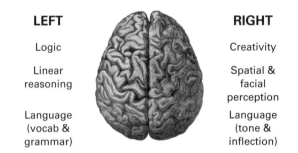

LEFT		RIGHT
Logic		Creativity
Linear reasoning		Spatial & facial perception
Language (vocab & grammar)		Language (tone & inflection)

Brand names conceived of logically reasoned, left-brain thinking invariably highlight a product attribute, or hark to their founders.

Product-based examples:

- Hotmail, as it included the letters 'HTML'.
- Sony, from the Latin word *sonus* meaning sound.
- Nikon (Nippon Kogaku), meaning 'Japanese optical'.
- Skype, from sky-peer-to-peer.
- Pepsi, from the digestive enzyme pepsin.
- Volkswagen, meaning 'people's car', so named in response to Adolf Hitler's want for 'cars for the masses'.
- Post-it, as in what you do with it, a brand name going straight after ownership of the verb.

Founder-based examples:

- Mattel, from founders Harold 'Matt' Matson and Elliot Handler.
- Adidas, the nickname of founder Adolf 'Adi' Dassler.
- DKNY, perhaps a brainwave while Donna Karan was once shopping in New York?

A brand's name is telling of the mind from which it came. The French chose to name one of their Citroën cars the *Picasso*, associating with one of the most inspirational painters of the 20th century. By stereotyping contrast, the Germans make the *Kompressor* available on some of their Mercedes models, denoting a turbocharger where air is compressed into the engine.

FIGURE 11.2 Brands and their 'brain-side'

THE NEXT FLUGELBINDER

A friend of mine, Adrian, broke away from agency life a good few years back to become an inventor and manufacturer. The idea of making something really appealed to him, as it of course does to many of us. There was, I suspect, also a 'get rich, and ideally quick' motive in the mix. Again, nothing wrong with that.

Over a beer in Wimbledon village one weekday evening in November, Adrian first pitched his idea to me, laid out the prototype and some early draft advertising.

'*Now try not to laugh…*'

A helluva way to start, particularly if you don't want someone to laugh.

'*This is either the most rubbish idea in the world…*' Adrian continued, as I thought, he maybe needs to work on his scene-setting, '*… or there's such a simple genius in it that it might just work.*'

Adrian has the touch of a young Hannibal Smith about him, a positive sunny belief that his plan will come together. He then showed me this small piece of transparent rubber, coin-sized, folded back on itself. It goes over the back of women's shoes, he explained, sits on the edge, to prevent an ankle blister. The name, he then added, with nice pause and gentle drama,

Shoelips. The adcepts Adrian spread across the table actually revealed *Shulips*, a trendy bit of spelling going on, taking it closer to tulips.

Adrian has now successfully taken his product to market, though the 'get rich quick' part remains a slower-burning work-in-progress.

I still don't know whether the world really needs Shulips, whether Adrian will become the next fluggelbinder billionaire, or if it's the kind of daffy enterprise that would get you fired on *The Apprentice*... but the name rocks. The name, I love. It makes me smile and (while on a miniscule level) I think the world is a *better* place for having the name *Shulips* in it.

BRANDS ARE THE PERFECT THOUGHTCRIME

Lewis Carroll's poem 'Jabberwocky' gave us 'chortle' and 'galumphing'. Two words, once upon a time 'nonsense', now bona fide.

The 'name' – a name, *any name* – is an opportunity to create additional layers of meaning. Lots of brands are 'nonsense names', out of which, over time, sense is made. People learn what a thing is. Lego, Accenture, Google, Pepsi, adidas – any name has the potential to work, so long as the product has the desirable chops.

Ultimately, there's really no such thing as non-words. A word either exists or it doesn't, and if a word is conceived and catches on, if it captures the imagination and drops into common usage, then it becomes a real word. New words, new meanings, new interpretations – 'neologism' is the word for it, though Dahl would have likely come up with something more rhyming.

One of the singularly most evil and terrifying thoughts I've ever read about comes courtesy of George Orwell's *1984*. *Newspeak*. Absolute iron-fist totalitarian control through the death of words. Take away the word for 'freedom', for 'rebellion', and it's so much harder to do it. To starve language; ultimately, to reduce understanding, through the removal of words that allow you to explain and express. The destruction of what it is to be human. To me, about as ghastly as it gets.

Brands are the opposite of Newspeak. In Newspeak, brands would be thoughtcrime on the broadest revolutionary scale. I love that. Brands are one-word bundles of all kinds of meanings. Their meanings are expansive, not reductive. Brands are born of invention, are neologism *expressed*. Figuratively, literally, brands can have a lot of 'OO' in them.

GROSS ASSUMPTIONS, CRUMBY CONVENTIONS AND THE CHURCHILLIAN VIEW

> " You get conventional brands.
> You get conventional advertising sectors. Typically they sit within that world of risk-aversion, of uncertainty and easy doubt, populated by journeymen and dullards.
> Coventions are the play-it-safe default that steps in the way of invention. "

> *Convention – noun*
> *a rule, method, or practice established by usage; custom.*
>
> SOURCE: DICTIONARY.COM

For me, an exposing definition. I thought *convention* would have more going for it. I'd have guessed there would have been some nod to best practice, understood *wisdom*, practices validated by past success. But no. The dictionary defines with no such glowing testimonies.

Convention is just as practised by a lot of people. Copied, replicated, mimicked, repeated. It's *same behaviour x 2*. The hope is that it's a smart behaviour, making for an impressive and proven convention – but that's one further and quite gross assumption.

Hey, it's a convention! It must *be the right thing to do! How could so many people be wrong?*

Of course, we know the answer to that one. We know that any amount of people can be wrong. Aggregate doesn't equal right. Aggregate just equals volume. And given that most pioneers have names – are individuals as opposed to steering committees and working groups – it's quite reasonable to propose that conventions are time-honoured practices in repetition, 'pioneering' little more than 'more-of-the-same'.

Yes, we've all taken a vote and we've decided to do the same thing again. Just like last time.

Well done all.

Conventions get in the way of invention. Invention is applying smarts, ingenuity, challenge to every and any given set of customs. Invention is that *want* to make something better, or at least try to, by challenging the status quo. Conventions uphold the status quo.

SOCIAL MASKS AND INSTITUTIONAL ADVERTISING

You get conventional brands, you get conventional advertising sectors. They sit within that world of risk aversion, of uncertainty and easy doubt, populated by journeymen and dullards. Conventions are the play-it-safe default.

Business-to-business (B2B) is one advertising sector where 'conventions' tend to be the order of most, and typically every day. In B2B, mould-breaking doesn't come easy, while conveyor-belt thinking is a customary walk in the park en route to possible promotion.

> *There is nothing sacred about convention; there is nothing sacred about primitive passions or whims; but the fact that a convention exists indicates that a way of living has been devised capable of maintaining itself.*
>
> GEORGE SANTAYANA

B2B advertising is a business that ticks over quite nicely, rocks few apple carts, instead spends a good while talking golf over expense-account lunches. For many of its practitioners, nothing feels particularly broken about the aforementioned kind of existence, and why should it? As Santayana observes, it is a way of living capable of maintaining itself.

Just occasionally, however, naming and shaming is a good thing, and this is such an occasion.

Flick through *Time, Business Week, The Economist,* or better still, go deeper into any business category, say grab yourself a copy of *Institutional Investor, IFR, Euromoney* or *Asiamoney,* and it's an advertising world of image and sentiment-based clichés. The financial services sector is guilty of many a malpractice. The advertising it briefs and buys has perhaps less consequence than sub-prime mezzanine-tranches, but it's still a guilty howler.

Too often in B2B advertising, brands forget the first principle, that they're still advertising to real people, to human beings. There's an odd assumption that because the advertising is talking professional-to-professional, it needs to be so much more serious, dry, ultimately 'more professional' than consumer advertising. It needs to be advertising *with reserve.* As if when people have their 'work hats' on their 'work heads', they're not the same people but are their 'professional versions', wearing masks of respectability and control, their behaviour measured and interactions managed. As if people then leave their desks and become unchecked, anarchic free agents amorally embracing each and every first impulse.

Okay, maybe some do, but you get what I'm saying.

Up to a point, in the Jungian sense, people do wear masks, but as the saying also goes, *'people are all warmed by the same sun and cooled by the same breeze'.*

Advertising must always be conscious of context, but where it speaks to the mask and not the person behind the mask, it will inevitably be guilty of falsity and deceit, its truth and humanity lost.

> We wear the mask that grins and lies,
> It hides our cheeks and shades our eyes,
> This debt we pay to human guile;
> With torn and bleeding hearts we smile,
> And mouth with myriad subtleties.
>
> 'WE WEAR THE MASK', PAUL LAURENCE DUNBAR (1872–1906)

From the B2B back-catalogue of print advertising, corporate personas and hollow truths are consistently de rigueur. The vast majority of examples fall into or span across one of four 'time-honoured' clichés – but in each case 'the institution' pushes advertising that merely provides paint and shape to its 'corporate masks'.

Cliché 1: skyscraper symbolism

FIGURE 12.1 Thrusting skyscrapers and high-fliers

Here we have *divine* skyscrapers, cathedrals to the worship of capitalism, spiking towards the heavens, doing as they say: 'scraping the sky'.

Here we have, *thrusting* skyscrapers, visual metaphors for the most vital symbol of male vitality. You can't rise too tall or be too big. The semiotics are not too subtle. This is advertising for men, produced by men. It doesn't come much more testosterone-packed, making for advertising that's as female-catered as a lap dancing club.

And for that extra little bit of ego-stroking, Credit Suisse choose to point out that their big-swinging high-flyers leave by helicopter. High-flyers, helicopters; oh dear, that clearly wasn't one of the better brainstorms.

Similarly, Credit Suisse's global strapline serves as proof that, in the wrong hands, a pen can be a truly dangerous thing. '*Thinking New Perspectives*' is about as clear to the ear as a Penrose triangle is to the eye. It barely makes sense.

Cliché 2: multiculturalism and handshakes

FIGURE 12.2 Ethnicity and visual cliché

I find the word 'internationalist' about as naff as these two print examples from Ernst & Young and Morgan Stanley. Where HSBC completely nails it with empathetic, imaginative, personable advertising fizzing from its '*World's Local Bank*' proposition, the above lives in that whole other world of painful visual clichés, of handshakes and studiously interlaced fingers, of boardroom smiles and Eastern skin tones. High Fives appear the only gesture omitted. In its over-effort to avoid being patronizing, it achieves the very opposite.

Let's move on.

Cliché 3: customer-centricism

FIGURE 12.3 Clients first

Capitalism is, by definition, self-interest. The cry that banking is a service-based industry that puts its clients first – makes them any kind of priority – rings absurdly hollow.

Imagine you're looking at a man who's grown the biggest beard in the world, and you're being told he uses Gillette every day. As Malcolm X more pointedly put it, '*You show me a capitalist; I'll show you a bloodsucker.*'

Of course, banks and their money-loaning clients have a *shared* interest, are bloodsuckers *united* in their lust for generating wealth. UBS might try to argue that '*real client commitment*' is about something other than shared bloodsucking, but I'm with Malcolm X on this.

We are further invited: '*Look into the centre of Barclays Capital and you'll find our clients.*'

From appearances, in the *centre* of Barclays Capital is a big dark atrium... into which, from a great height, it suggests they push their clients.

Cliché 4: literalism and deflection

FIGURE 12.4 Trust and 'fine-tuning'

I just love the idea of a Russian investment bank called '*Trust*'. I marvel even more at the idea that 'Trust Investment Bank' can run a press ad with copy that runs to a single word. '*Results*'. It's neither the subtlest nor the most sophisticated hook and bait I've ever seen.

Sometimes 'enough said' *isn't* enough. This is one of those times. Two words don't simply make it so. For me, there's a subtext here that screams its opposite, suggests prefixes such as '*Don't*' and '*Questionable*'.

By contrast, the way Julius Bär 'fine-tunes' their spectrum of financial products is either so (a) complicated, (b) dull, (c) both a & b: they use the manufacture of Mercedes cars to draw a deflective parallel. In fairness, I think this ad is quite charming, featuring Bernd Pletschen, the head of acoustics at Mercedes Benz, and his pursuit of 'perfect harmony'. But doesn't this ad say more about Mercedes Benz, and that bankers appreciate high-end automotive? And might it not further imply that Julius Bär thinks that what they do is simply a subject too boring to make decent advertising from?

FROM BAD TO BETTER

There are good, successful, high-performing examples of B2B brand advertising.

Great while it lasted: Accenture and Tiger Woods

When Tiger Woods's multiple infidelity scandal broke in late 2009, Accenture were the first major sponsor to walk, on the reasonable enough grounds that he was '*no longer the right representative*'.

Pre-scandal, however, Woods had been very much the *right* representative for Accenture, driving home their '*integrity*' and '*high performance*' values, and generating huge brand awareness and enquiries. Accenture's airport media was and remains choicely bought, securing key panels as close as possible to the in-terminal footfall of first-class and business-class flyers.

Quiet contemplation: Kaupthing bank

Another example of highly effective advertising... before it then went horribly wrong: Kaupthing bank.

Kaupthing bank ran a three-year campaign of single-page and double-page press executions, complemented with airport posters, that helped build their reputation as a thoughtful, considered, Icelandic investment house. The artwork sailed close to that of luxury brands, with a brand voice that asserted quiet power, implying that contemplation and inner dialogue was to account for Kaupthing's 'unconventional' and hugely lucrative approach to the money markets.

The advertising was a very direct and deliberate counter to any suggestion that Kaupthing were 'a bunch of Viking deal junkies'. History ultimately had the final say.

Actions over ads: Deutsche Bank and M&S

Brand actions typically speak louder than their press ads. Doing the right thing, for seemingly the right reasons, that's when B2B advertising really sings. By example, Deutsche Bank's cultural patronage of the Berliner Philharmoniker and the Frieze Art Fair (London) makes all the right kind of associations and sends the right kind of messages.

Consider further the scale and ambition of M&S's *Plan A*.

FIGURE 12.5 Quiet contemplation: Kaupthing bank

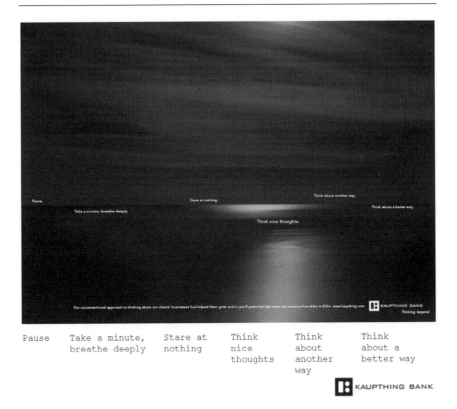

| Pause | Take a minute, breathe deeply | Stare at nothing | Think nice thoughts | Think about another way | Think about a better way |

KAUPTHING BANK

From the UK high street stalwart, Plan A was a £200 million environmental action plan; a bold, no-compromise, five-year commitment to sustainability, instigated by the then Chief Executive Stuart Rose at the beginning of 2007. At launch, it was toasted by all. 'The most progressive project of its kind by a mainstream retailer in the UK', hailed the *Guardian* newspaper (15 January 2007).

Plan A was M&S getting its house in order, a root-to-branch review of operations, declaring that it was doing its bit at least to make things better. Bravely, it was also an *outside-in* declaration, going public, making it 'real by announcement' and then trying to get on with the business of making it all happen. But I think Plan A always came from a sincere place; M&S and Rose really seemed to give a damn. By consequence, B2B brand-building was a tasty fringe benefit for the company.

*

Accenture, Kaupthing, Deutsche Bank, M&S, these guys are all convention-breakers. For each of them, it started with taking a risk. And risk-taking was, of course, first a decision they had to take, where the downside was failure – that dreaded of things, where people get to shake their heads, smirk, laugh, condescend you for daring to try something different.

Let me ask you this: *is disapproval such a big deal?* Some of that chorus and condescension will stem from the sheer fact that someone had the gumption to have a go, to dare to be different. Cowards love to criticize; the failures of others helps take the sting from their own fears and apprehensions.

Failure isn't something to be encouraged. But endeavour is. Failure is painful, but it should never be made to feel fatal. Even when a man stumbles, he at least continues to move forwards. It's progress of a kind. The occasional stumble seldom merits ridicule.

THE WORLD MUST ROLL FORWARD

It's telling how certain words get partnered with others. One word gets buddied with another. These are *word-play conventions*, no less. There's an association, an implicit transference of meaning, from which assumptions can start to sound like customs, and quickly can turn into rules.

'Time-honoured' conventions, two buddies right there, a common pairing, one happily helping out the other. Implication: conventions are something to *honour*, something folk have been honouring for a while now. So there's something to it. All those people doing it. For so long now.

I think and argue otherwise. 'Acknowledged' conventions, maybe? I could live with that tag team. I'll happily give convention a nod if I pass one on the street. *Acknowledge*, yes, but I'm not about to start *honouring*.

Honouring conventions is a nonsense pairing, like near-miss or friendly fire. A near-miss is an almost hit. Friendly fire still involves being hit by a bullet. Nice try, but I don't buy it. And I'm not buying advertising conventions either.

Conventions, customs – they're fine up to a point. They have a place, but they should also *know* their place. One man's comfort-blanket of tradition is another man's straightjacket. Every age has its rebels and misfits, its apparent follies and abject heresies.

The world was once flat, something you could sail over the edge of, if the leviathans didn't get you first. Then it was round, something for the Sun to revolve around, until Galileo discovered otherwise. Leeches cleaned the blood, later came penicillin.

Not so long ago, I remember being told that eggs were evil, spiked your cholesterol, that they sat in the bad-ass column up there with al-Qaeda and WMDs (weapons of mass destruction). Then eggs were our friends again, full of protein and vitamins, and all the previous was hogwash, forgiven and forgotten.

People, particularly en masse, can show real talent for parroting nonsense. Lemmings are very adept at jumping off cliffs. There's much to be said for the opposing view.

> *A love for tradition has never weakened a nation, indeed, it has strengthened nations in their hour of peril; but the new view must come, the world must roll forward.*
>
> SIR WINSTON CHURCHILL, SPEECH,
> HOUSE OF COMMONS, 29 NOVEMBER, 1944

'*The new view must come, the world must roll forward.*' Mr Churchill knew his mousetraps.

YOU ARE YOUR OWN MOUSETRAP

> " Successful brands know what they are. They are consistent. Deliberate when being inconsistent. They stand for something. They command loyalty and enthusiasm. People who buy into *their* brands do so passionately. Successful brands have fans and following. Successful brands are *winners…* and I'd argue that they are *happy brands*. Now who wouldn't want to be like that? "

I n my twenties I wrote a novel about being in your twenties. I'd moved to London; the novel was set in London. It wasn't autobiographical, but it was close to home in the way you can only write about what you know, and if you try and fake it, it comes out fake.

I was playing with the idea that your twenties are a time when you typically think you know everything, but know pretty much nothing. By consequence, you learn a lot, discover a lot, slowly come to gain some kind of appreciation as to the sense and scale of all the things you don't know.

I'm not trying to pitch the book to you, and this isn't the gratuitous plug you might suspect it of being. Truly. If you've read this far, I imagine we have an understanding by now.

My novel was about 'understanding', that we're on a lifelong journey to understand ourselves, others, the world around us, how it all works. I rather prescribe to the line, the older I get the less I sometimes feel I know. And that's not because I'm forever forgetting stuff, but because I'm only ever discovering more of the iceberg that sits above the water line. And I know what that means. Beneath the water lies the unknown majority that in absolute terms is even bigger than I'd previously thought. The average iceberg sits a good 80 to 90 per cent below the surface, in case you were wondering.

All the world may well be a stage, as Shakespeare 'metaphored' it, but it's a bloody big one. Actually, more like infinite. And in all our seven stages, as Shakespeare cited it, we change, evolve, grow, grow older and old, and I wager that there's a crazy amount to learn in each stage along the way. About ourselves, about others, about how it all works; about all the players upon this stage of ours and all those parts being played.

You can't understand *advertising*, understand *brands*, have any real clue, without committing yourself to the never-ending pursuit of understanding people (or at least trying to) and, within that, the pursuit of understanding yourself (again, at least trying to).

WE CAN LEARN A LOT FROM BRANDS

Advertising is about happiness – the suggestion of happiness – derived through purchase, through ownership, through affiliation to something. That happiness might be short-lived, but that's okay. Any dose of 'happy', over any time frame, is a gift and a good thing. The 'big H' (see page 174), that's what we're all after. 'All' in the sense that advertising is a very human discipline. It's why brands mirror people, assume human dimensions. Brands have physical attributes, are bundles of emotional meaning. They look to strike a rapport *with* people, their consumers, and seek acknowledgement and approval *from* consumers. Brands are created in our image; created by people, for people; wealth creation through *want* creation.

Looking at this in reverse, I think people are brands too. You. Me. Every one of us. A brand. The brand that is *you*. I think we can learn a lot from brands and branding, in order to learn a lot about ourselves.

Now some will latch on to this idea – '*You are a brand*' – with great enthusiasm. Others may feel it's somehow wrong, that it sounds like an affectation. *I'm not a brand, I'm a human being!*

I say you're both. I say that brands are very human things, and there needn't be anything contrived about any of it. In fact, I think it can be very healthy to think about yourself as a brand. (A little time in contemplation, given over to some personal honesty in the name of truer self-awareness can only be a good thing, whatever the supposition.)

CONSIDER THIS

Successful brands know what they are. They are consistent; they are very deliberate when being seemingly inconsistent. They stand for something. They command loyalty and enthusiasm. People who buy into *their* brands do so passionately, whether it's a brand denoted by an apple with a bite mark, a French crocodile, a five-pointed crown, or a white-and-blue rotating propeller honouring the Bavarian national flag.

Successful brands are *winners*. They have fans and following. I would argue that successful brands are happy brands. They are successful by being true to themselves and genuine with others. The love they receive from their consumers is genuine in return.

Now...

Who wouldn't want to be like that? Who wouldn't want to be like any successful brand? Who doesn't want to be more effective? Who doesn't want to be more effective at finding happiness?

This throws up some interesting questions:

 Do you know who you are?

 Do other people know who you are?

 Do people buy into you?

 How easily can you win people over?

 What are the headline ideas that you stand for and stand by?

Do you feel your actions and behaviours are genuine and authentic to who you are?

 Do you have a fan base of loyal loving friends, who genuinely love you for you?

What is your brand? Is it clear to you, is it clear to others?

How would others describe you?

How would you like others to describe you?

Much like a brand, you have a set of physical attributes, and you are perceived and judged and defined by others based on these. The same goes for how you talk, what you say, how you carry yourself, how you *project*. Again, these define you to others.

Given all this, given judgement and definitions are going to happen anyway, you might as well take control, ensure that what you do and say is on-brand and on-message, to build and re-enforce any definition of *you* that will make you most happy.

And then here comes the million dollar question: *do you know what makes you happy?*

I think branding yourself can help.

THE POWER OF BRANDING

> *Right from the beginning, I said I wanted to be more famous than Persil Automatic.*
>
> VICTORIA BECKHAM, *LEARNING TO FLY,*
> *THE AUTOBIOGRAPHY* (2001)

Posh Spice is one smart cookie. It's said that, in Japan, Coca-Cola is the most recognizable foreign word; 'Beckham' is the second. Spice Girl, football player, fragrance, fashion designer – it all helps fuel and refuel the Beckham brand, a brand that's estimated to be worth £145 million.

The fact is, highly successful people know, and are very conscious of, *their brand*. They understand their physical and emotional attributes, know their headlines, what they propose to the world, what they project. And they know *how* to project it.

Across social media, personal branding is becoming part of the mainstream. We see more and more people shaping their online identities, controlling the messages and impressions they put out there. They're building, defining, honing their brand. They are their own PR machines and spin doctors.

Branding is powerful stuff. It wields consequence, and when applied expertly, it creates powerful outcomes.

Saatchi & Saatchi became a UK household name, an agency your granny might have heard of. It brought fame to the industry of advertising through its role in influencing political history, by helping put Thatcher's Conservative Party into office in 1979. Saatchi's 'Labour isn't working' poster is hailed as a watershed moment in political advertising.

Alastair Campbell, spin doctor extraordinaire, picked up where the Saatchis left off. He acknowledged the potential, observed the rules, then moved the game on. Public influence... through media manipulation... through powerful branding. Campbell served as Director of Communications and Strategy within Tony Blair's Labour government from 1997 to 2003. Blair served as British Prime Minister from 1997 to 2007, and big brains like Blair and Campbell made sure that for as long as it could be spun, Labour *was* working. While it lasted, they were the Sun Tzu of sound bites, genius at being quotably 'on-message'. New Labour was a brand, The Third Way a headline proposition, both incredibly simple, designed to gain media traction, be 'catchy', and capture the public imagination.

I believe that thinking about *yourself* as a brand is very self-informing and, more importantly, can be a powerfully self-improving idea. It can work for political parties, and it can work for individuals. Applying brand-thinking will sharpen you, make you more effective, allow you to shake off the old aspects of yourself that didn't work so well, and amplify those elements that will help you succeed and be happy.

Hollywood movie stars are very aware of their brand potential, and (helped by their agents) are amongst the Svengali Masters of personal branding. To illustrate by way of opposite, look what happens when it goes wrong. Everything quickly goes horribly so, gets shaky and flaky in an instant. Jumping up and down on Oprah Winfrey's couch, Scientology: for Tom Cruise this stuff is painfully, awkwardly off-brand. Cruise doesn't play characters that 'lose it'. Coughlin's Law, *'never lose your cool'*, that's *on-brand* for Maverick: how people want to see him determines whether they want to see him take on another 'impossible mission'.

Now I'm not saying that Tom Cruise, or anyone else, should be two-dimensional. I'm not saying that building your brand self is somehow limiting. Far from it, and quite the opposite in fact.

What I'm saying is that everyone should consider their personal brand, all their brand's positive qualities, how they can fit together, and how as a consequence they can extend their brilliance.

BRING YOUR SELVES TOGETHER

Brands are multifaceted, just like people.

Straight-laced, buttoned-down accountant by day, party girl by night.

QC on the one hand, author of beach-read legal-eagle thrillers on the other.

A percentage-playing hedge fund manager whose cognition rolls on tramlines, with an obliquely intuitive understanding and appreciation of metaphysical poetry.

These kinds of people exist. Incongruous *selves* in one biological package, they are *not* contradictions. They are folk with differing qualities within each of their personas and, I would argue, different facets to their intriguing personal brands.

I discussed this idea with one colleague (quite recently, in fact), about how we could – *should* (in some cases actually do) – spend time on our personal brands. His response, 'Actually, I've got two brands. The me at work, the client-handler, what I do by day. And the other me. The graffiti artist.'

I knew he was also a graffiti artist. What I found curious is how he's a pretty mild-mannered, thoughtful, runs-deep, better at second-impressions kind of guy. And not that the 'graffiti artist' thing becomes a contradiction I can't then square away. More so, if you see his tag, his graffiti artist 'brand', the instantly impressive *first-impression* it creates, and you see his work – on his website, all over Flickr, blogged about, used commercially, commissioned for private collections – a niggling feeling takes hold that he's only being half-as-excellent as he could be.

This guy's graffiti artist alter ego is a strong flavour, edgily cool, and could really go places. By contrast, his day job self is doing... okay, ticking boxes, ticking over, but one doesn't smell early burning from any kind of sense that he's going to start some serious trailblazing. Now I'm not being mean, I like this guy, and I told him what I was thinking.

'I don't really spend any time on my personal brand', he acknowledged.

'But you've clearly put a lot into your other identity, as a graffiti artist.'

'Oh yes', he admitted. 'Lots.'

'Imagine if you were to focus on both, or just bring them together? What might happen then? What might you achieve?'

YOUR PERSONAL BRAND CAN START TODAY

I don't think there's any superficiality to this way of thinking, of spending time on and investing in your personal brand. Brands that succeed run deep. Brands that succeed are *true* to what they are. Even more, those brands that continue to succeed move with the times, as they move through time. Just like we all do. Invention, reinvention, improvement. Good words. Words that describe the human condition at its healthiest, at its adaptive best.

Developing your brand, layering it, adding meaning, but also decluttering it, maybe reinventing it, stripping away the negative attributes, amplifying the positive ones, it's all just an idea, but it's a proactive one, I think, which may just help on that path we all walk along of learning and under-standing. As a way of looking at yourself, I believe it will create personal momentum. I believe it will create clearer thinking. I believe it will create clarity of purpose.

Clarity, purpose, momentum: it's not a bad way to walk a path.

Take what Anthony Robbins has to say about getting stuck in, looking forwards and knowing about what matters:

> If you want to succeed in your life, remember this phrase: The past does not equal the future. Because you failed yesterday; or all day today; or a moment ago; or for the last six months; the last sixteen years; or the last fifty years of life, doesn't mean anything... All that matters is: What are you going to do, right now?

You are your own mousetrap, one that can liberate or limit you, one that can trap or release you.

I'll say it again.

You are your own mousetrap, and you can be a better one.

PART TWO

IN PURSUIT OF THE ACCELERATED CONSUMER

INTRODUCTION

> " The *fundamentals* will always slow The Accelerated Consumer in his tracks, cause us all to stand and stare; our want for material possessions, our possession and passing on of heirlooms, our want to leave a legacy; our base sexual drives, our wish to be the superior versions of ourselves; our desire to be happy, as an emotion and an idea, that ultimate phantasm. "

JOHN ANDERTON
Everybody runs.

Minority Report (2002)

The running man: I've always found the running man to be an incredibly evocative image.

A motif with all manner of potential meanings.

Running.

Running *towards* something.

Running *away* from something. Being chased. Driven by fear, the threat of capture maybe. Or more hopefully, being driven by one's self, to progress, succeed, to improve; the thing that *drives* not being a threat from behind but a goal in front, the horizon. A burning want to improve, this being mankind's perpetual forward motion.

Bannister breaking the four-minute mile (6 May 1954); Bolt devouring 100 metres in 9.58 seconds (16 August 2009).

Mankind. By brilliant example. Achieving. Always running. And always getting faster.

But don't get me wrong. Being the running man isn't all good. It just *is*, where *accelerated* is a very good word for defining our 'now', because it's what we all are doing, whether we like it or not: accelerating.

I suspect most of us are in a hurry most of the time. I suspect most of us feel rushed. I suspect few of us feel all the way in control of the haste and pace and to-do lists around us and the speed at which, complicit as we are, we race through our every day.

Digital technologies further play their part in hastening this world of ours, providing instant access and real-time digital interactions, feeding instant appetites and immediate gratifications.

Pause. Reflection. Contemplation. Patience, even. I'm not suggesting they're dying practices, but they don't feel very fashionably of the 'now'.

There is little in life that is getting slower. We don't find ourselves with more time to think, stop or stare. The poet William Davies may rightly ask, '*What is this life (if) we have no time to stand and stare?*' But the answer is pretty straightforward. A damned busy one. That's what *this* life is. That's the truth of it, whether you find that to be a sad reality or otherwise. And set against this sociocultural backdrop that's blurry, as if we're rocketing by in a bullet train, we have *brands*, their advertising asking that we pay attention, asking for our time. And we're so accelerated all of the time that we have no time.

What chance do brands have within this helter-skelter and hurly-burly?

How can any brand keep up with the running man, with each of us? In a lifelong game of kiss chase, brands are forever chasing after consumers, those faithful and those would-be, but most of us, most of the time, are too busy being busy, too busy running.

It's likely that because our lives have less sense of pause or contemplation that as consumers we act with greater haste, basing decisions on headline information. In our sound-bite culture, befitting of lives lived in fast-forward, we hunt out headlines and peddle 'short-form content'. Long-form content arguably demands that all too precious commodity.

Give me the lift pitch. What's the 30-second version? You're losing me. You want my attention? You're going to have to earn it. You're going to have to grab *it!*

You know how it is, and for brands this all means one thing: the absolute need for simplicity and ruthless single-mindedness: in intention, comment and deed.

'Marketing communications' need to be clear, concise and wholly single-minded in their pursuit of consumer preference. Consumers want to know near-instantly what a brand stands for, its reason for being, and its role in the world. Precision is the thing, where for all brands the advice can only be, say less, *never* more.

Because saying more ultimately means saying *nothing*.

Say less *better* than everyone else, and that's a conquering brand, winning of hearts, minds and market share. There are new rules to the game, rules upon which brands can not only survive, but thrive. This is the stuff of Part Two.

But it's also only half the stuff, half the picture. Imagine, say, the image of a running man that's painted *over* an earlier painting, where beneath there's a 'ghost' painting, perhaps a landscape, a forest maybe that evokes an enchanting and fundamental stillness?

I was in Vienna one time (stick with me on this), not so long ago, where I visited an exhibition of artworks by René Magritte. Magritte was a surrealist who wrestled with conformity and, as a result, produced a lot of paintings of suited figures wearing bowler hats, the surrealist touch being they were often headless. At the exhibition, I came upon a quote, a great quote that gave happier insight into that which drove the man, beyond simple inner conflict and a dark childhood:

> *I hate resignation, professional heroism, and all obligatory*
> *suavities. I hate the decorative arts, folklore, and advertising.*
> *I hate the odour of naphthalene and the topicality of the present.*
> *I like subtle humour, freckles, long hair on women, the laughter*
> *of children, a girl running in the street. I wish for myself true love*
> *and the impossible. I long for phantasms.*
>
> RENÉ MAGRITTE

Magritte was a gentle surrealist. Not an iconoclast. The Dada guys wanted to replace the surrealist's banana with a well-aimed bazooka, but not René. I liked this particular quote so much because it feels so very real and honest. 'Like' and 'hate'. These are powerful, self-defining ideas, passions that drive, coming from deep inside. These are not fashionable ideas. They're *fundamentals*.

And where I'm going with all this, is this: the running man is still a man. Literally, we're talking genetic building blocks, but in *essence*, I think we're more looking at a brickwork of *needs*.

Because I don't believe people fundamentally change, in terms of their needs, what they want, what *motivates* them to do what they are always going to do. I don't think that Maslow's 'hierarcy of needs' needs updating for the digital age, or that Freud and Jung require a reboot. People are fundamentally wired the way they've always been wired, however fast they may currently be moving. Like Magritte, everyone longs for their version of long-haired girls with freckles. Everyone fancies after a particular idea of *something*, their own phantasms.

The *fundamentals* will always slow us down, can stop the accelerated consumer in his tracks, cause us all once again to stand and stare: our want for material possessions; our possession and passing on of heirlooms; our want to leave a legacy after we've shuffled off our mortal coil; our pursuit of instant gratification; our base sexual drives; our wish to be the superior versions of ourselves; our desire to be happy, as an emotion and an idea, that ultimate phantasm.

So we firmly remain in the land of constants and change, of 'change within the frame' (see 'Everything changes, everything stays the same', page ix), the stuff of Part Two being wholly about how two overlaying images sit within a frame, how fundamental human needs are addressed and satiated by brands reacting to ever-changing contexts.

If you're reading this, you've found the time. And I appreciate what that's worth. With hope, may it meet some kind of need, even if then following this brief moment of pause it may help you to run that bit faster.

WE ARE ALL CONSUMERS

> " There's nothing very voodoo about consumer understanding.
>
> I think insightful consumer understanding typically comes from being un-clinical, from being emotive.
>
> Great agency planners have to draw on raw first-hand experiences, on 'feel' and intuition, of head, heart and gut. "

once had a lively debate with a pretty high-profile industry commentator who continues – good on him – to make a happy living teaching MBA modules, writing articles and giving lectures on most things marketing.

He argued (no doubt still does) – that the moment you work in marketing – on any side of the corporate/agency divide, but where you're ultimately mixed up in the big selling machine – then at that point in time... 'you' and 'the consumer' forever divide. Like a split atom.

His stance was that once you're working 'on the inside', a practitioner in the dark arts of persuasion, you forgo all rights to simply *being* a consumer. All past man-on-the-street innocence and naivety are lost for good. You sit *behind* the mirror, and *they* sit in focus groups, a circle of mysterious abstract alien beings.

Ah, look, do you see, there's one, 'a consumer'!

I said I thought that was bollocks. And I still do.

There's nothing very voodoo about consumer understanding. I think *insightful* consumer understanding typically comes from being *un-clinical*, from being emotive. Great planners know people, like people, *want* to know people, want crucially to know them better. They want to know about foibles, quirks and traits, about motivations, about the internal swirl of anxieties, fears, hopes and dreams; they want to better understand the things that can round the shoulders and leave someone skulking; they want to understand what puffs a chest and makes a person walk a little taller.

Great planners are *people people* and they have to draw on raw first-hand experiences and encounters, on 'feel' and intuition – of head, heart and gut – in order to then make the empathetic leaps they make.

How can you build a brand, come up with a great campaign thought, a killer social media idea, make any of it compelling, and believe deep down that your ideas are really good and really going to work... if you can't first empathize with your audience? I don't see how it's possible.

When I buy one brand over another, I do it as a consumer. When I smile at a great ad, get hooked in to what a brand is up to, cheer at the smarts involved, I initially smile and cheer just as anyone else would. Any appreciation and professional level of understanding... that comes after.

Folk who work inside the selling machine, they may be better equipped to unpick and dissect what an ad says and why it's doing what it's doing, but I believe we're all prone to the sucker punch and purchase when we see something that rings our bell.

Robert McKee, the guy who wrote *the* book on how to write a screenplay (*Story: Substance, Structure, Style, and the Principles of Screenwriting*) gladly admits that when he sits down in the dark and those opening credits roll, he's prone to enjoy a movie and experience just the same ride as the next guy. His knowledge of theory doesn't get in the way of his inner child, he's as bewitched by movie magic as anyone else.

Advertising / comms / account / brand / digital planners – whatever the prefix – all planners need to have heart, not clinical detachment. They cannot be at a remove, looking down from on high, urging the mouse along the maze. It's not how you build a mousetrap. If you cannot *relate*, or cannot at least try hard to relate, you're surely in the wrong business?

Please. Always consider the mouse's view.

IN STRANGERS WE TRUST

" 'Who's there left to trust?'

The answer has reflexively become...

'Anyone just like me.'

Y'know; ordinary, nice, normal, everyday people with no ulterior motive or hidden agenda. "

You win a brand war by winning hearts and minds and you win those hearts and minds by stimulating 'comment and conversation'.

Everyone at the front, and at the back; yes, we're all smiling in agreement.

The original 'one-to-many' advertising model naturally assumed the 'one' to be the brand, and *what it had to say for itself*. 'One-to-many' *still* holds as a conversation and influence path, only the 'one' is now 'the vocal consumer'.

You could argue that ours is a *post-naive world* (or at least a world that likes to believe it's not naive). 'Straight advertising' is received and digested like propaganda, *knowingly*, where the deal going in is that there's virtually nothing and no one left to trust, where you must always interrogate the source, and where every interest is vested. Institutions, banks, world leaders: it's all ill-gotten, where the lie–truth border has so blurred that it's fine to fib and call it 'spin'.

A bleak picture, perhaps, but it's surely *one picture* of the world today, and one that in relation to the question of, '*Who's there left to buy into?*', the answer has reflexively become... 'anyone just like me'. Read: ordinary, nice, normal, everyday people with no ulterior motive or hidden agenda.

A Nielsen Global Consumer Survey in 2009 found the following:

> *Opinions posted by consumers online are the most trusted forms of advertising globally. 90% of consumers worldwide trust recommendations from people they know; 70% trust consumer opinions posted online.*

For me, the above finding has two components: the blindingly obvious... and the actually quite remarkable!

People trust the opinions of people they know. I get that. They'd be some kind of sociopath if they didn't, but '*70% trust consumer opinions posted online*'! As in, 70 per cent of people trust the opinions of complete strangers, people who very easily could be complete idiots, as well as being completely sociopathic for all anyone knows.

FIGURE 15.1 Would you trust a complete stranger?

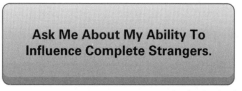

Average Customer Review: ★ ★ ★ ★ ☆

Who ludicrously suggested we live in a post-naive world? In reality, welcome to 'the new naivety', where you no longer have to earn trust, you just need to be any ordinary Joe with a keenness to comment through a keyboard.

FIGURE 15.2 AN Other is happy to post their opinion: do you trust it?

THE AGE OF THE ACCELERATED CONSUMER

> **"** More than ever
> before, 'Time' feels
> like it's bolted
> out the gates and
> building to
> break-neck.
>
> And we are right
> along with it,
> keeping pace,
> flying just as fast.
>
> How can brands
> 'create time', in
> a world where
> no one has much? **"**

> *Sed fugit interea fugit irreparabile tempus.*
>
> GEORGICS, VIRGIL

The long short: *time flies*. Actually, the closer translation is *time flees* (an interesting side bar for those so interested.):

> *But meanwhile it flees: time flees irretrievably, while we wander around.*

Flies, flees, same difference. Neither means insects, which would at least require a misspelling, and the *meaning* remains. More than ever before, 'time' does feel as if it has bolted out the gates and is building to break-neck. And we are right along with it, no longer wandering, but keeping pace, flying just as fast.

The following quote is from the well-known psychiatrist Ronald Laing (1927–89), who spent a lifetime studying the environmental triggers of mental illness (which is telling in itself)...

> *We live in a moment of history where change is so speeded up that we begin to see the present only when it is already disappearing.*

What I think Laing fundamentally means by this is that modern life too often feels like a constant bewildering blur. That everything is happening faster and faster. That it invariably feels like today is already out of date and tomorrow is already upon us, like we're getting to the future too soon, that we no longer find any time to stop and stare or contemplate.

Okay, let's all breathe. But it does sound rather familiar, doesn't it? I know you're with me on this one. I know because I have bar charts to prove it.

Really, take a look, these are actually quite good ones.

Figure 16.1 shows that it took 71 years for telephones to make their way into 50 per cent of homes. It took radios 28 years. It took MP3 players just six years. The speed at which we embrace new technologies is accelerating. Compared to the increasingly distant past, now we're all early adopters.

For me, there's a stat in Figure 16.3 that says so much. Suddenly given a 'spare 20 minutes', less than 5 per cent of us can find it in ourselves to 'just relax'. We struggle to switch off, prefer to remain ON, connected, tuned-in. We're culpable in all of this, all this speed and haste and growing blur.

FIGURE 16.1 Bar chart 1: the number of years taken for major technologies to reach 50 per cent of homes

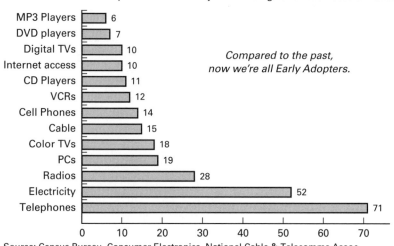

1. Pace of change (tech take-up) is accelerating

Number of years taken for major technologies to reach 50% of homes

Compared to the past, now we're all Early Adopters.

Source: Census Bureau, Consumer Electronics, National Cable & Telecomms Assoc.

FIGURE 16.2 Bar chart 2: we face a growing time famine

2. We face a growing time famine

% agreeing 'I never seem to have enough time to get things done'

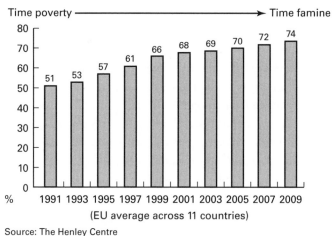

Time poverty ⟶ Time famine

(EU average across 11 countries)

Source: The Henley Centre

FIGURE 16.3 Bar chart 3: dead time... is officially dead

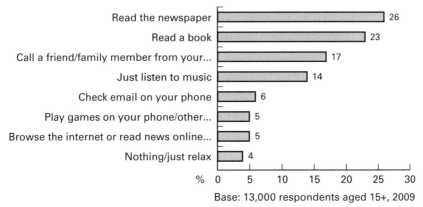

3. Dead Time is... Officially Dead

'If you had 20 minutes "to spare" while waiting for a bus/train, which of the following would you prefer to do in that time?'

% who would prefer to do the following

Activity	%
Read the newspaper	26
Read a book	23
Call a friend/family member from your...	17
Just listen to music	14
Check email on your phone	6
Play games on your phone/other...	5
Browse the internet or read news online...	5
Nothing/just relax	4

Base: 13,000 respondents aged 15+, 2009

Source: nVision, 2009

The late great George Carlin paints it best, better than any bar charts ever could, even good ones. Here, the first two paragraphs of a nine-paragraph soliloquy of comedic genius, entitled 'I am a Modern Man':

> *I'm a modern man, a man for the millennium. Digital and smoke free. A diversified multi-cultural, post-modern deconstruction that is anatomically and ecologically incorrect. I've been up linked and downloaded, I've been inputted and outsourced, I know the upside of downsizing, I know the downside of upgrading. I'm a high-tech low-life. A cutting edge, state-of-the-art bi-coastal multi-tasker and I can give you a gigabyte in a nanosecond!*
>
> *I'm new wave, but I'm old school and my inner child is outward bound. I'm a hot-wired, heat seeking, warm-hearted cool customer, voice activated and bio-degradable. I interface with my database, my database is in cyberspace, so I'm interactive, I'm hyperactive and from time to time I'm radioactive.*

So what does all this mean, what's George looking to say, what am *I* looking to say here? I'm bemoaning *what* exactly?

In truth, I'm not bemoaning anything, not giving anything 'the big neg'. I'm just saying this: getting attention isn't easy. People have less time to listen. In terms of commercial messages, they filter, edit, ignore more than ever before (see also 'Brands must behave, must woo', page 15).

As consumers, we're in an almost permanent state of acceleration.

As brand-builders, therefore, the question becomes: how can our commercial messages carry sufficient weight to stop the accelerated consumer in his tracks? Where consumers are constant motion, how can brands become immovable objects?

Nigel Morris, CEO of Aegis North America, puts it very simply and very shrewdly when he offers this on what brands should stop being and start being:

> *Stop interrupting what people like and want. Be what people like and want.*

I really like this thought. And I like the implications just as much. It means the marketing-communications model is facing an epic overhaul. From *push* marketing and interrupting people to *pull* marketing: to drawing people towards a brand with content and ideas that are attractive, sexy, curious and the kind of thing people naturally want. Because while so few of us feel we have any time these days, we still *find* time, when possible, to continue doing what we like and want.

SIMPLICITY, SOUND BITES AND COMING OVER ALL STURM UND DRANG

Even when a brand is something people like and want, how does it then ensure it's heard loud and clear?

I think the answer to how brands can effectively communicate to a fast-moving audience, an audience busy filtering so much competing brand noise, lies at the centre of three interlinking imperatives:

 The need for simplicity.

 The need for concision.

 The need, on occasions, to be provocative.

Simplicity

> *60% of Europeans agree when making an important decision there is too much information.*
>
> SOURCE: NVISION RESEARCH

We're all such wonderfully hypocritical contradictions. We love 'lots of choice', because we want to feel in control and unlimited. And yet, we hate 'choice overload'. Too much choice freaks us out, fries us, freezes us, brings on decision paralysis.

Tech brands and software-makers are becoming increasingly sensitive to how they present themselves, and ultimately in how they look to meet and resolve our want-more-want-less contradiction.

Take Bing, a good example. Behind the curtain, Bing is a wealth of complex calculations and algorithms and the latest search technology. In front of the curtain, it's a few words and, in the example below, a friendly family of meerkats. Bing's 'shop front' couldn't be more approachable (unless one suffers an inexplicable phobia of meerkats).

FIGURE 16.4 Bing's friendly shop front

Away from our screens, in physical 3-D form, more and more tech design is about 'complexity on the inside', with an external presentation that's friendly, human, welcoming and always boiling down the number of buttons.

John Maeda in his book *The Laws of Simplicity* (2006) toasts the iPod wheel as a design triumph in the ongoing pursuit of reduction and simplicity. Maeda's law: 'SHE' – shrink, hide and embody.

FIGURE 16.5 Maeda's law, 'SHE': shrink, hide and embody

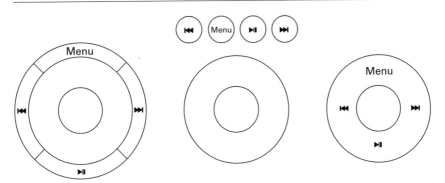

Sound bites

'Less is more' applies to words too. Delivering high-impact messages is about economy and precision. People may like reading novels and luxuriating in 'long form content', like motion pictures and TV season box sets, but our day-to-day lives are defined by headlines. It's single, snappy sentences that tend to move our world. We all like dealing sound bites, like school kids trading baseball cards. In our sped-up society, the ideas that influence and take hold are the ideas quickly told and easily retold. 'Catchy' is almost always good. Catchy catches on. Smart sound bites are so very spreadable.

> We devour pop culture the same way we enjoy candy;
> in conveniently packaged bite-size nuggets made to easily
> munch at maximum speed. This is snack culture.
>
> SOURCE: *WIRED* MAGAZINE (MILLER, 2007)

We're starting to see advertisers really responding to our accelerated world and lack of time. Microsoft's '8 second demo' campaign from 2010 was all about 'elevator pitching' us the benefits of Internet Explorer 8. Multiple

10-second TV spots, actors delivering to camera in a first person testimonial style, were favoured over the conventional 30- or 40-second launch ad format. Microsoft figured they might just be able to say more, and get more people to listen, if they gave themselves less time to say it.

The fact is – young and old, male and female, erudite or less so – we all love our headlines. We love quotable slogans. It's not that we wield the mental agility of goldfish. Simply, we are impatient, easily distracted and quite often lazy when effort or genuine concentration is asked of us.

In 1968, presidential candidate Robert Kennedy, in the midst of his campaign, startled his staff by saying he would rather have 30 seconds on the national evening news than a full-page ad in the *New York Times*. Robert Kennedy was ahead of the game and ahead of his time. The average political pitch ran to three minutes back in 1968. By 1988, that running time was down to one minute. By 2008, politicians were working their message to an average of 30 seconds. It seems only bad guys, evil geniuses and megalomaniacs 'monologue'. By contrast, politicians want to be heard, and they appreciate what that means.

Old-school cynics would, I imagine, glumly shake their heads at the death of discourse, the thought of political rhetoric being reduced to a car bumper sticker. I'd counter that such head-shaking is a deliberate refusal to move with the times.

Rhetoric can take many forms. It's only purpose, in whatever form, is to inspire and influence, to be *effective*:

> A speech can broaden the circle of people who care about this stuff. How do you say to the average person that's been hurting: 'I hear you. I'm there. Even though you've been so disappointed and cynical about politics in the past, and with good reason, we can move in the right direction. Just give me a chance.'
>
> JONATHAN FAVREAU (B. 1981), OBAMA'S DIRECTOR OF SPEECHWRITING

There is no question in my mind that Jonathan Favreau is a gifted, insanely clever guy who understands word-craft and the potential power of words. It is oddly ironic that one of the greatest successes of Obama's presidential campaign, an initiative that so embodied Favreau's stated view of politics and speech-writing, was a music video produced independently by Black Eyed Peas front man Will.i.am.

'Yes, We Can': the slogan, the song and the music video did not originate from the Obama camp, though the lyrics are all quotations from Obama's concession speech in the New Hampshire presidential primary, much of which was written by Favreau.

Released 2 February 2008 and uploaded to Dipdive.com and YouTube.com, by 22 July 'Yes, We Can' had been watched online more than 26 million times. 'Yes, We Can' subsequently became a secondary slogan for Obama's campaign.

Change. Hope. Obama. Those were the subtextual beats. 'Concision-in-action' became a different three words. But still just three words. 'Yes, We Can' showed that three words can make all kinds of difference. Rhetoric can be a music video, a way for politicians to say to someone hurting, 'I hear you'.

Sturm und Drang

Sturm und Drang, meaning *Storm and Urge*, was a counter-cultural movement that gained some following in Germany in the 18th century. It was a movement in literature, music and across the arts, which hailed 'subjectivity' and encouraged unchecked emotions, spontaneity and all the liberation that comes with not being stifled by rules, dogma and people trying to paint the world in black and white.

Aesthetic rationalism, empiricism, universalism, these were straight-jackets to the Sturm und Drang crowd, a bunch who just wanted to let their hair down and go a little crazy.

Feeling provoked through the presence of constraint, Sturm und Drang looked to provoke back, be a bit extreme, ensure it made an impression. How far apart is Sturm und Drang from shock and awe? I wouldn't say there's much in it.

In today's world I think there's a lot to be said for brands storming and urging and shocking and awing. I think in order to win, brands need to start from a place of already feeling provoked and needing to poke back.

I love how BBC World announced themselves when they launched in the US. To me, the outdoor work, as produced by BBDO New York, stormed. The central premise: 'see both sides of the story' – that BBC World represents balanced journalism that reports and debates both sides of the argument. Where the campaign got a little bit brilliant was in its use of posters depicting hot-topic issues, which *asked* those walking past them to vote with a text, to state upon which side of the fence they stood. Iraq: American imperialism or liberation? China: a new friend or eternal foe? Bird flu: avoidable or imminent?

FIGURE 16.6 BBC World: 'see both sides of the story' (2007)

Posters for BBC World stopped being posters for BBC World – 'a British news channel' – and instead became a mirror on the world, reflecting back the opinions of the people they advertised to.

Provocation, revelation, creating talking points and polarizing (see 'Curve, contour and come-on', page 134): sometimes brand invention is about rattling society in the smartest kind of way.

BRANDS NEED TO BE EVERYTHING, THEN MORE

Time is only ever going to continuing fleeing. I wish it wouldn't, but it's not something I have a say in. It's something we all have to deal with. Brands have to deal with it too, and have to move as fast as the consumers they're chasing.

For brands, I think the message is loud and very clear. Brands need to be loud and very clear. They need to be very concise, and be all about the benefits. And beyond being all these things, they have to be more besides. Brands have to stop trying to get *in the way* of consumers. They need instead to get in their cross-hairs. This is how a brand stops the accelerated consumer in his tracks. This is how brands 'create time', even in a world where no one has much time.

Brands need to ensure they are what we *like and want*: it's something to think on the next time your train is running 20 minutes late. Assuming, that is, you're not already doing something you like doing more.

THE BRAND COMMUNICATION MODEL: A BIT LIKE A TIME-TRAVELLING DELOREAN

" I love this idea,
that
Brand Communications
should be about
prompting
conversations,
which consumers will
then want to have…
with other consumers.

It's a really open-
ended-very-human-and-
who-knows-where-
we'll-end-up? kind
of idea. "

> MARTY MCFLY
> Are you telling me that you built
> a time-machine... out of a DeLorean?!
> *Back to the Future* (1985)

Every model can benefit from an upgrade. Very few designs, almost none, are timeless and at their evolutionary summit of perfection. Sharks... maybe sharks are one, but it's not a long list. In advertising, there's no model of such streamlined refinement as to be near-perfect. There's no one brand communication model that's the equivalent of *Jaws*.

Consider B2C, namely 'business to consumer', as a communication principle. It's one of the tablet-inscribed commandments of advertising. B2C, where a business has brands – brands that advertise, promote themselves to consumers who listen, hopefully go wide-eyed by what they hear and run out to the shops, *craving*. As models go, it's an okay one. It's simple and straightforward. It has more presumptive holes than a slice of Swiss cheese, but it's very logical, also like the Swiss.

Now 'success', as derived from the original B2C communications model, depends on a couple of heavy-duty assumptions:

1 that the brand message is a real thriller, exactly what people want to hear, delivering exactly what they need, meaning they'll be motivated to gladly crack open their wallets;

2 that consumers are *passive* enough to embrace said brand message, without question or recourse, and yet are *active* enough to then purchase as a consequence of it.

First, and for the record, old school B2C *can* work. Produce a dazzlingly brilliant enough piece of creative, a 90-minute spectacular on a production budget inevitably north of £1 million – the commercial equivalent of *Dr Zhivago* or *Lawrence of Arabia* – and then play it in the darkened hush of a movie theatre, on a massive screen with a thumping THX sound system, and sure, people are going to sit forward. Guinness's *Surfers* (1999) by AMV is one such example of brand film awesomeness.

Drop the audio, just go with static visual, and the likes of Wonderbra, *The Economist*, Silk Cut and Nike are sterling examples of poster genius that ably prove the merits of push-based advertising.

But let's face it, any creative genius is a point of exception, set against the dishevelled norm of mediocrity.

B2C WITH UPGRADES

B2C, as a *one-way brand monologue*, lives in the nice picket-fenced sub-urban homes of the 1950s and 1960s, a world of mass-media reaching an easily impressed population of couch potatoes. The TV set was a huge novelty back then. TV ads were part of that sensation. *Honey, did you see that! A washing powder that washes three-times whiter!*

The world has subsequently turned. A great number of times.

There are more competing brands chasing after audiences who are increasingly running in the opposite direction. And it's not a game of kiss chase. Many audiences are simply *repelling*, have become ad rejecters, able to pause 'Live TV' and skip at will and whim those expensive ads occupying those expensive airtime slots.

By necessity, today's B2C model has undergone two significant upgrades. And we're not talking a subtly streamlined shell on the same old chassis. We're talking complete overhaul, like turning a DeLorean into a time-machine that runs on nuclear fusion.

First, B2C isn't just one-way any more; it's *two-way*, monologues becoming *dialogues*.

Why so necessary?

Four good reasons, right here:

1 Because brands, just like people, who only *bang-on* about themselves without pause or reaction, are unattractive bores.

2 Because brands need to *listen*, to pay attention, and will learn considerably more from listening than just listening to themselves.

3 Because consumers emphatically have the right to reply.

4 Because B2C is ultimately about brand's nurturing and evolving a *relationship* with their consumers.

And while this may sound like a very obvious list of 'becauses', it isn't being so very obviously done. Campaigns that are *dialogue-building*, that endeavour to prompt two-way conversations between brands and their consumers still remain part of the exception than the norm. A lot of ad agency creative briefs start with: 'We'd like to make a TV ad.' A lot of ad agency *solutions* to a myriad of marketing problems remains: let's make a TV ad.

'Open conversations' will likely be a nice-to-have afterthought, following the development of creative work – quite possibly a TV ad – rather than a direct input into the initial creative brief. Theory and practice rarely nestle together as yin and yang.

The second upgrade of B2C is even more radical than introducing a feed-back loop. Ready?

The shark-like-natural-born-killer evolution of B2C is... C2C.

FIGURE 17.1 B2C... with upgrade

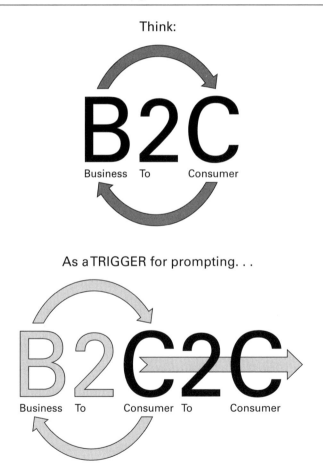

BRANDS NEED TO CREATE CONVERSATIONS

I love this idea, that brand communications should be about prompting conversations, which consumers will then want to have... *with other consumers*. It's a really open-ended-very-human-and-who-knows-where-we'll-end-up kind of idea.

Today, brands need to be conversation triggers. People don't tend to trust 'advertising'. If anything, they tend to *distrust* its all-too-often slick and oily charms. But people do incline to trust their fellow consumers, even if their fellow consumers are absolute strangers (see also: 'In strangers we trust', page 94).

But in a C2C dynamic, there's no suspicion of ulterior motive. Personal advocacy is not perceived as harbouring any underlying commercial agenda. Consumer recommendations are deemed truthful, involuntarily offered as open and honest advice: 'I liked this; got excited about this; benefited from this... and I wanted to tell you about it.'

Consider the folk an advertising campaign reaches by way of the media it buys, the TV airtime, the billboards, the print space, the online activity. Then consider who those folk then reach, should the advertising give them something to say and do. Great (as in very clever) advertising looks to exploit the available degrees of separation, to extend *beyond* its initial reach.

The desperate want and keen hope of every advertising campaign is that the message will spread. Much like a contagion, or a spore. From the Latin *propagare* you get, 'to propagate', from which derives propaganda, which we tend to couple with 'lies'. More accurately, though, propaganda is an attempt to *influence*, to steer people towards a cause. In this regard, advertising is no different.

In one sense, C2C is not so revolutionary.

Brands have always wanted to be talked about. Ad agencies have always wanted their work to be talked about. Being talked about, being relevant and contemporary, is oxygen to a brand – any brand, every brand. This particular goal – to be talked about – is always the same. There's but one difference, and it's a big difference. The means available by which the goal can be achieved has changed.

What David Ogilvy and the Saatchi brothers accomplished with TV ads and posters is a reflection of the tools available within the analogue world in which they operated. Today's world is deterministically more digital.

FROM BENT ADVERTISING TO BEING BRILLIANT COMPANY

People aren't as easily impressed as they were in Don Draper's day. People have seen more, had more sold to them. They're not so gullible. And much of today's 'straight advertising' can feel a bit bent, come across like it's selling door-to-door. Straight advertising was once very sexy. By contrast, in these more cynical, more credit-heavy, recession-weary times, a kind of ugliness lies beneath many a TV spot and billboard. Straight advertising is often an interruption – unwelcome but editable thanks to TiVo and PVRs.

For people to get excited by a brand, it increasingly requires a different bag of advertising tricks. These tricks don't place brands in a pulpit, safely removed but within preaching distance of an impressionable congregation. Brands no longer have the self-ordained role of preacher, and they need to stop preaching. They need to start whispering and gossiping instead. Forget pulpits; think garden fences, bus stops and coffee shops – because to interact, *to natter*, is human.

FIGURE 17.2   Google logo is made 'playable' to celebrate Pac-Man's 30th anniversary

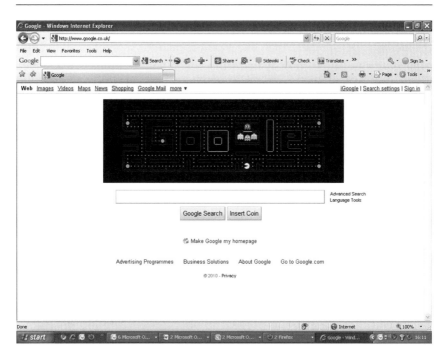

People enjoy having something to do, even when it's a distraction from whatever it was they were originally doing. Hence, to celebrate the 30th anniversary of Pac-Man (21 May 2010), Google made their logo 'playable' for the first time, turning it into a 255-level Pac-Man game, just like the original coin-op.

Suddenly, Google's home page wasn't just the means to a search-satisfied end, but a satisfying end in itself, a fun and welcome Pac-playing distraction. The dip in workday productivity on the Friday in question became a point of considerable Tweet and tabloid speculation.

FIGURE 17.3 Google Pac-Man causes dip in workday productivity

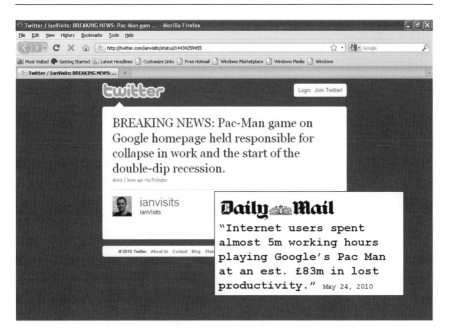

If the best company is that which we leave feeling most satisfied with ourselves, it follows that it is the company we leave most bored.

GIACOMO LEOPARDI, *PENSIERI*

For brands to succeed, they need to be brilliant company, like Google's Pac-Man day. Brands need to indulge their consumers, to listen more than talk, to make their consumers the centrepiece of proceedings, the headline star of the show. Why have social media brands become so addictively popular? Because they take a back seat in their relationship with consumers. The consumer is the one in the spotlight, *not* the brand.

Successful brands allow their consumers to do what they do best and what comes most naturally. To talk, create, imagine, invent and play. There is a child in all of us. There is an inventor, a Dr Emmett Brown, in all of us.

The future of successful advertising lies in the active participation of people. With ever-growing consumer sophistication, audiences are on to the brand 'Bootleggers & Bores'. But give people a role, a *starring* role, and they will love their brands all the more. B to C to C.

ALLOW ME TO PROPOSITION YOU

> " Brand propositions don't have to be melon-twisting. But they do need to be shrewd as hell, and very clear about what they mean. They need to convey a single-minded, super-seductive, utterly captivating idea that people can really latch on to; because successful brands are all about seduction; a brand's advertising about permanent courtship, ongoing campaigns to forever keep the fires burning and the passions alive. "

> *Every man is to be had one way or another, and every woman almost any way.*
>
> LORD CHESTERFIELD, *LETTERS TO HIS SON* (1750)

When were you last propositioned?

More accurate a question would actually be, how many times do you think you've been propositioned *today*?

Subject to where you are on the planet – deepest rainforest, remotest desert, most bustling metropolis – you're subject to as many as 5,000 commercial messages a day. That's the top-side figure. Some studies put it closer to 2,000 commercial messages per diem for the average city dweller. At even 2,000 commercial messages, that's quite a bombardment. And given that more than half the world lives in cities (3.3 billion of us), that's quite a few folk on the receiving end of a good many sales pitches. And each sales pitch is *more* than a sales pitch, more than a quick-buck, small-con attempt to get you to open your wallet, grab the money and run. Brands are ambitious. They see the long game. They look on their customer base in terms of lifetime value. Brands are proposing to you, maybe 2,000+ times a day, and they want you any way they can.

Who knew you were so popular?

PROPOSITION, POSITIONING: YOU SAY POTATO, I SAY TOMATO... BECAUSE THEY'RE DIFFERENT

In marketing circles, mainstay words such as *proposition* and *positioning* are banded around with daily frequency, often used interchangeably.

'*What's the* proposition?'

'*How are we going to* position *this to consumers?*'

Proposition and positioning *are not* the same, and innumerable books have been written on both, but it's a telling remark on 'marketing' generally that it can operate perfectly well without exactitude. But let's get exact, and say it again.

Proposition and positioning are not the same. But they are interlinked, one existing in relation and reference to the other.

First, *proposition*: I take it to simply be what a brand proposes to the world, its enthusiastic pitch to woo an audience. Then *positioning* simply places the brand proposition within market (and mental) context.

Positioning, by implication, is about where a brand sits, relative to others. Brand positioning is a compare-and-contrast juxtapositioning, an attempt to carve out a point of difference and competitive advantage versus the brand pack. Positioning, if you like, is looking to find that 'gap in the market'. Proposition then, is hoping to attract that 'market in the gap'.

And I like this word, proposition. To my way of thinking, it's actually a very shrewd, apt way of talking about brands. What is the brand proposing to consumers, and how is it a mind-opening, heart-thumping, pheromone-releasing trigger sufficient to create consideration and trial?

The proposition may be tactical, opportunist, say born of economic context. From M&S, a recession-busting: 'Three-course meal for two... for £10.' The New Citroen Xavia... 'now available with 0% finance.' Buy a new sofa this weekend from DFS and 'pay nothing for 12 months.'

Tempted?

Tactics aside, brand propositions are (fundamentally) long-term strategic stances looking to address deep-seated and perennial yearnings. For the family man, *familia defensor*, who needs to know he's doing all he can (and maybe has a need-to-be-needed thrown in for good measure)... there's Volvo... a family car that's the closest thing to driving a tank on the open road.

THE BRAND GAME

Every brand message is a proposition, a take it (or leave it) appeal, with the hope that it'll be a 'Yes, I'm buying whatever it is you're selling. Which room are you in? Let me get my coat and do you live near?'

It's all about attraction, seduction, wooing, about making it hard to say no. Ideally, making it almost impossible. (See also, 'Brands must behave, must woo', page 15.)

Religion is pickup. Politics is pickup. Life is pickup.

NICK STRAUSS, *THE GAME* (2005)

Advertising is pick up. Brands are pick-up artists. But not in the traditional sense. Brands are pick-up artists that actually want you to marry them. They want your lifelong commitment, your fidelity, forsaking all other brands in favour of them. They want your monogamy... only they want everyone else's monogamy too. Brands want it all.

Brands don't just want to play the field. They *want* the field, the whole field: complete market share, total domination of their category, without any other suitors or Don Juans getting a look-in. But no brand knows for sure whether they'll get lucky, whether they'll bag the babe or land the hunk.

In much the same way, with no marriage proposal does any guy know for sure, not with absolute-iron-clad-this-can-only-play-my-way certainty, that she'll say *Yes*. You may have been together for years, may have children together, may have *raised* children together, or raised not so much as a window ledge display together; whatever your circumstances, I don't believe you can *know* for sure. You can't guarantee the reaction of others, not until after the fact. You ask the question – '*Will you...?*' – and it can go one of two-ways. Joy, tears, tears of joy, laughter, hysteria, shock, derision.

When you're mining emotional depths, almost anything can happen by way of instinctive, unchecked reaction. Who knows what you're drudging up? Any sort of monster can rise out of the deep, whether happy monsters or otherwise.

People are reliably unpredictable, is what I'm getting at, and this is hugely relevant to any understanding of how brands work – to the brands we buy, those we remain loyal to, and those we promiscuously flip. There are, however, many things brands can do to maximize their chances of success. I'd argue that an effective proposition, achieving a *desired effect*, needs to be a killer one-liner. It needs to look you in the eye with intensity and openness. It needs to be honest, human, inviting, utterly assured.

Writers Ronald Shusett and Dan O'Bannan pitched their screenplay *Alien* (1979) to studios as 'Jaws in Space'. For the *Deep Blue Sea* (1999) aqua-action movie about three scientifically altered sharks made super-smart, think 'Mensa Jaws'. Self-proclaimed 'Hollywood pitch maestro' Robert Kosberg sold New Line Cinema the story of a blood-lusting canine on the loose. The title: 'Man's Best Friend'. Kosberg's opening line: 'Think *Jaws* on paws'.

I'll quit referencing killer fish, but my point is that brand propositions are all about finding the right human hooks, about getting people excited about an easily graspable 'one line idea'. That's really what – and all – a strapline is.

Snakes on a Plane (2006), *Cowboys & Aliens* (2011), *Indecent Proposal* (1993): consider the central premise of these three movies. All are brilliant because of their simplicity. Their gift is that they strike near-instant intrigue.

From 2006, *Snakes on a Plane* – and it's all in the title! Just imagine? *Snakes...* on a plane. Thirty-thousand feet, a captive audience travelling inside a metal tube... with all those fangs around. Who doesn't want to see that? You sure don't want to be *on* that flight, but you sure as hell want to see someone else go through it.

Cowboys & Aliens: hands up who wants to see some cowboys fight some aliens? I'll stand and wait in that line. Sure, this is likely to be more one for the boys than the girls, but that's a broadly three billion target audience.

Indecent Proposal: as in, would you sleep with someone, be unfaithful to your spouse, for $1 million? Would you? Quite the proposition and, back in 1993, it was intriguing enough to make a lot of people (including me) want to see what Demi Moore would do.

Now those who are quick to debate will be keen to stress that both *Snakes on a Plane* and *Cowboys & Aliens* were box office underperformers. Yes, they were, and with one very good reason: neither were particularly good films. They didn't draw the crowds... because neither of the films were great products.

There's little point having the best chat-up lines in the world if you're no great shakes in the sack. If you're a brand, there's little point prompting trial if it's a one-time-only purchase. Brand longevity and market share is all in the repeats. Every proposition needs to be able to deliver. The brand's advertising needs to talk a great game. The actual *product* or brand *experience* then needs to be able to play a great game. Because the thing with word-of-mouth is that it flows in both directions.

THE BEST PROPOSITIONS ARE BENEFIT-BASED

Yes, brand propositions say something about the brand – but they must also say something fundamentally true about the consumer, about their audience. The really great brand propositions convey consumer benefit. Great brands spell-out the buy-in. They make it easy for people, give them the 'Why?'. Brands need to (and successful brands *do*) play to the needs of people.

Take BMW, L'Oreal, Apple and at&t. In my opinion, four of the best propositional straplines of all time:

- *BMW – The Ultimate Driving Machine*
- *L'Oreal – Because I'm worth it*
- *Apple – Think Different*
- *at&t – Reach out and touch someone*

And why are they so great? First, they're brilliantly written, beautifully simple, unequivocal, highly quotable and memorable. Second, they instinctively appeal to their audiences because they implicitly spell out *benefit* in their subtext. These straplines codify and acknowledge deep-seated human needs. They are not merely brand-centric messages.

FIGURE 18.1 The best brand headlines address fundamental human needs

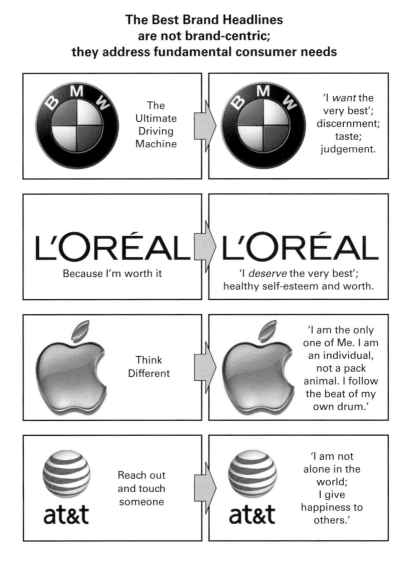

The Best Brand Headlines are not brand-centric; they address fundamental consumer needs

BMW	The Ultimate Driving Machine	BMW	'I *want* the very best'; discernment; taste; judgement.
L'ORÉAL	Because I'm worth it	L'ORÉAL	'I *deserve* the very best'; healthy self-esteem and worth.
Apple	Think Different	Apple	'I am the only one of Me. I am an individual, not a pack animal. I follow the beat of my own drum.'
at&t	Reach out and touch someone	at&t	'I am not alone in the world; I give happiness to others.'

THE FIRST RULE

You give them half a chance and 'propositions' *per se* can be a philosophical minefield. A minefield of the mind, that is, wrapped up in any number of melon-twisting neo-positivist concepts, around *language, meaning*, the meaning of *being*, distinctions of an analytic and synthetic nature. All good stuff, but a complex web in which to get easily tangled.

You see, propositions strike right at the heart of what we mean, and what we say by what we mean. It's a debate without a lid; not the sort of thing anyone's going to square away any time ever. And when it comes to brands, it's smart not to get too strung-up.

Brand propositions don't have to be melon-twisting. But they do need to be empathetically as shrewd as hell, and very clear about what they *mean*. They need to convey a pretty single-minded, super-seductive, utterly captivating idea that people can really latch on to, because successful brands are all about seduction. A brand's advertising is about permanent courtship, ongoing campaigns to forever keep the fires burning and the passions alive.

Wikipedia defines propositions as a 'meaningful declarative sentence'. *Will you marry me?* There's one right there. *Come to bed with me.* There's another. '*Meaningful declarative sentence*' is what a brand's proposition must be all about.

Bertrand Russell took the view that propositions are 'structured entities with objects and properties as constituents'. This is also helpful; he could have been defining what a brand is.

What is any brand's start point? Personally, I'd look to the advice of the Roman poet Ovid:

> ❝ *Women can always be caught; that's the first rule of the game.*
> OVID, *THE ART OF LOVE*, TR. ROLFE HUMPHRIES

Women, as also true of men. In the brand game, all can be caught.

Good hunting.

THROUGH A GLASS CLEARLY

> **"** Language is
> a beautiful thing,
> and fortunately
> robust enough to take
> the slings, arrows
> and occasional atom
> bombs of abuse aimed
> at it. **"**

Is ecosystem the new road map?

This, from a colleague of mine recently, in derision of all things jargon. At the time, the tongue was firmly in the cheek. One eyebrow Roger Moore-high.

And yes, maybe you had to be there. And maybe you wouldn't have smirked or sniggered even if you had been. But the underlying point still stands. Language is a beautiful thing, and fortunately robust enough to take the slings, arrows and occasional atom bombs of abuse aimed at it.

'Ecosystem' is the term *du jour* in many quarters of Adland. And the line of forbearers goes back a long old way. Steve King is associated with starting the ball rolling with his invention of brand (or account) planning. Understand the brand; build the brand; give it form, meaning and reason. Give it emotional depth to equal its physical dimensions. And, ladies and gentlemen, we'll have lift off! And just watch 'em flock!

Account planning exists for the sole purpose of creating advertising that truly connects with consumers.

JON STEEL, AUTHOR & WPP WORLDWIDE PLANNING DIRECTOR

For me, Steel's '*What's it all about?*' definition is not just on the money, but swarms all over it. Advertising that truly connects with people. Therein, I suspect, a very deliberate inclusion of the word 'truth'. Planning exists to find truth, human truth, upon which advertising is a creative expression and appeal to that understanding.

THE BRAND-CONSUMER VENN

Brand. Consumer. Join the dots. How I see it, that's what advertising does. It's that simple. Because on paper, the theory is simple. Or think two circles, apart, then bring them together, make them overlapping and Venn-like, so that each inhabits the world of the other. Intersecting, 'truly connecting', equals brand purchase and preference. A simple principle. It's the 'making it happen' that can get tough. Like boy meets girl. Again, a wonderfully simple premise. Boy meets girl. Love ensues and all ends well. Easy on the page indeed, but a low-percentage outcome in the real world. Even with Romeo and Juliet, love may have ensued, but then too did tears and fatalities. Note to all: brands can't afford fatalities.

COMMUNICATIONS PLANNING

I think *communications planning*, a late 1990s early noughties new-view of advertising did (truly) move the thinking game on. Naked Communications were the guys who pioneered and pushed it hardest, and arguably had the greatest successes, building a global network from London to Tokyo, New York to Sydney, with everyone involved swaggering and grooving to the same brand of self-belief.

'Comms' planning takes the consumer as the start point, rather than the brand, and acknowledges that people don't experience brand messages in neatly wrapped and singular packages. People build an overall and ever-shifting impression of a brand through a non-linear set of messages, whether that brand exposure is a million-dollar TV ad, a beer coaster, bumper sticker, or an editorial piece they read on the train. It sounds pretty obvious, but the folk commissioning the advertising, thinking it up, making it and getting it out there, can be so wrapped up and so close to the process that anyone can lose sight of the bigger picture and the audiences viewpoint.

Naked's stance remains 'channel agnostic', where anything (any 'touch-point') can influence, big or small. Giant billboards through to fly posters, online chatter through to front-page headline news, *everything* communicates, sends a message, can make and does make an impression. Brand communications is therefore the sum total of all points of contact with consumers, how they join up, interplay and write themselves large and compelling, adding (with hope) to a significantly greater whole.

DISRUPTION PLANNING

Disruption planning sets out advertising's role as a kind of intervention, a thud, a message delivered that will stop people in their daily tracks, and wake them up to the sudden and absolute merits of, say, a washing powder (or dental whitener) claiming 'twice as white for twice as long'. Ad agency TBWA are big exponents of a good disruption.

TBWA helps brands to grow by identifying Disruptive strategies and developing Disruptive campaigns. Disruption is no corporate buzzword.

SOURCE: WWW.TBWA.COM

I don't know about you, but whenever someone actively stresses that something is not a buzzword, somewhere I hear this very loud and not very grand symphony of alarm bells. With no conductor.

From advertising as a disruption to our everyday – such as public transport workers striking, or a volcano suddenly erupting – hot on the heels came the counter-thought that people *don't* want to be disrupted, that brands *aren't* such a big deal for people, that they'll *resent* the intrusion by any brand that attempts to get in their way, even if that brand is serving up a washing powder (or tooth whitening) epiphany.

The solution to advertising as 'a resented intrusion'? For brands to fit in, to accommodate, to be of use. I've always liked this elegantly simple idea, of being 'useful', of brands that provide clear evidence of their *utility*. Advertising doesn't have to be a hard sell; it can be a gentle sell in a timely manner, there only when people need it.

Only the *what*, *who* and *why* should dictate whether advertising should stir or shake us.

ENGAGEMENT PLANNING

Of the planning prefixes, *engagement planning* is the nonsensical one, the one that I've always struggled with the most. Why? Because when did advertising, any advertising – from any age, conveying any kind of message – look to *disengage* its audience? As in, messages designed to consciously fall on deaf ears, meet indifference, be incidental, unappealing and easily dismissed?

When exactly was advertising ever in the disengagement business? As prefixes go, it's utterly superfluous, like prefixing 'plane' with 'winged'. I'm ready to go bare-knuckle on this one – and I suspect there are a few guys over at ad agency BBH, the gang pushing engagement planning for a good few years now, who might be keen.

Ever-new labels (most likely) add new layers of ambiguity, to consciously mislead through some snazzy verbal-dancing. I guess, hell, I know – we all know – everyone's looking for an angle. The labels that orbit the thinking that goes into the making of advertising each tell a story, and unpacking their meaning can help explain how the industry does what it does. And derisory as I may be of the unnecessary 'engagement' prefix, 'to engage' *does* serve as a spot-on descriptor for the purpose of any and all advertising.

> *Engage – verb*
> *To occupy the attention or efforts of a person (or persons), causing emotional response and a change in behaviour(s).*
>
> DICTIONARY.COM

Attention-grabbing. Triggering emotional response and behaviour change. Now that to me is *advertising* by definition! That's the definition of advertising done right!

So let's park the 'fashion for words' for a moment and talk ultimate purpose. All brand communications look to engage an audience in *purchase*. Whatever the prefix, whatever the eulogized philosophy of the industry moment, it's all about getting to the same destination, achieving the same desired outcome.

Any ad campaign and every piece of brand messaging is a direct or indirect, explicit or implicit invitation for an audience to *act*. Smart planning is smart planning. It's about inventing new and inspired ways to inspire audiences to 'trial and buy'.

All advertising must fundamentally be...

FIGURE 19.1 All advertising must fundamentally be an...

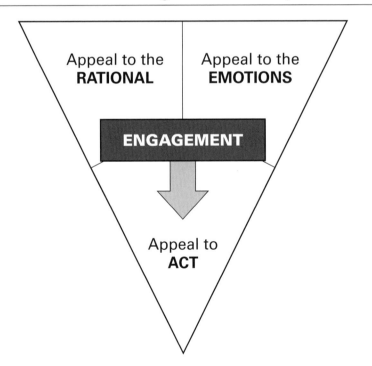

Advertising is a war on passivity, each sortie an attempt to stimulate, pro-voke and arouse people into doing *something*. And ultimately into *buying*. Adverting looks to lift us from the couch, from our slothful, apathetic, mild boredoms; it wants to slam an adrenalin shot straight into our slow-beating hearts, making us sit bolt upright, excited and keen 'to do'.

And what, finally, of these new ecosystems mentioned right at the start? What of them, and do we need a road map to find one?

ECOSYSTEMS

Agency R/GA is one of the more public industry pushers of 'ecosystems'. It's through ecosystem thinking that R/GA is actually trying to define their business future, their role in the world and the road map they need to get there. And there is, of course, nothing wrong with any of that. What busi-ness doesn't want to future-proof itself?

For brand-builders, creating 'ecosystems' feels like a potentially big idea, one where brands can be important to people, play a central part in people's everyday lives and, at a commercial level, generate 'repeat fees'.

Ultimately, 'ecosystem' thinking is a play on product versus service. You buy a product, even a beautifully branded one, and it's a one-time buy. Whereas you can keep buying services, time after time. So why not merge the two, have the consumer sit within a 'life sphere' of branded products *and* services, all of which they love using – use all the time – and keep spending money on?

The Apple ecosystem is a within-easy-reach example. Its hardware, its software – it's beautifully branded stuff that people naturally like to use. It is for people's everyday use, and if you took it away from them they'd get more than a little upset. Think: your iBook, iPad, iPhone, iTunes, iCloud. Think: all those Apple-badged staples, whether physi(cal) or digi(tal) in form, that all compliment, harmonize and synch, and that build an Apple-branded universe and tech-life support for people.

Building ecosystems might not be the whole answer to the future of branding, but it could well be a part-answer. Take Nike, once the manufac-turer of running shoes, now arguably a 'brand provider' of all things run-ning, fitness and even wellness related. From 'a product', you blow it out, to a genre, a lifestyle idea that people want to wrap around themselves, out of which forms a happy dependency and sense of 'can't live without'.

A brand ecosystem may well just be a new way of looking at an old set of ideals, founded on wanting to make brands important, useful and desirable to people, but it's a long way from being a bad way of looking at the fundamentals of brand invention.

JUST PLANNING

> *Chess is as elaborate a waste of human intelligence as you can find outside an advertising agency.*
>
> RAYMOND CHANDLER (1888–1959)

Much as I like his books, I can't quite bring myself to agree with Chandler's take on Adland (I also like chess.) I do acknowledge that ad agencies, without exception, consist of some very smart people, some of whom spend a lot of time trying to reinvent what it is to *think smart*. Smart thinking doesn't need reinvention. It just needs to be smart. It is its own invention. I say, ditch the labels, jettison the spin. It's all about the ideas. Great, inventive ideas born of truthful insights; there's your golden ticket.

'*All veils and misty*', sang INXS ('Mystify', 1987), but not everything has to be.

Brand planning, communications planning, disruption planning, engagement planning, influence planning, persuasion planning, participation planning, momentum planning.

Here's an idea. What about *planning* planning?

Or, better yet... Just *great* planning.

COLOUR ME HAPPY!

> 'Why BLACK suits?'
>
> Man,
> what's cooler
> than a black
> suit?
>
> Quentin Tarantino

W hat's your favourite colour?

C'mon – it's *not* a boring question – and everybody has one, and whatever you say says something about who you are... or at least about the particular *mood* you're in at the time of asking.

The whole field of colour psychology, the 'language of colour', the implicit *meaning* we take from every colour, and therefore how we can pointedly *use* colours in branding and advertising to evoke a potential set of responses really fascinates me.

As a field of advertising it may be well-furrowed and clod free, but it's eternally relevant to the cause.

> *People make a subconscious judgment about an item within 90 seconds of initial viewing, and up to 90% of that assessment is based on colour.*
>
> SOURCE: INSTITUTE FOR COLOUR RESEARCH

Louis Cheskin was one of the early greats; he founded the Color Research Institute of America in Chicago in the 1930s. A clinical psychologist, he really moved the game on in terms of 'motivational research', an early days' account planning approach anchored in psychological understanding.

> *Cheskin observed that people's perceptions of products and services were directly related to aesthetic design, and named this relationship sensation transference. He was one of the first marketers to use customer-centric methods, and to value direct customer input above marketers' expectations or guesses about customers' needs.*
>
> SOURCE: WIKIPEDIA

Did everyone catch that line about 'customer-centric'? The next time someone argues that 'comms planning' started in the late 1990s, that for the first time the big difference was that consumers were put 'at the heart' of the planning process, ask them if they've ever heard of Louis Cheskin or *motivational research* or ever read anything by Vance Packard.

Colour psychology and branding goes hand in hand, like holy matrimony and brides wearing white, which happens to be a favourite example of mine. (How was that for a clunky segue?)

In a Western Judeo-Christian context, take the symbolic meanings associated with white:

FIGURE 20.1 The psychological properties of white

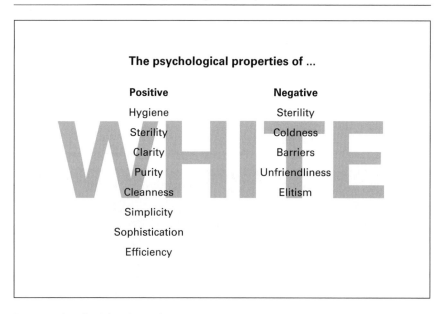

The psychological properties of ...

Positive	Negative
Hygiene	Sterility
Sterility	Coldness
Clarity	Barriers
Purity	Unfriendliness
Cleanness	Elitism
Simplicity	
Sophistication	
Efficiency	

Source: Institute for Colour Research

Then, think Apple.

In their early noughties renaissance, Apple applied *white* to create tech-sex desirability. *Be* different: sell technology based on aesthetic. Create pure form, so pure that it has to come... in white. Apple made white... the new black.

(Trust me, that segue made the first segue look slick.)

I once worked for an investment banking client who came in with 'the dream brief'. They had a name, they traded aggressively, they had high-achieving staff, but all that they had... was far from all that they wanted.

They wanted to be a brand. They wanted to have values, meaning, stand for something in the world. They wanted to buy a vision. And they had deep pockets and a willingness to invest in order to make their vision real. In other words, they were the dream client. (That type doesn't come along often, and you grab them with both hands and a grappling hook when they do.)

If you're going to build a premium global banking brand, one that inherently appeals to the corporate banking fraternity, that transcends borders and cultures, and instinctively compels ultra high-net-worth individuals, then it makes solid sense to speak in a brand language they already understand and respond to.

Don't think Apple this time. Think *black*.

FIGURE 20.2 The psychological properties of black

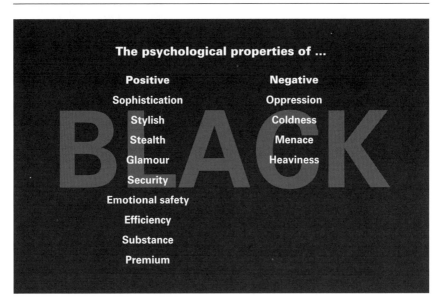

Source: Institute for Colour Research

No colour is 'all upside', but you naturally look to exploit the positive properties of a colour. For black, the positives are many.

For our dream client's brand creation, we played heavily on black. Very deliberately: black. With every execution and creative asset thoroughly thought through, because quite (in)arguably, black is cool; glamorously dangerous; dangerously glamorous; the most aspirational colour of any colour, shade or hue. Simply, nothing does black like black. (And yes, it's no coincidence that the cover of this book is predominantly black.)

FIGURE 20.3 Why black suits?

```
                              FADE IN:
              Eight men dressed in BLACK SUITS sit
              around a table at a breakfast cafe.
```

"What is the Matrix?
Hell knows! I just
know they dress well."
Keanu Reeves

"*Why* black suits?
Man, what's cooler
than a black suit?"
Quentin Tarantino

So let me just end with this: colour counts, really counts. When it comes to branding, it pays to know your colours.

CURVE, CONTOUR AND COME-ON: HOW PERSUASIVE IS SEXUAL PERSUASION?

> How much do you enjoy the ad of the hot brunette in the skimpy tank-top winking at you? How much do you enjoy that image of the college hunk with the cubed abdominals blue — steeling into the breeze? Once you make the link that it's *American Apparel*, or *Abercrombie & Fitch*, or whomever, how do you then *feel* about that brand?

SEX!

I'm betting that got your attention.

MONEY makes the world go round, but it's not the only irresistible force. SEX gives more than a helping hand, populates the place as it turns. It's why there's so much sex in so much of our advertising.

The adage 'sex sells' is etched in the earliest-inscribed tablets of advertising theory to make their way down off Mount Madison... but the perennial doubters and new order thinkers remain justly entitled to ask, *'But does it?'*

Does sex persuade purchase?

*

I can think of two very logical reasons for using sex in advertising as the preferred tool of persuasion.

Logical reason 1: taking advantage of what's already front-of-mind

Men think about sex every seven seconds. That's the popular myth, buoyed by all those rotating articles in *Maxim* and *Cosmo*.

Research carried out in 2010 scaled it back: 'the average male turns their thoughts to sexual intercourse 13 times a day – a total of 4,745 times every year. (In comparison, women think about sex just 5 times day – or 1,825 times a year.)' (*The Telegraph*, 8 Jan 2010).

Marketeers talk a lot about getting their brand front-of-mind. Given that we are sexual beings, prone to preoccupy, some even obsess about sex, it logically plays that a brand might as well give itself a head start and slip-stream the preoccupation.

Logical reason 2: cutting through the commercial din

Marketeers and their brands also face the daunting challenge of rising above 'the noise'. Depending on the study, researchers claim that the average urban dweller is assaulted with between 2,000 and 4,000 commercial messages every day. The figure, of course, can be sliced and diced by compass point, maturity of urban environment – all number of variables – but the point is, even if the low-ball figure of 2,000 stacks up, that's a lot of noise. And how much of this is just white noise and wallpaper, messages that miss the mark, that are blanked by commuters on autopilot, by savvy and cynical consumers numb to a never-ending deluge of oversell? Using sex in advertising should help a brand cut through, leapfrog and rise (the pun's there if you want it) above the commercial din.

Using sexual content is a simple and sure-fire ploy for attention; that against a backdrop of 2,000 commercial messages or more, we'll still halt in our tracks, crane our neck, give ourselves whiplash even so we can (figuratively) check out 'the woman in the red dress'.

For these two logical reasons, the following is true:

> *One fifth of all advertising today uses overt sexual content to sell its products.*
>
> SEX IN ADVERTISING: PERSPECTIVES ON THE EROTIC APPEAL (2005)

Then there's the counter-argument. The one that says one-fifth of all advertising today has got it... all wrong. In *Buyology* (2008), citing brand recall studies performed by MediaAnalyzer Software & Research, Martin Lindstrom proposes that ads with sexual content are half as effective as non-sexual ads:

> *9.8% of the men who had viewed the ads with sexual content were able to remember the correct brand or product in question, compared to almost 20% of men who had seen the non-sexual ones.*

Consistently trending with female viewers too, the stats read 10.85 per cent and 22.3 per cent audience recall respectively.

It's a pretty crotch-grabbing headline Lindstrom's shooting for.

Guess what, sex does NOT sell after all! One-fifth of advertising is grossly misguided. The more distracting the image, the more likely our cognitive abilities are also *disarmed*, leaving viewers unable to, as it were, process the main thrust of the ad, the actual 'brand sell'.

I accept that sexy ads using distracting images... can distract. This is their very purpose. And I believe there's a strong *counter* to Lindstrom's counter-argument.

THE COUNTER-COUNTER-ARGUMENT

People aren't typically exposed to ads (whether TV commercials or big posters) *just once*. Almost no ad campaign is designed to be seen once, and once only. Blink, gone. No, that's not how it is. Outdoor posters are posted in two-week cycles. It's common for some advertisers to buy certain poster locations on a long-term holding.

FIGURE 21.1 Fashion brand Sisley 'doing a Wonderbra' in 2007

FIGURE 21.2 And that Wonderbra poster, by TBWA (1995).
Market: UK

The media planners go to great pains to stress 'effective frequency', simply the optimal number of times an audience should be exposed to a commercial message so that it may 'stick', prompt 'consideration', serve as a 'purchase-trigger'.

All that the MediaAnalyzer study really suggests is that a higher average frequency (multiple exposure) needs to be set in order for audiences to 'take in' curve and contour AND word and logo, thus connecting all the message dots.

FIGURE 21.3 Just in case you weren't looking bottom right, this ad is for Lynx shower gel. Print ad, 'Get Dirty' (2007)

There's a second point too, beyond frequency of exposure, that's far more interesting. What happens once brand atribution is established? How do audiences then *feel* about that brand? I'd argue they will be more passionately disposed (or disinclined) to an emotionally charged, heavily sexualized brand gesture.

How much do you *enjoy* the ad of the hot brunette in the skimpy tank-top winking at you? How much do you enjoy that image of the college hunk with the cubed abdominals blue-steeling into the breeze? Once you make the link that it's American Apparel, or Abercrombie & Fitch, or whomever, how do you then *feel* about that brand?

FIGURE 21.4 Abercrombie & Fitch. Print ad (2007). Flagship Store Opening, Savile Row

Because we *do* enjoy some of these ads, are aroused by them. We're sexual creatures with button-pressing physiological responses.

FIGURE 21.5 Calvin Klein's Obsession for Men. Print ad (1993) with Kate Moss, aged 19, shot by then boyfriend Mario Sorrenti

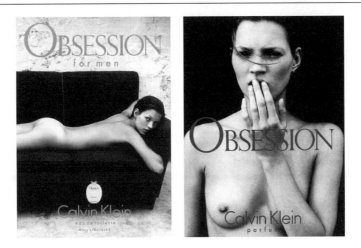

There's no question that the use of semi-clad, half-naked and evocatively posed models is going to cause strong physiological and cognitive responses in any viewer with a heartbeat. A rise in skin temperature, pupil dilation, increased heart rate, all are quite likely – and likely hoped for by those responsible for making the ad.

This flavour of advertising very consciously tries to put its viewer 'in the frame', creates a mental scenario and 'implies outcome'. From adidas, the close-to-surface subtext: *look what will happen to you when you wear our trainers...*

FIGURE 21.6 adidas: the first thing she notices... are your shoes

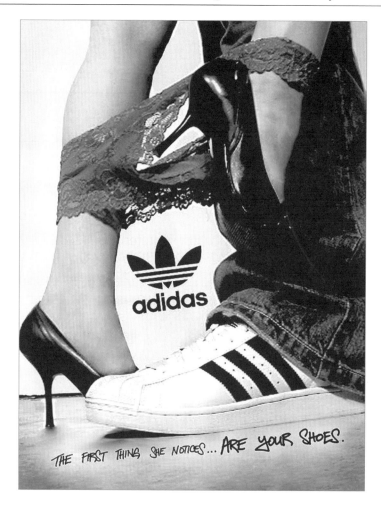

The more suggestive, more explicit, more provocative, more indecent, the stronger the reaction, whether favourable or negative.

A scandalous, sensationalist campaign can wake up the world, get the blogosphere spinning, the whispering classes whispering, the tabloids in a tizz. Create buzz, and you've got people actively looking for 'that ad... with the guy... with the enormous...'

You get the idea.

People talking about and *hunting out* a campaign – so they too are in the know, able to make up their own minds – that's 'brand nirvana'.

Tom Ford was clearly comfortable with the prospect of a little controversy when he signed off this 'visually arresting' print campaign for his men's fragrance launch in 2007:

FIGURE 21.7 Tom Ford went for images of the explicitly eye-popping variety

More than a little obvious maybe, Ford went for images of the explicitly eye-popping variety.

Explicitly *suggestive* is an equally popular ploy. From nearly 40 years ago, National Airlines were only too happy suggesting how men should feel and what they might like to do to their stewardesses.

FIGURE 21.8 I'm Jo, fly me (1970s)

From the same era of less reformed gender politics, Tipalet cigars proposed that female dotage and devotion was simply a matter of blowing (smoke) in her face.

FIGURE 21.9 Tipalet: blow in her face and she'll follow you anywhere (1970s)

One feels for all those suffragettes!

While it's easy to marvel and appall at the social mores of decades past, how many leaps and bounds have we truly made in the name of sexual equality?

In 2009, Burger King went the none-too-subtle route when suggesting what would happen when confronted with their new 'Super Seven Incher'.

FIGURE 21.10 Burger King (2009). Market: Singapore

And maybe that's the thing with sexual innuendo and suggestion. It doesn't work if it's too subtle. It can only be, by definition, really rather obvious.

I suspect really rather obvious is fine by Irish low-cost airline founder Michael O'Leary. Putting 'Fly Me' in a two-piece, we have Ryanair's annual charity calendars, toasting the clear talents of some choicely chosen cabin staff.

FIGURE 21.11 The Girls of Ryanair charity calendar (2011). All proceeds go to charity.

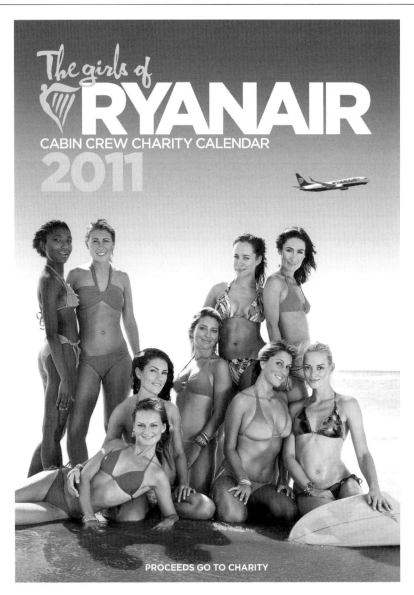

Fundamentals such as 'know your audience' clearly apply, clearly remain fundamental. Men and women don't, of course, respond to the same universal set of turn-ons. One man's 'bit of healthy fun' can easily be a woman's lifetime crusade for legislation change. As Billy Crystal puts it far better: 'Women need a reason to have sex. Men just need a place.'

One of the big fears is that a campaign will be a turn-off, or worse still, achieve public outcry and backlash... but I think the brands who operate in this space do so comfortably, happy to polarize, even keen to offend, intent on dividing audiences into titillated onlookers and outraged objectors.

Luxury brands, for example, aren't *mass* brands. Indeed, they're snobbish without apology, more than implying that if you're so easily offended – a prude – then you're really not for us, not *our* sort of consumer. If you don't 'get it', it's proof you're not really a 'Tom Ford' kind of person, one of the Emanuel Ungaro in-crowd, not fit to be seen in American Apparel.

Take this press and poster work for travel brand Club 18–30, all visual innuendo and double-take.

FIGURE 21.12   Club 18–30, by Saatchi & Saatchi (2005). Market: UK

When we first sat round a table and pitched this work to the Club 18–30 client, our line of argument was that it was cheeky, playful, really quite hilarious, and anyone who felt otherwise just 'didn't know funny' and was simply, painfully, without humour. The Club 18–30 marketing director at the time barely broke a smile. Not even a grin. Perhaps a slight facial suggestion of constipation, but it was hard to tell. We could have all been playing poker. The work was shelved, but not forgotten; file-tagged to fight another day. A few years later, a new marketing director, and an agency with a long memory scheduled a fresh meeting. The work was bought, and a new campaign created some shelf space in the agency.

SEX IN ADVERTISING: WORKS FOR ME

> *I wouldn't recommend sex, drugs or insanity for everyone, but they've always worked for me.*
>
> HUNTER S THOMPSON (1939–2005)

Hunter was keeping it personal, he wasn't of course referencing the world of advertising, but he could have been. It's not such a stretch.

Sex, certainly, does work in advertising. It works to promote and deliberately provoke in equal measure. The line from the movie *Heathers* (1988) applies: 'the extreme always seems to make an impression', and the advertising community knows this all too well.

Of course, the question and concern is how far is too far? When is close-to-the-wind unacceptably too close? Because each 'latest extreme' raises the average, sets a new normal, and ups the stakes in order for a brand to trump its competition and achieve the same level of reaction next time round. The advertising community has a responsibility here. Material that's 'plastic-wrapped and on the top-shelf' shouldn't translate to the side of a skyscraper. Even advertising isn't immune to the observance of 'everything in moderation.'

In the case of advertising, the headline holds firm. Sex sells... so long as you do it well. Life and advertising has many a parallel.

TRUTH, LIES AND ADVERTISING

" Anti-Capitalists may view advertising as packaged lies in a damnable word, but the world we live in *is* a capitalist one, where buying is a key driver, and advertising is the necessary flux.

I don't see 'advertising' as the bogeyman telling tall tales.

Effective advertising acknowledges some kind of prevailing truth about 'how things are'. "

How's this for a 'Debating 101'?

> *To what degree does advertising bare any resemblance to*
> *reality? Brands, are they street-selling naked truth or*
> *the emperor's new clothes?*

And away you go.

I believe it's a compelling polemic, partly because it doesn't immediately conjure an image of there being a pole with two ends, of there being two sides to this debate.

Advertising: any resemblance to reality? Intuitively, the knee jerk would be no, not much.

'Truth and advertising' doesn't exactly roll off the tongue. In fact, it comes out more like a spit, possibly followed by a guffaw. Fred and Ginger, Butch and Sundance, Crocket and Tubbs: those guys all fit, complemented, made sense, were magically compatible. Truth and advertising, by contrast, doesn't sound like a speed date with much potential for any fireside follow-on.

Advertising, by definition, makes truth its natural antonym. The dictionary definition of advertising is a telling one:

> *To 'advertise' – the verb:*
> *to call attention to, in a boastful or ostentatious manner,*
> *in a public medium; to induce people to buy.*
>
> SOURCE: DICTIONARY.COM

Boastful. Ostentatious. Not exactly 'positives', are they? Neither are they qualities that we keenly seek out in others, toast them for, use as illustrative labels of someone's easy appeal. Boastful and ostentatious, read: wankers you wouldn't invite to a dinner party.

But the dictionary definition isn't a surprising one, because to *advertise* is to promote something with an *agenda to sell*, and that de facto brings into question the credibility of the promotional message.

> *We tell you it's great... because we want you to buy it.*

Advertising, as defined, has all the tact and sincerity of, 'Trust me, I'm a salesman'. 'Trust me, I'm a gynaecologist' conjures the same essential suspicion.

And yet this is what brands are known to do, *to advertise*, and this places them under instinctive suspicion, where consumers know they're being *advertised to*, and by consequence their 'brand barriers' are up, which is very understandable. Anyone feel like we've just fallen through a time tunnel and into a frontier world of carpetbaggers, con artists and quacks selling snake oils?

Equally derisory, but again revealing, is the belief held by some that advertising takes a tone that is, let's say, far from personable.

FIGURE 22.1 Advertising deserves a punch in the face

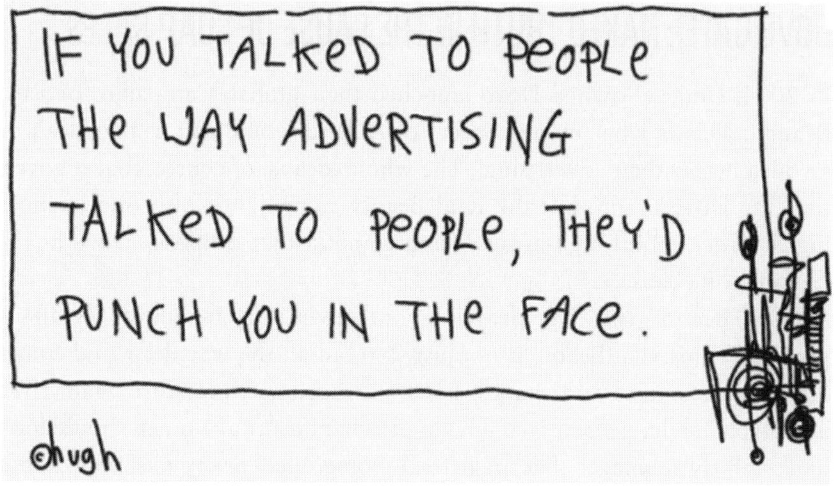

There we were, as brand-builders, wanting our brands to disarm, when instead they're provoking people to take up arms.

So advertising is a bluff and blag, the ignoble exploitation game, where its only salience is that it has no virtue. And yet... This isn't going to wash with me. It's not going to wash because, frankly, it's a flaky witness that crumbles under cross-examination.

Good advertising has to be a reflection of life, of some kind of reality, meaning it has to be anchored in truth. The truth is, good advertising can only work if it's a comment on life, on people, on some kind of human understanding. Because the brand sell is based on the understanding of a problem and the proposition of a solution.

Effective advertising acknowledges and addresses some kind of prevailing truth about 'how things are'. The only disrepute deserved is if the proposed brand solution is illegitimate, is fraudulent. In other words, if it's a big fib. And while advertising has, from time to time, been busted for fibbing, fibbing isn't tenable as a long-term strategy for keeping a brand afloat, because every brand will get found out in the end. So advertising has to be based on the honest answer to a truism. Making advertising and reality closer, more logical buddies than instinct would first have us believe. Meaning brands are more honest than they are the purveyors of pretence.

Let's consider two successful examples that have embraced 'real': Dove and The Kooples.

DOVE(GATE): NAKED TRUTH IN THE CAUSE OF SOAP SALES

In 2004, Unilever-owned Dove launched their global 'Campaign for Real Beauty'. This is what many corners of Adland would call a 'Big Idea', or an 'idea bigger than advertising'. The whole idea is, of course, that it advertises the Dove brand, but the Real Beauty campaign is also one of those higher order, moral high-ground kind of ideas that proposes Dove as the crusader of a cause.

'Real Beauty' (the big idea) is about celebrating femininity in all its physical forms, that beauty is not just skin but all-the-way deep, and comes in many ages, hues and shapes. It's a suffragette-style gesture against the archetypal media-perpetuated images of 'what beautiful women should look like' – all those images that make 'real women' feel pretty miserable about themselves.

The jewel in Real Beauty's campaign crown came two years after its launch, with Dove's 75-second online film, *Evolution*.

Ogilvy & Mather used the budget offcuts from a completed project, and for a reported C$130k (that's Canadian dollars), shot the time-lapsed journey of a model's face, from make-up chair to billboard.

FIGURE 22.2 Split screen 'after and before'. *Evolution* by Ogilvy & Mather (2006)

Evolution is whistle-blowing derision at how far advertising stretches the physical truth in order to create 'unnatural' beauty. It's clever stuff. So clever, in fact, that it went on to take the Epica D'Or at Cannes (the first online film ever to do so), and is estimated to have generated $150 million (that's US green) worth of free media coverage.

Dove's Real Beauty campaign started out as a full-tilt feminist charge against all those glossy and unreal images, exposing the clear wrongs of a system that produces 'visual lies'. The campaign has since softened, but retains its sentiment, turning soap-box stance into a positive, saying to women everywhere: join us, and feel good about you.

Of course, 'Real Beauty' is no different to any other kind of advertising, in its endeavours to sell product and grow market share, by inviting you to buy into a brand that makes you feel good. Dove is selling women happiness; the invitation to feel happy about their bodies and how they look. To the principle that you sell the sizzle and not the steak, this is soap sold as self-esteem. Put another way, this is advertising sold as 'anti-advertising'.

THE KOOPLES: TRUTH, WELL-DRESSED

The Kooples is a French rag-trade brand that came to London in late 2010, having only launched in France two years prior. Selfridges described them as 'the chic new Parisian export'.

Parisian chic is just about spot-on as far as helpful descriptors go, but what helped their get-noticed cause more than anything else was an ad campaign that purported to use 'real couples'. This was Dove, done the couture way.

FIGURE 22.3 The Kooples, UK print campaign (2010)

> *... a very clever advertising campaign, which you might have spotted on the sides of taxis and buses if you happen to live in London, featuring real-life couples looking drop-dead cool in their Kooples gear.*
>
> THE TELEGRAPH, 3 DECEMBER 2010

'Very clever', suggested the *Telegraph*. I'm not sure I'd agree it was *that* clever, but at the time it was very noticeable, and getting noticed is always half the battle.

What I found wryly amusing at the time (and still do) is how advertising can only *sometimes* do reality, can only do real people, if they already *look like* advertising. Here we have real 'Kooples', 'real people', who do really good impressions of models.

Real-life couples posing as models really just felt like a cheap way of getting models, when the real people in question looked the way they did. But let's not lose sight of the fundamentals. The very-good-looking-though-not-actually-models remain pretty effective 'drop-dead cool' clothes horses. The ads showed an undeniable truth: they're 'giving it' and wearing it well, the way anyone would *want* to wear it. By extension, Kooples gets to imply it's 'as worn by the cool kids', even if they're beautiful people *not* signed to Elite, and all this might somehow serve as an even more effective message to aspirational lovers of glad rags, in some pseudo-authentic kind of way.

At the risk of over-analysing this far too much, I'll move on.

CRAZY BUT TRUE

Advertising, reality and how they rub up against each other was the central premise of the movie *Crazy People* (1990). Starring the late Dudley Moore, it pitched itself as 'a comedy about truth in advertising'. As a movie, it's sadly less than the sum of its parts, but some of its parts are, to me, little comic gems. Moore plays a disillusioned copywriter who wants to 'level with America', and conceives a series of ads that don't hold back in their levelling:

> *Jaguar – For men who'd like hand-jobs from beautiful women they hardly know.*

> *Volvo – they're boxy but they're good.*

Movie launches and tourist boards also get the treatment from Dudley: for *The Freak*, a new horror flick: 'It won't just scare you, it will fuck you up for life!'; for the Greek Tourist Board: 'Forget Paris. The French can be annoying. Come to Greece. We're nicer'; for the Bahamian Tourist Board: 'Come... in the Bahamas.'

The funny thing about all the spoofs in *Crazy People* is that they're all actually really good pieces of advertising... that really just mimic what the best 'real world advertising' does. The spoofs simply spell out the subtext, put it on the page – which, of course, is what makes it funny – but 'real advertising' *is* like the movie's spoofs.

Take this execution by Euro RSCG in 2005, for the launch of Jaguar's new 'XK'. It's 15 years on from *Crazy People*, and you could argue it's just a new execution working from the same consumer insight.

FIGURE 22.4 The launch of Jaguar's new XK in 2005

On the 'DVD Dungeon Night' that they popped *Crazy People* into the tray, one imagines the guys from Jaguar were sharing popcorn with the people from Aruba.

Nassau may be nearly a thousand miles north of Aruba, but both islands can play the same card. Aruba Tourism Authority won the 'Best Poster' category at the 2010 Travel Marketing Awards for their 'Oooh' campaign, inviting tourists to come to their 'happy island'.

FIGURE 22.5 Aruba's 'Ooooh' campaign wins 2010 travel marketing award

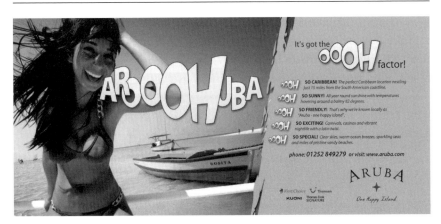

THE REAL TRUTH OF IT

Advertising makes its own bed. The bad wrap and vile rep occasionally placed at its door is sadly an earned one, a function of past follies and some very gross misdemeanours. Selling cigarettes 'for their flavour' is one 'guilty as charged' that's pointless taking to appeal. From half-truth can sometimes come whole-lies.

While advertising today is not akin to the cigarette advertising of yester-year, the ad industry remains a convenient scapegoat for all things demonized as 'abhorrently capitalist'.

To be anti-advertising is to be anti-capitalist. The anti-capitalist 'demon-strates' (with placards aloft) that we don't need *all this stuff*, that it doesn't make us happy, and so let's zero the clock, stop buying, and see what happens (it's a big placard and they abridge). Keep buying, or the house of cards tumbles, they suggest, before then adding, let it tumble.

Many people want to make the world a better place. An evil few may rather like to see it burn. The trick is to make sure good intentions don't fan flames. I don't think the world's quite that bad, or in that bad a shape, and I don't see 'advertising' as the bogeyman telling tall tales.

The truth is, while anti-capitalists are wholly entitled to their 'right-to-reply', and will view advertising as packaged lies in a damnable world, the world we live in *is* a capitalist one, where buying is a key driver, and adver-tising is the necessary flux.

And I don't see how liking and buying things has to occupy a moral low ground. Since when did liking stuff, enjoying material things, automatically make someone shallow? Having possessions does not dictate that people can't also run deep. It's a non sequitur. People with no material goods aren't automatically spiritual by nature of their not owning anything.

It's the responsibility of the pro-advertising camp to ensure the observ-ance of a moral code; a code whereby products are promoted and brands built on a foundation of truth. This is in everyone's interest. More and more often, advertising and reality are twains that *do* meet. Good advertising, *effective advertising*, necessitates their union and their working together. I think that's the real truth of it.

IRRATIONAL REASONING, MAGPIE DESIRE AND THE WATCH FROM OUTER SPACE

> " The Human Condition
> is a Constantly
> Unsatisfied one.
> This is not
> a bad thing.
> We are all in
> a permanent state of
> desire, of wanting,
> for one thing or
> another. 'Desire'
> exists to address
> a deficiency, whether
> for food to appease
> hunger, or a luxury
> handbag, to imbue
> social standing.
> Both desires are
> for a 'return to
> balance', where
> a current imbalance
> exists. "

> *The marketers decided it is dangerous to assume that people can be trusted to behave in a rational way... If people couldn't discriminate reasonably, marketers reasoned, they should be assisted in discriminating 'unreasonably', in some easy, warm, emotional way.*
>
> VANCE PACKARD *THE HIDDEN PERSUADERS* (1957)

O r as my granny, Marjorie, used to say, 'Tha's now't so queer as folk.'

A common expression in the north of England, and a statement of truth, albeit from the mouths of those likely born sometime around the beginning of the last century, and unlikely to still be with us. Of course, it's a statement of truth that still applies, however thick or thin the accent involved. And while queer may now assume rather different connotations, few would be wise to challenge Marjorie's meaning. There's nothing odder, nothing stranger, than folk.

We are a curious and compelling pick 'n' mix of issues and motivations, a never-ending riddle, constantly surprising, so often unpredictable.

And I love that. It's one of the reasons I work in advertising.

> *Why do we do what we do? Why do we behave the way we behave? What motivates us? Drives us? What issues lie beneath?*

Fine questions, all of them. People are a mystery... and yet... they are also not.

Given the right triggers, the right stimulus, people can be quite predictable. With the exception of impulse behaviours born of clinical madness, all behaviour is with reason.

Every reason provides a guilty tell into the inner workings of the human heart or mind. What's so compelling is that only occasionally is human reason anchored in straight, neatly tram-tracked logic. Human beings we are, Vulcans we are not – meaning, there's method to almost all our apparent madness, but Mr Spock would have a hard time joining the dots.

Whenever research investigates people's media habits, it always reveals a massive over-claim in the declared reading of the more cerebral and high-brow titles. *The Economist, The Times, Business Week*: all are examples that would punch double their circulation if everyone who said they read them actually did.

FIGURE 23.1 *The Economist*: one of the many brilliant print executions by AMV

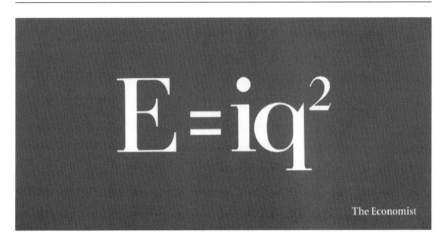

We're not good at admitting our guilty pleasures, but white lies that portray us as wider-read and better-informed come easy. We reason, why should a modest thing like honesty get in the way of a more impressive self-image?

VEBLEN GOODS

The first time I came across Veblen goods, I had to marvel at how it so succinctly illustrates 'irrational reasoning'. Veblen goods, aka: 'I WANT to pay more! The MORE expensive it is, the MORE I LIKE it!'

> *Veblen goods are a group of commodities for which people's preference for buying them increases as a direct function of their price, as greater price confers greater status.*
>
> SOURCE: WIKIPEDIA

Wanting to pay more is, at face value, absurdly irrational – but face value and snob value are very different beasts. With Veblen goods, the notion of value is reinterpreted, is no longer literal, meaning snob value is simply a different kind of ROI (return on investment).

What does the purchase of luxury goods afford? Potentially a concise and consciously indiscrete badge, screaming, 'I'm a success, have money, can afford this! Acknowledge me!'

Our conspicuous consumption is now so evolved, so beyond blushing, that it can even afford to be ironic and still maintain the ticket price. Consider *Bling H₂0*: $40 bottled water decorated in Swarovski crystals.

We can all be ('thieving') magpies in our fancy for shiny trinkets, in our lust for jewellery and gems and all things bling. And if 'bling banditry' is a touch vulgar for our particular strand of materialistic snobbery, alternatives remain to still tone-down *and* overindulge. We may walk the line signed stealth wealth, of discrete luxury and inferred 'high quality', so displaying our impeccable taste, as to be similarly appreciated by a 'good taste set' of fellow lux goods in-the-know-ers who are *just like us*.

FIGURE 23.2 Louis Vuitton, print ad (May 2010)

Following complaints to the ASA, the Louis Vuitton ad in Figure 23.2 – Louis Vuitton, print ad, May 2010: 'The seamstress... A needle, linen thread, beeswax, and infinite patience protect each over-stitch from humidity and the passage of time.' – was pulled for being misleading. Louis Vuitton handbags are in fact machine stitched.

STELLA ARTOIS

Placing economic theory in the hands of a copywriter, Stella Artois' UK strapline (from 1982 to 2007) was a sharp, snappy salute to Veblen. 'Reassuringly expensive' was a brilliant piece of copywriting, but the real genius lay in the fact it was referring to a lager, *and* in that it needed to slight-of-hand drinkers into being happy to pay more for it, given the heavier duty applied to higher ABV beverages.

Feel reassured by the expense. Enjoy paying more! What an awesome head space for any brand to occupy. On trade, at the bar, Stella Artois became the gold standard for what it was to be a 'Premium' lager.

FIGURE 23.3 Stella Artois print campaign, 'Reassuringly expensive', by Lowe Lintas. Two fine examples (2000)

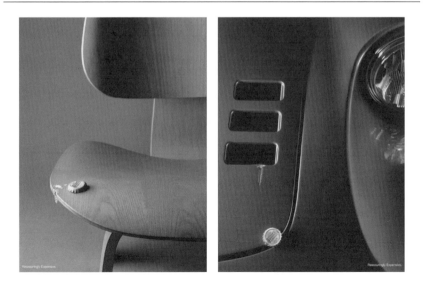

Crisply ironic and largely unappreciated, up and down the supermarket aisles of Britain, Stella Artois (in bottle and can) ran close to a 52-week-a-year promotional discount. 'Reassuringly expensive'... and 'always on offer'.

For a good while, Stella Artois got to have it both ways, with their off-trade discounting seen by shoppers as an opportunistic 'deal' rather than a contradictory pricing strategy that devalued brand perception. It was all very clever stuff, with Stella Artois 'marketing' showing all the wiles of a seen-it-and-sold-it-all rug trader in a dusty souk.

PATEK PHILIPPE

Patek Philippe's advertising also makes its pitch to offer the best of both worlds. It's all treat, no guilt, for the high-income family man who wants to feel *selfless* about indulging more than £10k on a wristwatch: 'You never actually own a Patek Philippe. You merely take care of it for the next generation.'

I once worked with a creative director who had a borderline physical reaction every time he saw this Patek Philippe campaign. And no, it wasn't a positive physical reaction, more 'big red welts of contempt' – but, like Stella Artois, here too there is a blend of genius at work.

Diametrically opposing a world of fast consumerism, of layer upon layer of consumer landfill made ever deeper by so much disposable material goods, we have Patek Philippe. We have quality, craftsmanship; we have a sense of true timelessness. A wildly self-indulgent luxury article becomes 'an heirloom'. *For your son*, where selfishness is flipped as familial benevolence, materialism as a mortality dampener.

The 'social sciences' may just text-book this up as 'over-justification', but it's quite brilliantly effective. No one likes to be in conflict (*cognitive dissonance* is no fun), and no one has to be with this kind of easy, multi-levelled justification from the knowing pen of Tim Delaney (of Leagas Delaney).

Surely any advertising that manages such a blatant and effective guilt-appeasing hustle, and sugars the purchase by implying a small shot at remembrance and immortality, has to nail a few jury votes?

FIGURE 23.4 Patek Philippe, print ad (May 2011)

HALDA

Authenticity and rarity are, of course, among the more rational high-price-point justifiers.

A friend of mine, a senior partner at the seriously hot and seriously cool Forsman & Bodenfors, also sidelines in the watch business. Hans helped his friend Mikael develop a watch prototype that they then sent into space, aboard *Discovery*, decorating the wrist of Swedish astronaut Christer Fuglesang.

'The Halda Concept' is a 128-piece wristwatch that comes with two interchangeable 'modules', one mechanical, the other digital: the former for planet Earth, the latter for those moments spent journeying the Final Frontier.

Made from NASA certified TECAMAX, it's very lightweight, resistant to extreme 'space-like' temperatures, and the Vertu-like digital module also measures G-Force. All in all, it's all rather James Bond.

The primary target group for a 'space tested' Halda wristwatch? The 5,000 people who've made a down payment on a US$200k ticket to travel by 'the world's first commercial spaceline', Virgin Galactic. And the secondary target, as Hans put it best, 'someone who wants the ultimate bar-side conversation piece on their arm.'

Some may dispute whether 'ultimate' is to the exclusion of anyone dating a supermodel... but then, sporting supermodel arm-candy is still more

FIGURE 23.5 The Halda Concept: built for time and space

commonplace than a wristwatch that can boast of your endurance to G-Force acceleration.

PERMANENT WANTING

Headlining Maslow's 'hierarchy of needs', Wikipedia runs with: 'Human beings have wants and desires which influence their behaviour. Only un-satisfied needs influence behaviour, satisfied needs do not.'

I say that the human condition is a constantly unsatisfied one. This is not a bad thing. This is not a cynical statement. We are all in a permanent state of desire, of *wanting*, for one thing or another. 'Desire' exists to address a deficiency, whether for food to appease hunger, or a luxury handbag to imbue social standing. Both desires are for a 'return to balance', where a current imbalance exists.

Advertising is 'the business of selling'. To do this well, it must appreciate what people are *really* buying. Typically, they're buying gestures, gestures that contribute and compensate, that return balance. They're potentially buying social status and self-esteem, recognition and respect, belonging via 'clique approval'. They're buying individualism, or maybe the short-term 'feel good' of accumulation. All advertising is an appeal to act, so behind the appeal is a clarion call to our most rooted human desires.

Does advertising create desire, or does it merely play to those perennial needs that exist within us? Is *effective* advertising the sinister science of hidden persuasion, or simply an empathetic mirroring of the human condition?

Advertising that *works* knows its audience all too well. Advertising makes most sense when it has the clearest sense of its audience, however irrational, conflicted or seemingly queer that audience may be.

'WITH GREAT POWER...': ADVERTISING TO OUR INNER SUPERHERO

```
BOURNE  I fought my way out of
        an embassy. I climbed
        down a fifty-foot
        wall — I went out the
        window and I was doing
        it — I just did it.
        I knew how to do it.

MARIE   People do amazing things
        when they're scared.

BOURNE  Why do I? — I come in
        here, and the first thing
        I'm doing is I'm catching
        the sightlines and
        looking for an exit.

                (He leans in.
                Flat out now.)

BOURNE  I can tell you the
        license plate numbers of
```

```
all six cars outside.
I can tell you that our
waitress is left-handed
and the guy sitting up at
the counter weighs two
hundred fifteen pounds and
knows how to handle
himself. I know the best
place to look for a gun
is the cab of the gray
truck outside, and at
this altitude, I can run
flat out for a half mile
before my hands start to
shake. Now why would
I know that? How can
I know that and not know
who I am?
```

The Bourne Identity (2002),
                    Pre-shooting script

Secretly, maybe not even that secretly, most grown men on the planet also wish they knew the stuff Jason Bourne knows. Bourne is a classic hero archetype, a capeless strain of the superhero variety. Utterly resourceful, awe-inspiringly capable... but also an insomniac who slowly discovers he's a highly trained super agent.

In *The Matrix* (1999), Keanu Reeves is Neo, an office-cubicled nobody who has the faintest itch of a suspicion that his world might not be all it appears, and that his name could just be a letter-jumble. After much self doubt and gunplay, and having Kung Fu mastery brainjacked straight into his prefrontal cortex (or somewhere), it all comes good. 'Bullet time', for him, is slow time, and he quickly rearranges Neo to appreciate he's 'the One'.

Journeys of self-discovery are just great when you end up in a place where you're some kind of James Bond or Cyber Superman. I find hero mythology fascinating.

I think brands help with our self-constructed inner superhero, and that a certain sub-genre of advertising is there to knowingly appeal and feed the Batman within us.

TV ads for Snickers, the Ford Focus and Universal Studios are all recent-past examples of really charming and very knowing nods to the superhero we all want to be, wish we were and believe that maybe, somewhere inside, we actually are. Escapism, wish-fulfilment – for brands, these are associational levers within easy reach.

PERSONAL FABLE

> The Personal Fable, a term coined by David Elkind (1967), is used to describe a form of egocentrism normally exhibited during early adolescence, characterized by an over-differentiating of one's experiences and feelings from others to the point of assuming those experiences are unique from those of others. A person might believe that he is the only one who can experience whatever feelings of joy, horror, misery, or confusion he might encounter.
>
> SOURCE: WIKIPEDIA

They say our egocentricity dilutes as we pass through childhood, as with greater sense of self we develop a wider sense of other(s). We gradually, begrudgingly learn that not everyone is purely here for our own amusement or distraction. It's a tough dawning. Maybe even a lesson that doesn't find its footing with everyone. Does ego diminish that much with maturity? Consider the various egos that have ever orbited your working world. How many, past or present, have really developed cognitive range beyond that of a six-year-old struggling to 'de-centre'?

Take it as rhetorical. Response unnecessary.

My point is this: we all like the idea of a universe existing for and serving our ends, where we're the heroic central lead in our own remarkable life narrative. Being 'the One' is a play-theme impossible for our egos to tire of.

Adolescent or not, we're all very capable of dreaming up and living out personal fables, of feeling and wanting to feel 'unique'. In many ways, I'd argue this is pretty healthy: to feel special, of worth, have a little self-esteem going on.

A little like Neo, for the vast (male) majority, 'all things hero' brain-jacks wirelessly into whichever parking bay of the encephalon is responsible for wish-fulfilment.

FIGURE 24.1 *7-Up* 'Get Real Action', by Bob Peak, plays like an action scene from a Steve McQueen movie

The American illustrator Bob Peak was a grand master at overlaying glamorous, dynamic scenarios on basic 'product sell' print advertising. Peak's illustrations are all very alive, but highly stylized. They're less 'real world', much more about a seductively cartoon world, of action and sass and sex appeal. From the vaults: 7-Up, Winston cigarettes, Diners Club: three examples from his prolific canon.

FIGURE 24.2 Winston 'Flavor your fun...' press ad, by Bob Peak, shakes (not stirs) memories of the Bond movie *On Her Majesty's Secret Service*

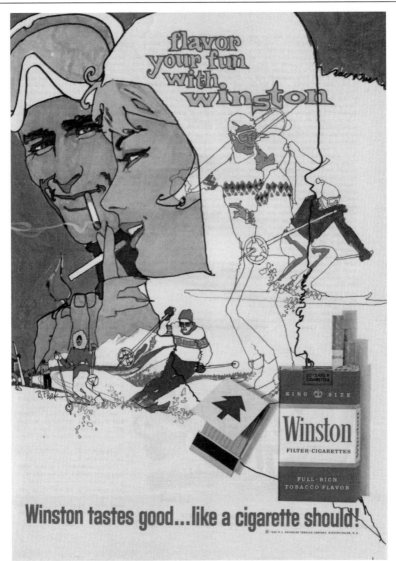

FIGURE 24.3 Bob Peak's 'Diners Club Guy' is *classic* ad invention. A strong-lined, cool-cat archetype alluring to any who felt they could roll with the Rat Pack

Fast-forward fifty-some years and the same rules are still conscientiously observed. Here we have Jude Law as... 'Dunhill Guy':

FIGURE 24.4 Jude Law in Dunhill – Spring/Summer 2009 advertising campaign

And here's the question: when we look at these kinds of ads, are we looking at Jude, or looking at Jude and then transposing ourselves on to the scene, imagining how cool we'd look in the dune buggy or safari suit? (Okay, maybe not the safari suit.)

THE PRETENDING LAYER

Agency über planner Russell Davies uses a terrific expression: 'the pretending layer'. Davies talks about how using a product, a computer for example, should contribute to our moment of private role play:

> *It's not just a useful or beautiful or functional object – it's got some little nod to who we're pretending to be when we're using it... for the imaginary me.*

This is something that Apple's advertising understands supremely well. Their silhouette device is a very shrewd one, a cipher for audiences to place themselves in the scene, to jack right into 'the feeling of using' Apple, of *living* Apple.

The 'pretending layer' plays to our eternal inner child, to that five-year old within who liked dressing up in primary colours and perhaps a cape. And as we grow older and grow up, our imaginative play goes sub-surface, but stays close, finding subtler forms and assuming more implicit brand costumes.

We still self-define. We are cool, trendy, maybe edgy. We are chic, a geek, possibly geek-chic. We're going places. In-places where It-people go. Etc, etc, etc. For going and being any, some, all of these things, brands help build our personal narratives and bolster our pretences.

Where we choose a Swatch over a Seiko, a Panerai over a Rolex, it all says something, and it's all very deliberately *meant* to say something. We have Boden family moments; we have Butlins family moments; we're an upscaling Prada couple; we're a downshifting Primark couple.

We buy into brands because they're signifiers. They signify a whole bundle of values that we *buy into*, believe *define us* and our view on the world. 'Our Brands' echo our definitions of who we are and who we want to be, and at a more playful extreme, the brands we assimilate help sharpen the resolution on our superhero projections.

MENTAL PROPS FOR WALKING TALLER

Bond film director Lewis Gilbert once said that the magical effect of a Bond movie is that you leave the theatre walking that bit taller. All boys, of all ages, deep down, want to be 007.

Dodge bullets, fly, always get the girl: we know we can't but we still like the idea, and there's nothing wrong with dreaming, of still feeling like a kid from time to time. Advertising knows this and is here to help, here to fuel our escapist flights of fantasy with suitable mental props, a fictional scenario here, a role-model outline there, an invitation-to-regress served on the side.

Once equipped, how far we go with our superhero role play is really up to us... though a little moderation is probably advisable.

DAVE LIZEWSKI

I always wondered why no one did it before me. I mean, all those comic books, movies, TV shows... you think that one eccentric loner would've made himself a costume. I mean, is everyday life really so exciting? Are schools and offices so thrilling that I'm the only one who fantasized about this? Come on, be honest with yourself, at some point in our lives we all wanna be a superhero.

Kick-Ass (2010)

THE BIG H

DON DRAPER

Advertising is based on
one thing:
Happiness.
And you know what
happiness is?
Happiness is the smell
of a new car.
It's freedom from fear.
It's a billboard on the
side of the road that
screams with reassurance
that whatever you're
doing is okay.

(Almost to himself)
You are okay.

Mad Men (2007)
Season 1, Episode 1

Don's right.

At least, he is about the first part. Maslow, for one, might want to challenge on what happiness 'is'. (It partly depends on how much you like cars and how they smell.) But happiness as a central, emphatic pursuit – happiness as an undeniable, unfaltering, ultimate human goal – I'm very down with that.

For all of us, happiness is our *one ultimate end*. Boil it right the way down, reduce all those different motivational drivers, and sitting right there at the centre of our very human hearts is our yearning to be happy. Happiness is sitting there, knowingly smiling back at us, the reason behind all the things we do.

I believe this.

Flip it round 180 degrees. I won't stretch it so far as to say that the human condition is driven by cowardice... but our deliberate avoidance of discomfort features pretty large and centre stage.

The human condition is smart enough to know that feeling miserable (slightly or acutely) is no fun condition to be in. It's undesirable because it's simply so very *unpleasant*. And no one *likes* unpleasant.

In the presence of 'the unpleasant', we physically react. We fight, we flight, we respond instinctively, viscerally, we catch-up mentally, and then it's a serious mental strain to stop ourselves from turning and running if things look ugly or threaten to turn nasty.

Flip it back again, back to the positive.

Innately, we *pursue* happiness. It is the perfect, desirable state of being. For all of us. Masochism? No contradiction here. Masochists *enjoy* misery. A little pain makes them happy. No need to baffle at the surface contradiction. Just roll with the root motivation.

Context and circumstance, of course, set the scene. Maslow, 68 years on, remains on the pulse.

'Happy' is food and shelter if you're hungry and cold. Happiness is benevolence and giving if you personally have so much. Billionaire philanthropists are philanthropic for a reason. Once you have everything that a Hollywood movie star has then you typically find yourself wanting an audience with the Dalai Lama. Existential angst only tends to follow once your tummy doesn't grumble and you potentially have a star on Hollywood Boulevard.

So if happiness is what it's all about, the Big Question is a rather specific and obvious one. *'How do I get there? What's my line of pursuit? How do I get close, lock it down?'*

Because happiness can be pretty slippery, damnably elusive, would be quite the dodge-ball opponent. As Don Draper appreciates so very well, this is where 'advertising' comes in, to 'show the way' – because advertising silver-platters the oh-so-many routes, signposts by easy means of pretty pictures and seductive words. Advertising is *based* on happiness – and the one thing, therefore, that every powerful piece of advertising must imply?

Hope.

I once pitched a big insurance company that had recently renamed and needed to build some emotional value and high-recall into their brand. Our big idea was beautifully simple: 'Own Sunrise'.

Associate with sunrise, make the brand – in name, whenever heard or seen – utterly synonymous with sunrise. What better visual device? Pure hope. A new day. Renewal and possibility.

FIGURE 25.1 The hope of a new day

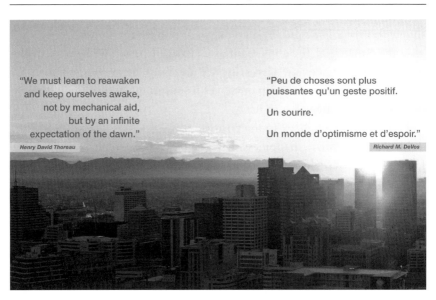

Reframe insurance 'in the positive'. Insurance: *not* a hedge against a worst-case scenario... but 'personal future-proofing', affording peace-of-mind for today, meaning you're covered, smart, have done the right thing, are providing for you and your loved ones. 'Having insurance' should mean one less thing to worry about, should make you feel happier and free you up to worry less and pursue more happiness.

They loved it.

We loved it.

We didn't get the business. It's still the best pitch I didn't win.

Brands need to be 'happy hits' of short-lived feel good. A Molton & Brown soap dispenser on your bathroom sink; an iPod in your pocket; the feel of a Mont Blanc pen when I first wrote this sentence on a scruff of paper on my journey to work. Brands are made to make us *feel better*, to help give us what we *want*.

For many, *happiness defined* might be as clear-cut as wanting to be a rock star. For others, maybe happiness is a simple concept but an opaque and moving target, where owning a new car and enjoying its smell just won't quite cut it. It's fundamentally because happiness is a whole lot easier said than done that we have advertising. Because Advertising is Hope, the largely unsubstantiated hope that everything really will be okay. That before things turn bad, there can be a heap of good stuff. That happiness isn't about chasing the horizon, but running towards a fixed point. That we are born to live, and the objective of any lifetime is to cram it with as much happiness as can be found.

Advertising is the offer of hope, that happiness – however temporal and potentially fleeting – is at least touchable and wholly real. You just have to believe and buy.

BUYING WINE, GETTING HER TO DRINK IT AND OTHER ADLAND MISDEMEANOURS

> " Adland is no different to any other industry badlands. There are rednecks with shotguns, for sure, just like anywhere, and maybe some hungry tigers too, but also like a Narnia, there are friendly lions and new frontiers forming all the time, where you get to play explorer, pioneer, and cartographer. That can be thrilling. "

I n the movie *Jerry Maguire*, Jerry succumbs to a nocturnal bout of con-
science and a slice of 'bad pizza'. He spends the night writing '*The Things
We Think But Do Not Say*', which he then circulates to all his colleagues.
And then he gets fired.

This isn't one of those times. This isn't about the things that ad folk dare
not say. They're a pretty opinionated, vocal, often bolshie lot even at the
most demure of times. But to write about brand invention, I think it's worth
briefly making a practitioner's address to some of the barriers. If you're
going to talk about outward-facing brands that ace it in the real world,
I figure it's helpful to pass comment on a few themes and debates that go
on behind the gate and inside the chocolate factory. Such as, if we're going
to talk strategy, let's be clear on what we should mean. Like, what is the
role of the ad agency and what kind of relationship should an agency have
with its clients? Squaring away this kind of stuff allows the smarts and
magic to happen, while getting bogged down and giving it a Sisyphean naval
gaze will, I believe, only guarantee mediocrity.

Here we go.

STRATEGICALLY SPEAKING... IT'S ONE

When we say 'strategy'... just what do we *mean*?

And, more crucially, what *should* we mean? Because I hear it way too
often, that word 'strategy', and it happens far too often, how everyone *needs*
a strategy, a separate strategy for *everything*.

You have one campaign, one brief, and before anyone has conceived the
first half-baked first draft and most likely wildly off-beam idea... there are
half-a-dozen different 'strategies' being needed and coveted and banded
about the place.

There'll be an express-and-urgent-and-heartfelt need for... a *brand* strategy;
a *creative* strategy; a *communications* strategy; a *media* strategy; a *digital*
strategy; a *PR* strategy; a *below-the-line* strategy...

And some of the aforementioned may be blended or replaced (depending
on the in-vogue parlance or a given agency's 'world view') with an 'engagement strategy', a 'disruption strategy', a 'dissonance strategy', an 'activation
strategy'... and the list I assure you doesn't end there.

How can these 'strategies' all help? How do they all align? How are they
all different but wholly vital to the cause, while still being... crucially...
complementary?

They can't be.

Ego-feasting, posturing and land-grabbing, unilateral authorships and cluttered thinking; all get in the way of purpose and of developing great strategic thinking. Let's take a moment, a breath, a pause and apply some clear thinking.

And breathe in.

And out.

Okay.

I love language and I love words, but 'strategy' is a real front-runner for chronic abuse through overuse. In so many hands, 'strategy' has assumed so many meanings as to become potentially meaningless.

When it comes to definitions, dictionaries are a pretty good place to start, and I'd suggest the following two definitions are rock-solid:

Strategy – noun:

1 *Long-range planning and development to ensure victory.*

2 *A plan-of-action intended to accomplish a specific goal or result, using all disposable resources to execute as effectively as possible.*

So, where does this clear and defined start-point then take us?

Ideally, there should be a *business strategy*. That's the best place to start. And then... that's where brands come in – because brands, done right, build business; they grow the bottom line.

To build a brand you need a plan, which involves a whole host of people, of professional specialists, all pulling together in the same direction, behind a common purpose, setting out and holding hands along a common path... and that's 'The Strategy'. (As well as being a beautiful image and a little slice of wishful Adland nirvana.)

There is, therefore, only one strategy.

> One Ring to rule them all,
> One Ring to find them,
> One Ring to bring them all
> And in the darkness bind them.
>
> JRR TOLKEIN, *THE FELLOWSHIP OF THE RING* (1954)

Just replace *Ring* with *Strategy*, and we're there. Creative, digital, PR, direct response, experiential, ambient, etc: it's all about linking into that one given strategy and expressing it through any given specialist, contributing strand. One strategy, *One collective intent*.

I've too often sat around a conference table where everyone starts talking a strategy for this and a strategy for that. It may be a touch gothic to suggest my blood has boiled and my urge to decapitate swelled, but trust me the restraint needed has at moments been quite Herculean.

One strategy, *multiple* and many expressions, activations and amplifications, with all moving parts always and completely aligned. Simple, uncomplicated, how it should be.

FIGURE 26.1 One insight, one strategic platform, multiple expressions

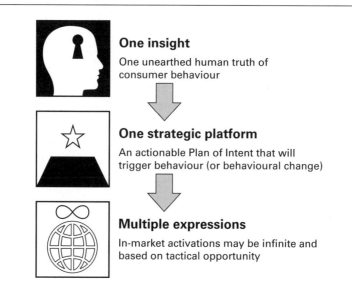

One insight
One unearthed human truth of consumer behaviour

One strategic platform
An actionable Plan of Intent that will trigger behaviour (or behavioural change)

Multiple expressions
In-market activations may be infinite and based on tactical opportunity

Of course, square away the definitions, stop sitting round abstractly debating what a strategy 'is and isn't', and then the real tough thinking starts. The real trick is ensuring that any plan is a good one, and then in finest *A-Team* style, making sure it comes together. Benjamin Disraeli warned of flawed, broken thinking in the planning process...

The most dangerous strategy is to jump a chasm in TWO leaps.

No arguments there; all the more reason to get it right upfront. Realizing the strategy sucks only when you come to execute it can lead to some rather nasty falls.

But the even better word on this goes to the English comedy writer Frank Muir, who clearly knew the score:

> Strategy *is buying a bottle of fine wine when you take a lady out for dinner.* Tactics *is getting her to drink it.*

SYSTEMIC THINKING... IN THE NAME OF STRATEGY

> *STRATEGY is: A style of thinking, a conscious and deliberate process, an intensive implementation system, the science of insuring FUTURE SUCCESS.*
>
> PETER JOHNSON, AUTHOR AND HISTORIAN

Most agencies implicitly acknowledge Johnson's definition of 'strategy'... because every agency feels the heavy need for an 'implementation system', a 'planning process', a 'tool to call their own'... that they can wheel out in pitches (wheel-shaped visualizations are common), use to assert how they are different from the pitching field, use to internally train their planning staff... and use to demonstrate how they can both embrace best practice *and* remain permanently on the cusp of innovation.

Yes, betwixt the above lines you will have felt a needle of sarcasm, so for balance, let me add this. Best practice is *best* and having a *process* is how you get there. But there are also caveats, otherwise (back to Johnson's definition) all 'style of thinking'... ends up losing all style.

Planning is only *part process*, and over-fixation with 'the process' is to the distraction and detriment of desired outcome. And a desirable outcome – *smart thinking, great work* – is the only reason for championing a process in the first place.

An agency's planning process, or 'system', or 'tool', may well be an acronym. Big organizations (agency and corporate alike) tend to be utterly adoring of acronyms. Consider 'real world' examples such as:

- TCP (Total Comms Planning);
- IBM (Integrated Brand Marketing);
- IBC (Integrated Brand Communications);
- ICP (Integrated Communications Planning).

All are absolutely harmless, so long as no one goes confusing them with WMD's symbol variants:

FIGURE 26.2   WMD symbol variants: not to be confused with ICP, TCP, IBM *et al*

Cheap acronym gags aside, all four of the aforementioned are fine and decent planning processes as long as they're taken with a pinch of human-istic perspective. All are very systemic left-brain carefully plotted and con-veniently linear road maps to – *and here's the thing* – a fundamentally more right-brained, intuitive, zig-zaggy discipline. Yes, you've got to learn the rules in order to then start breaking them, but once you know the rules it's wise to recognize that everyone has the same toolkit back at the ranch, and it's the human dimension that makes or breaks a good piece of communica-tions thinking. Because there ain't much imagination born of mechanistic thinking.

Some agencies go a step further, dodge the acronym pratfall. Planning systems have been known to be named after volcanoes (no copyrights on 'Etna'), winning chess moves, or consciously treated with cheeky post-modern irony – 'The Big Tool' remains a personal favourite of mine.

Whatever the volcano, irony or acronym, a tool is a tool is a tool. And while there's nothing wrong with a good tool, there's also a clear bottom line.

Use a tool, don't be a tool.

WHAT THE @#$&...?

Here's one of those moments where you might even feel like a bit of a tool. It's one of those moments to avoid. Where it's a big joke and you have the disagreeable feeling that fate has made you the punchline.

The moment goes something like this. You've had an epiphany, a moment of blinding clarity, been left dumbfounded by your own smarts. You've looked into the darkest potholes of the human condition and seen truth, felt genuine understanding; surfaced into the light, articulated your beliefs with crisp, elegant simplicity; concocted a quite brilliant plan for contriving the spiritual confluence of 'brand' and 'consumer'; and the end product is... a TV ad that looks just like the director's last TV ad. And, in truth, like the one before that.

Your strategy has just fallen off a cliff. A big cliff. You can't even make out the busted-up remains at the bottom. It may even have evaporated on the way down.

At best, there'll be a TV ad, some TV airtime; someone, somewhere has bought some poster sites; and sometime soon after the brand and campaign tracking needle goes marginally up, or down (either is statistically irrelevant), and it's really a 'planners' debate' (read: exists in a vacuum, like the original strategy) as to whether the sales figures are causal, coincidental, or may, in some near-to-far-off future *become* causal... or not.

All in all, it's a less than great day in the office. I suggest you try to avoid it. Try to avoid having *that day*.

How?

Well, have you ever thought about Sales? No, really, I'm serious.

'SELL IT TO ME' – THE CONSIGLIORE POSITIONING

As far as I'm concerned, everyone in advertising is 'a suit'. Everyone's accountable. Everyone's in Sales. The client pays the bill, you get your salary. No client, no gig, no money for Smarties. Just long, lonely, contemplative walks in the park. Without any Smarties to munch on. This is the cause-effect equation.

I believe that good agency planners are *only* as good as their ability to sell their thinking, agency creatives only as good as their words and pictures. McCann-Erickson headlines what they do with *Ideas Well Told*. That's their mantra. I think 'Ideas Well Sold' is pointedly even closer to the mark, and I see little wrong with this emphasis. Have a great idea; selling it should be easy, but still make sure you do it well.

Of course, 'sales', 'selling', 'salesman', these are dirty words to some. They come with ugly baggage. The salesman is desperate, is dishonest. Self-interest is his eternal ulterior motive.

> BLAKE
> A-I-D-A. Get out there — you got the prospects coming in. You think they came in to get out of the rain? A guy don't walk on the lot lest he wants to buy. They're sitting out there waiting to give you their money. Are you gonna take it? Are you man enough to take it?
> *Glengarry Glen Ross* (1992), Writer: David Mamet

With David Mamet's words at his disposal, Alec Baldwin's cameo as Blake in *Glengarry Glen Ross* is pure, uncut, cinematic cocaine. But it's no role model for any Ad Man, even if you are taking it and giving it daily, feeling the heat of the punks to the left of you and the pugilists to your right.

Certainly, the litany of external 'suppliers' orbiting a company's marketing function will be numerous, borderline comical: Advertising, Media, Digital, PR, Below-the-line, maybe throw in a 'Planning Boutique'. Typically, where the number is any greater than one (and it's almost always greater than one), it's a lot of egos, some chancers, and a whole lot of posturing, politicking, undermining and destabilizing. It might all be very exhausting, but it's 'the game', and to prevail you've got to be happy (enough) to play the game all day every day. Because everyone wants the 'ear of the client'. Everyone ideally wants the ascendant role, to be the lead agency, to sit top of the tree, be the one orchestrating manoeuvres and calling the shots.

> *In terms of the relationship between many advertising and media planning agencies, it's a little like watching porcupines mate. Who is in the lead is often not clear, it is painful for everyone and no one is really sure when the mission has been accomplished.*
> DICK METZLER, EVP DHL EXPRESS

There's only one way to gain trust, earn confidence and get to call the shots. Don't hustle. Play it straight. Sell what you *believe* is right. Because I say there's selling... and then there's selling. The great thing about the ad industry is, when it's done well, you're selling and your client's buying, and there's not some tug-of-war across a ravine of suspicion. The agency work is produced *for* them, based on what you think they need and what you trust will work.

With hope, you want to sell your client the equivalent of a Ferrari, that's really reliable, with great mileage, cheap parts and the kind of roll cage that goes into a Volvo.

'Sales' is never ugly or ulterior if you're selling an idea you truly believe in.

So in the best client-agency relationships, there is no them-and-us. You don't sit across a table from one another, *opposing*, brokering a ceasefire or resolving a trade union dispute. You occupy the same side of the table as your client. You trouble and preoccupy about the same issues. You go to bed and worry the same worries – and if you're good at what you do, you wake up in the morning with a few ideas. *That's* your value. That's your contribution to the relationship. Your role, *my role*, I've always thought, is that of consigliore.

Agency planners, client handlers and creatives who roll up their sleeves, sell well and make it happen, who get the job done – they're worth their salt (and their smarties).

Because these are 'our times': life within a capitalist structure, post-industrial, mostly light industry, light on manufacturing. It pretty much leaves us with our ideas, our conviction and our ability to bring our thinking to the table and hypnotically to life.

Audacious ideas, genuine innovation, so-sharp-it-might-cut creativity: that's *The Ad Industry Well Told* (and well sold), and that's no bad thing. In fact, it's the complete opposite. It's all good and as it should be.

So, I say go sell it.

AND FINALLY, JUST REMEMBER...

1   Wearing black does not make you smarter or create an air of mystique around you (despite what I said about black on page 132).

2   'Ceiling-staring' and looking into middle distance does not convince that you are deep in deep thoughts.

3   Wearing thick-set glasses, shaving your head, driving a Vespa maybe, and drinking espressos in Soho neither makes you a pseudo-intellectual nor of a form 'more cool'.

4   Having a business card with a job title that suggests world leaders seek your counsel does not put 10 points on your IQ.

Being smart and doing humblingly brilliant work is *not* determined by your job title, business card or wardrobe selection.

Now, we all understand that everyone, by degree, can feel a need to compensate, to compensate for whatever anxiety or perceived inadequacy they fear they're carrying around with them, perched whispering on their shoulder, vibrating from inside an emotional closet deep inside their palpitating heart. As long as *you* know it, it doesn't matter what *they* know. If their particular set of compensatory emperor's clothes is working out for them – the self-contrived pantomime they've got going on is salving their soul and stabilizing their wobbles – then let 'em roll with it.

I enjoy a fine caricature, and the ad industry is full of every two-dimensional stereotype pretty much ever conceived: geek chic, power player, super suit, Napoleon complex, posh boy, wide boy, barrow boy, ivory tower intellectual, straight shooter, overachiever, slacker, silver fox, ladykiller, ball breaker, marriage wrecker, rainmaker, and the beat goes on.

I'd argue that it's best to get on with 'being you'. If you can square away what being you means, you'll be a good length ahead of most of us.

Adland is no different to any other industry badlands. There are rednecks with shotguns, for sure, just like anywhere, and maybe some hungry tigers too, but also like a Narnia, there are friendly lions and new frontiers forming all the time, where you get to play explorer, pioneer and cartographer. That can be thrilling.

Good luck and be safe out there. And remember: lions good, tigers bad.

PART THREE

DAWN OF A MEDIA DEMOCRACY

INTRODUCTION

> **"** We are waking to
> the dawn of a Media
> Democracy.
>
> Digital Media is
> changing the way
> we live our lives.
>
> Social Media is
> personally liberating
> and collectively
> empowering, a means
> to political regime
> change and to people
> more able to express
> who they are. **"**

> " *I have a vision. Television.*
>
> U2, ZOO TV TOUR, 1992

I'm pretty sure everything works to a system, an order of one kind or other. The natural world, natural selection, evolution, survival of the fittest, a hierarchy of ascending prey and predators. A very clear order, where it's very clear that you want to be hanging out at the summit.

Replicating the natural order, we have social and political hierarchies, some with clear demarcations, others more subtle, but all rigid in how they are observed by the powerful, the empowered and the powerless. There are triangles everywhere.

The communication landscape – the world of media – has its own system, its own natural selection. TV sits top of the tree. As Nicole Kidman observed in *To Die For* (1995), 'You're not anybody in America unless you're on TV.' Gus van Sant's movie darkly satirized the idea that just about everyone wants to be on television, because television *validates*, imbues with importance, makes significant. It *justifies*. This was, at least the long-held thinking, the convention, back in the *Mad Men* days of Don Draper and company. People want to be famous. Brands want to be famous. Ergo, television.

Jump forward half a century, and within some (make that many) marketing circles, not so much has changed. The vision remains. Television. A brand that advertises on TV is a brand that is justified, is credible in people's eyes, making it worthy of their attention and consideration. Television makes an impression; people are *impressed* by who and what they see on television.

But times, it is fair to say, they are a-changing.

We are waking to a new dawn, the dawn of a media democracy. I believe this and I think it's a truly, 'no-spin-required', remarkable time with untold and yet to unfold possibilities for how society will evolve. It's a speculator's paradise. No one knows for sure, but everyone's entitled to a view and it's no bad thing if everyone has one.

But what do I mean by a *media democracy*? I mean that there's *inclusivity*, that everything's up for grabs and everyone's invited. I mean that digital media is changing the way we live our lives. I mean that social media is personally liberating and collectively empowering, a means to political regime change (see 'Web 3.0: regime change', page 199) and to people feeling closer, part of something, and more happily able to express who they are (see 'Teen alienation is so analogue', page 226). This media democracy is allowing people to mobilize in a very physical sense – in 2011's case of Libya, for example – and it's allowing anyone to upload their creations and potentially find their audience (see 'A pop culture where everyone's invited', page 213).

As US President Barack Obama acknowledged and put so very simply in his UN address of 21 September 2011, *'Technology is putting power in the hands of the people.'*

We're post Web 2.0. There's some toying with its logical successor, Web 3.0, because everyone likes a good label, gets keen when it comes to pigeonholing in order to easier understand the way the world is and the direction it's marching in. However you want to label it or slot it, this is cheerful stuff, an adrenal-pumping time we're living through, as long as you're willing to ride it and let the wind trash your hair.

I remember vividly watching news footage of the Berlin Wall falling (9 November 1989) and US President George Bush saying everything and nothing with the remark, 'We live in fascinating times.' Twenty-three years on and we don't have a bold image of Berliners standing on a wall, punching the night sky and clawing at the brickwork, but I think we live in similarly fascinating and potentially liberating times. I suspect we're only scratching at the surface of what the internet – what an instant access and connected world – *means* for us. It's a whole lot bigger than just being able to buy coffee with your phone.

The analogue wall has fallen. And while this is a dawn with one hell of a distracting sunrise, I think perhaps the outline of a bridge is forming.

It was out of this thinking, the notion of this grand sunrise, of walls replaced by bridges where the vision is no longer *just* television, that this book came about. The cusp of *something*. A time of potent and tangible change, the digital age, with rule book rewriting implications for how brands advertise and behave and ply their dark arts and voodoo charms, *this* was the start-point for the pages and dispatches that followed.

I've always seen my business – the business of brands, advertising and media – as being an interconnection of three points. Like I said, there are triangles everywhere. The start point is human understanding, some kind of genuine *insight* into the way people are. I see people, all our failings and fulfilments, as being 'the constant'. Our relationship with technology and media is then the moving feast, the table at which we all sit, to an infinite tasting menu where each course is something new and there's never a repeat. Eager to join the table, we have brands, hoping to bring their best conversation, their finest anecdotes, all the charm they can muster. Brands need to be the perfect company, disarming and winning, while deftly complementing each course.

FIGURE 27.0 The 'brand invention' triangle

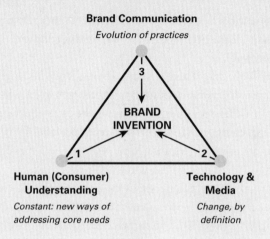

In this very new 'now', the call to brands – to how they are built and how they must behave across media – is increasingly bold and clarion. 'Media mix' is becoming limitless. Advertising is no longer primarily all about making TV ads and buying TV ad-breaks; no longer about then running big posters by the roadside, smaller versions in magazines and, to complement, maybe some newspaper space; no longer about airing radio ads, if budgets are tight – that poor media relation because radio doesn't boast pictures; and no more about debuting in cinema before the trailers, if budgets are fat and the audience is right.

Because along came the '*interweb*' and the old media triangle toppled, definitions altered, a clear hierarchy giving way to a bright and shiny new democracy. 'TV' is no longer TV, no longer singularly associated with the box in the corner or the screen on the wall of our living rooms. TV broadcasting can be watched on our phone or tablet or laptop. We no longer think '*What's on?*', more so, '*What do I want to watch right now?*' And we don't have to be anywhere near our living rooms to watch it.

We live in a world of screens, whether we're at home or out of it, where a TV ad has become AV content that needs to transcend our many screens – 'content' only worth a damn if it entertains and inspires and is *worth* watching, just as much as all the other content out there, as made by you, me and anyone else. Advertising has to be of ultimate worth, equal to the value of someone's time taken to watch it.

All meaning that brand success and survival can come from only one thing: constant invention. From ongoing adaptation as brands must campaign with heart, soul and devilish smarts within this new media democracy, where every vote counts and no number is high enough.

We have a new vision.

'DIGITAL': WHAT IT IS, WHAT IT ISN'T

> " Digital now
> pervades everything.
>
> Our TVs are digital.
>
> Our streets are
> populated with
> digital billboards
> showcasing
> advertisers who buy
> 'dayparts'.
>
> We have become
> digital beings. "

*'W*e need to improve in digital.'

I hear this a lot from clients.

And here's the thing. Digital is too often talked about like it's someone's tennis game, or golf game; like a handicap that needs shaving. 'Digital' is not something to get *better* at. Digital is not something to improve at, like your golf swing.

FIGURE 27.1 Digital is not something to improve at, like your golf swing

Digital is zeros and ones. It's a technology, by extension an opportunity. 'Digital' is NOT a practice. 'Digital' is not an expertise.

Controversial?

Not really.

Digital now pervades everything. Our TVs are digital. Our streets are populated with digital billboards showcasing advertisers who buy 'dayparts'.

'We' are digital, have become digital beings, and by virtue of 'digital' now 'being everywhere', digital's role as a descriptor is arguably redundant. Our world, as a digital playground, can really just be termed a playground, and 'digital' simply offers new means by which to play... in a bigger playground with more distractions.

So now for the '*what digital really is*'... the exciting bit.

What a post-digital world *does* represent is a world of considerably greater marketing opportunities, a genuine surfeit of possibilities. There remain old ways of thinking and acting, and there are now new ways of thinking and succeeding.

The brand communication model is changing, has changed (see 'The brand communication model', page 107). With ever-greater enthusiasm, we're shifting from making ad messages that intrude into people's lives, to producing content that people enjoy and share and (even) rework. All this means that 'digital' sits *inside* the 'big picture challenge' of making brands meaningful in people's lives.

And for marketing practitioners, this further means that digital 'pure-play' is purely naive. Cold truth: digital-centricity is blinkered, silo-thinking. Digital solutions are an exciting new set of answers that serve as part-response to an age-old set of marketing questions: How do you build my brand? How do you make my brand famous? How can you compel and excite people to buy my brand? How can you reveal something of human nature that motivates it to *want*?

'Improving at digital' is really about capitalizing on new ways to improve at the fundamentals.

WEB 3.0: REGIME CHANGE

" Social Media is
becoming a
geopolitical
change agent;
the means to
mass-mobilization
of a citizenry
even under
dictatorship.

In 2011, in Egypt
and Libya, we saw
a Flash Mob capable
of making history. "

What we're seeing right now on our TV screens is no less significant than the images of 1989 in Berlin.'

Francis Fukuyama, author of *The End of History*, speaking on current events in North Africa (*Newsnight*, 24 February 2011).

*

These are crazily fascinating times. We're playing witness to some real melon-twisting moments.

'The digital revolution' is ours to work through and figure out. It could go in so many directions; it'll probably end up going in all of them, all at once. And it is a 'revolution' (I know, you weren't necessarily challenging otherwise), but a revolution that's only just revving up.

Web 2.0? Well, we're post *that*, but you still get a sense that the dawn light hasn't yet melted away.

The events of 2011 in Egypt, later Libya, the long shadow of implication and the dominoes that still may subsequently fall across the Middle East: is *this* the digital 'revolution' everyone's been speaking of? Is the digital revolution only now starting to find its wider stride?

When uprising and regime change started to take hold in North Africa, there was much talk of how it had been 'made possible' by social media. When agency planners talk about '*how media can be used to facilitate people's lives*', seldom is the 'facilitation' in question one of revolution and potential shift in a nation's political ideology. That's typically a lot to ask of any media vehicle.

But the question has now become... Are we seeing an evolution of the internet medium, and an eye-widening sense of its true potential?

Is this Web 3.0? Not a tech-upgrade, a smarter algorithm, slicker fibre optic or better Bluetooth beam. Instead, Web 3.0 as in an *outcome*, the demonstrated *consequences* of being able to access information? Specifically, the demonstration of how an oppressed majority living under dictatorship and state-controlled media can 'socially network' themselves into mobilization and revolt?

'Social media', by means of the internet, can be a geopolitical change-agent; the means to mass-mobilization of a citizenry, even under a dictatorship. In terms of cause and effect, one wonders just how much bigger can the internet get?

Very simply (because on one level I think it is very simple), we're witnessing an evolution of the internet in three very quick steps.

FIGURE 28.1 The internet: from search to social to social mobilization

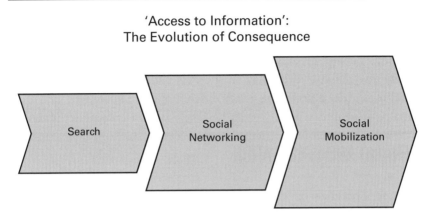

'Access to Information':
The Evolution of Consequence

Search

Social
Networking

Social
Mobilization

FIRST CAME 'SEARCH'

From a primordial superhighway of disaggregated information and cyber chaos, there quickly came structure and internet 'order'. Google, Bing and so many like them kindly provided a torch and shone the way.

Search was for simple, utility-based tasks. Book a restaurant, find a good plumber, look at porn. The internet, for the late majority, was the Yellow Pages, but one where you typed into a search box and didn't have to turn any pages. (Not that the Yellow Pages had ever been that great for pornography.)

From an internet that was search-based, then came social. The internet found its mojo (Mark Zuckerberg will happily testify), became 'social outreach', and on one kind of slightly weird and oxymoronic level, we saw the death of loneliness. For a permanently 'on' society, staying in provided all the fix of going out.

Ian Nathan (writing in *Empire* magazine, March 2011) hailed Facebook as the act of a '*monomaniacal genius, smelling oil in the digital landscape; a brilliant exploitation of the internet generations bipolar status as voyeur/ exhibitionist*'.

We're now witnessing the rise of the voyeur/exhibitionist/*revolutionary*. One simple step on, it stands to reason that a social network can be rallied, can be mobilized into a collective force, for collective action.

What took place through 2011 in Egypt and Libya was no more than a flash mob with a considerably higher purpose; a flash mob with geopolitical impact, capable of making history.

Living in a digital age *has* meant reading your morning commute in hi-res on your new iPad, but that's a very Western take on digitally afforded benefit, as defined by how many screens you need in order to pass more happily through your every day. In societies under State lock-and-key, the digital revolution is providing a very different kind of liberation.

SCENARIO AND SPECULATION

When we speculate on the consequence of humankind converging with technology, the alarmists and storytellers in us frequently see that convergence as a grizzly collision. So many juicy and rather literal doomsday motifs: mice with human ears, bug-eyed scientists playing God, cybernetic organisms that enjoy killing people. We can get very Mary Shelley about the whole thing.

But here's the other thing. There's an upside scenario to humanity's handshake with technology, one that's a good deal more utopian in potential. For those who live without the freedom to exercise voice and vote, 'technology' may give them means.

Historian Simon Schama passed comment, 'You can't make power out of Twitter', but it appears you can use it to take power away.

TRANSMEDIA...
IN A TUBE CARD

> " Transmedia theory,
> applied to a movie
> launch, is all
> about promoting
> 'The story'.
>
> Set against the
> convention of
> Stars Sell Movies,
> Transmedia thinking
> is near-heretic
> and boldly purist. "

> *In his book* Convergence Culture: Where Old and New Media Collide *(2006), Henry Jenkins describes transmedia storytelling as storytelling across multiple forms of media with each element making distinctive contributions to a fan's understanding of the story world. By using different media formats, transmedia creates 'entrypoints' through which consumers can become immersed in a story world.*

SOURCE: WIKIPEDIA

It was in the middle of 2011, coming at me out of nowhere (which is how it should happen), that I had a 'transmedia' moment. It was during my morning commute by Tube train, while deep in the clay strata of London. A transmedia moment, no doubt, and the first time it's so obviously happened to me, which says everything, given that 'transmedia' as published theory is more than half-a-decade old.

There was a new movie coming out that I hadn't heard of, and what I saw adjacent to the Tube panel ads for adult education courses, Wellman vitamins and the latest techno-packed tablets was... *The Clear Pill.*

FIGURE 29.1   *The Clear Pill* – Tube card panel... as story-world 'entry point'

My thought process went something like this...

That's the guy who was in *The Hangover* and *The A-team*, B-lister Bradley somebody. He's in a new movie called *The Clear Pill*? Or he's 'face-ing' some pharmaceutical pick-me-up? If the latter, surely his agent has dictated a European ring fence so it doesn't trash his Stateside movie star image?

Two seconds more reading and a spoof ad, tactically placed, became clear. Only, *The Clear Pill* is not the name of the movie. The only piece of copy that wasn't pure fiction is where it suggested I visit **www.showfilmfirst.com**, type in 'Limitless', and nab me some preview tickets. For the record, '*Limitless* is a 2011 American techno-thriller directed by Neil Burger, starring Bradley Cooper and Robert De Niro. It is based on the 2001 novel *The Dark Fields*.' (Source: Wikipedia).

What I liked about my one single Tube card experience is how it fluttered at the edges of a still very buzzy idea. The fact that 'transmedia' is still buzzy has (I suspect) everything to do with it being a 'broad beam ambition', and that few-to-none have really cracked it. Jenkins's *Convergence Culture* is no by-the-numbers *How To* guide. Putting transmedia theory into practice remains largely unsatisfying, much like humanity's attempts to conquer outer space.

THE BOW TIE MODEL

Transmedia thinking anchors itself to the world of story, the ambition principally being one of how you can 'bring story to life' in different places, in a non-linear fashion. The marketing of motion pictures is the most obvious application, where transmedia maintains that there's a 'bigger picture opportunity' to punting a big picture.

Transmedia theory, applied to a movie launch, is all about promoting the story, not the 'due date of a movie starring...' In an industry built on the conventions of 'stars sell movies', where their name sits above the film's title, transmedia thinking is anti-conventional and boldly purist.

People crave the ride of a great story. Transmedia purports: start the ride early, way before the journey to the movie theatre. Hook people in with 'the story conceit'. Turn any number of media 'touchpoints' into a non-linear narrative ecosystem. Media becomes a tapestry. 'The story' is a golden thread stitched in any number of directions to create an immersive, multi-sensory shroud.

But you see what just happened?

Yes, in that last paragraph. The common transmedia trap, getting all giddy and overexcited and 'metaphoring' like crazy, still fixating on the 'big vision' as theory and not practice. And what was that about a shroud?

Let's back it up a bit. Simplify.

I call it the Bow Tie model, which I think can rather neatly map the delivery of a transmedia solution.

FIGURE 29.2 The Bow Tie model

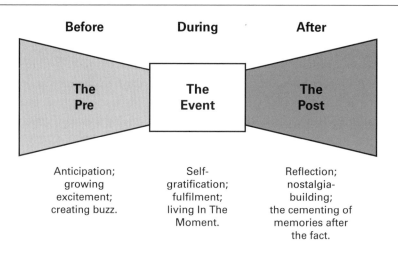

The Bow Tie model structures every event into three parts – a Before, During and an After. Every event – as common-garden-variety as going to the movies – has a 'pre' and a 'post' – and both can be used to serve the marketing endgame of box office takings, of getting popcorn-munchers into seats.

Consider transmedia and the marketing of movies within the Bow Tie model. In the 'pre' it's all about mystery, tease, some reveal, and reward through discovery – the marketing equivalent of studio-pitching early-adopting consumers with a movie idea (only one that's already been turned into a movie).

The story 'outside' the movie theatre: the story in 'bite form', like a Tube card snippet, and maybe some choice semiotic seeding, guerrilla stencilling some story emblems perhaps, all serving to build intrigue, and hype and fan-boy cyber chatter.

In the 'pre moment', you want people to know everything and nothing about the movie. You want them exposed to any collateral that creates a vivid sense of the movie's style and its premise. You don't ideally want them exposed to the film's major visual moments and killer lines. These should all come in the context of 'the event' – sitting in the dark, marvelling in-the-moment of watching.

A movie producer/director such as JJ Abrams thinks like his fans. *Cloverfield* (2008) and *Super 8* (2011) both showed that JJ is not capable of launching a new movie without loading the 'pre' full of transmedia fizz-bombs. Of course, Abrams has a devoted following, and his transmedia wiles conform to fan expectation.

Christopher Nolan is another maestro of drip-feed-intrigue. For the final instalment of his Batman Trilogy, shooting on *The Dark Knight Rises* started 19 May 2011. On 20 May, Nolan posted an on-set photo of Batman bad guy Bane. The image was virally released via a Twitter #tag, TheFireRises. *The Dark Knight Rise*s had a Summer 2012 release date, with Nolan clearly confident he could feed the flames of fan frenzy over a 12-month 'pre'. The point is worth making, however, that Nolan was working the pump of a hugely successful movie franchise.

The danger with oblique (read: obscure) transmedia gestures supporting a movie no one's heard of (so, not a franchise affair like a Bond or Batman) is that no one will get it, because no one will have the first clue what you're up to. The thing about clues is that you still have to spell out that a clue is what it is.

Transmedia should never be too smart for its own good, specifically too smart for its own audience.

The 'post' is a very different kind of messaging opportunity. It's all about self-perpetuation, indulging the feel-good of in-the-know early adoption; encouraging all those good pass-it-on behaviours and 'OMG!' first-person proclamations. More fizz-bombs, but these from the early adopters stoking the pre-moment for the late majority.

I also don't think it's such a stretch to export transmedia beyond the marketing of movies, say into a broader entertainment space, into the story-telling of, for example, theme parks, public attractions, zoos and aquariums. It is very possible to take the theme park beyond the walls of the theme park, to create 'virtual experiences' that ghost the real thing.

Imagine roller coasters with mini-cams mounted to the front carriage, beaming first-person experiences direct to digital escalator panels. One ride, juxtaposed against another. Imagine projecting real-time images of a shark tank in an underground Tube station.

Rather than taking the park *beyond* the park, Disneyworld focused on capturing the emotions of the 'pre' in their 2011 UK TV campaign, 'We're going to Disneyworld'. The TVC was a home-recorded montage of children being told that they were off to the magic kingdom. The reactions filmed are so innocent, wide-eyed and utterly thrilled that I defy any parent to be immune to their heartstring tugging.

WRESTLING THEORY

On 6 April 2010, the Producers Guild of America announced the addition of 'Transmedia Producer' to the Producers Code of Credits. A big deal that some termed 'unprecedented', it marked the first time in the guild's 60-year history that a new credit had been added to the list.

At the time, I suspect few suspected that an 'unprecedented' role could be so effectively delivered through the simple booking of a few Tube card panels. And I think that's a rather pleasing thought, because getting to grips with any theory is often a challenge. Theories have a habit of wanting to remain vague and theoretical, but they can be pinned down, grabbed by the throat, but not so tightly that they lose the voice to explain themselves.

Over-complicating transmedia theory only gets in the way of being able to take it off the page – and any theory is arguably worth considerably less than a hill of beans if you can't apply it. On those occasions where you can apply it, however, the opportunities might just be limitless.

IS SOCIAL MEDIA JUST A BIT ANTISOCIAL?

> We're developing a 'curator's conceit', our 'Life Experiences' only made 'real' once they're logged, tagged, uploaded, shared.
>
> 'The Moment' is serving as 'Exhibited Proof' of the Socially Rich and Rewarding lives we're clearly leading. Are we only enjoying the fun once someone else can see how much fun we had?

THE CULT OF ME

In Part One's 'Yours digitally: brand charisma's second coming' (page 48), I make the comment: 'we *use* our digital brands to help express who we are [...] They allow us to vividly *be*, to hold a mirror up to ourselves. And it is clear that we like what we see.'

When a very good (though sadly ginger) friend of mine, John Paul, first read the above, he was quick and keen to offer that we so '*like what we see*' because it's narcissism of the contrived kind, a self-manufactured pixelated reflection of the cooler, better-looking, more impressive version of ourselves.

'Yours digitally' is a pretty positive commentary – acknowledged – and every upside invariably has a downside, every upbeat a corresponding downbeat. To even things up, JP's comments got me speculating on the downbeat.

Has Brand Charisma's second coming brought on the Death of Social Innocence?

For 'social innocence', I mean this: innocent as in to happily portray yourself for who you are, and to live genuinely *in the moment* – as opposed to at a *remove*, self-conscious to whether and when a moment can be tweeted or uploaded.

Social media is turning private lives into public 'factions'. (This theme has got me tinkering with some new descriptors.)

LIFE FACTION A personally portrayed existence that is 'digitally enhanced' and favourably abridged; augmented reality applied to one's own life.

The criticism is that we're developing a 'curator's conceit', living so much after the fact, with 'life experiences' only made 'real' once they're logged, tagged, uploaded, shared.

The 'moment' is no longer reflective of what occurred, because it only serves as 'material', as 'exhibited proof' of the socially rich and rewarding lives we're clearly leading. The puzzler then becomes: are we only enjoying the fun once someone else can see how much fun we had?

For, 'the man who wasn't there', we now have, 'the life that wasn't really lived'. Like being the photographer at somebody's wedding, the experience is through a lens, within a frame, 'outside the moment'.

 DIGITAL DETACHMENT The primary urge to document and share, to the sacrifice of ever being openly in the moment. As in: 'I'll drink my cocktail once I've uploaded these photos of us rocking-it at the bar just now.'

For a while now, an old secondary school buddy of mine has appeared to be 'living through Facebook'. He was always a bit of a Walter Mitty-type, inclined to flights of fancy and exaggeration. All judgements aside, social media has become a quite major channel for him, as the self-appointed 'biographer' of his own digitally documented life. Fulfilling as it may be, I can't help wonder, for just how long is he out-of-body – in the third person, applying an observer's eye upon himself?

As Peggy Orenstein put it in 'I Tweet, Therefore I Am', there's becoming a quite extreme blurring of 'the line between person and persona'.

 SELF-BRUSHING The act of polishing and buffing your more desirable online self. The airbrushing of person, act, or event to stylized and self-flattering effect.

Few of us are so evolved as to be fully accepting of who we really are. 'Being selective' is too big a temptation for almost everybody – but social media allows us to busily build the avatar of our ego.

EGO-AVATARING

Online, the short and the fat can walk taller and feel thinner. Online, we can be 'all ego', can be our own Dorian Gray.

DIGITAL DORIAN-GRAYING The digital image we most care others to see. The preferred version of ourselves; narcissism with artistic license; a contrivance; positive hyperbole; personal spin-doctoring.

Most extreme, perhaps, social media allows us to even have 'followers', which is ego-fuelling on a wholly higher level. Is a Messiah-complex now within easy reach of everyone?

No question, social media taps deep into the human condition. All the upsides and downsides aside, let us ultimately hope it will bring out not only the best but also 'the real' in us.

A POP CULTURE WHERE EVERYONE'S INVITED

> The *lumpenproletariat* is no longer a 'raggedy' crew of non-achievers.
>
> Jedi-Wannabees the world over are now showing everyone else their moves. They're firing up their Macs, sharing the life they've got, and leaving it in the hands of their fellow Jedis to decide whether it's a thumbs-up.

Not so very long ago, I came out with a line that was, I have to admit, a little on the lofty side:

What we're seeing is the democratization of popular culture.

Lofty, right? It just slipped out and it rightly rolled a few eyeballs in the room. (I can do that sometimes; I'm working on it.) On this occasion, though, I was still very down with the sentiment behind it.

You might ask what prompted it. If you didn't, I'm still going to tell you. I'd just seen the Tipp-Ex 'White and rewrite' campaign (2010) running on YouTube. The interactive video *A hunter shoots a bear* lets you change the ending, by replacing '*shoots*' and typing your own choice of verb. You type 'kiss': bear and hunter get it on. You type 'dance': bear and hunter get down. And if you type 'tickles', then a hunter '*tickles* a bear', specifically in the fashion of *Surprised Kitty*, that cutely ridiculous (or ridiculously cute) and very popular YouTube video from October 2009.

Hence, you see, '*the democratization of popular culture*', which put another way, is where advertising acknowledges, pays homage to, plagiarizes, repurposes (the word you prefer is a whole other debate) popular content that's *out there*, anywhere, as made by *anyone,* whether they're cute kitten-owners or not.

The ad industry is a wonderfully creative one, but it's also guilty on occasions of unimaginatively jumping on and all over pop culture's latest bandwagons. The popular stuff that comes out of Hollywood – makes money, has a good 15 plus minutes of fame – all too often becomes rich pickings for that new car, bank, travel-operator campaign.

Sometimes this is okay, sometimes just sadly lazy, but this is not a moment to name and shame. Conversely, what I do rate is when UGC (User Generated Content) gets picked up on and reworked. It means that anyone who wants to sound off, go nuts, rant, rave or praise can put it out there. Anyone, anywhere, born of talent, imagination or sheer dorkiness can capture the moment, gain a voice, an enthusiastic following, and contribute in some small way to the canon of popular culture.

STAR WARS KID AND SIMILAR FOOTSTEPS

Remember *Star Wars kid*, and its companion piece, *Drunken Jedi*?

FIGURE 31.1 Star Wars kid

Here was a 15-year-old Canadian tenth grader who back in 2002 achieved over 1.1m downloads. It's impossible not to love *Star Wars kid*, and there are many who've deliberately, or otherwise, followed in his Jedi footsteps.

When Lauren Bernat's boyfriend sat innocently on the sofa, watching her gyrate to a Wii Fit hula-hoop game, he didn't have to start recording her bottom with his mobile phone. He also didn't have to upload the video, or add the title, *Why every guy should buy their girlfriend a Wii Fit*. But these things he did do. And as a by-product, true to Warhol's observance, Lauren Bernat (and her impressive bottom) became famous enough to land a talk-show slot and feature in subsequent advertising for Wii exercise games.

The internet gives form to the fact that we're crying out to be entertained and easily distracted, just as Lauren Bernat's boyfriend was.

Why it is that we are preoccupied with cat's doing stuff – flushing toilets, jumping, falling, riding robotic vacuum cleaners – may forever remain a deep mystery, but that's part of the internet's charm, that it spawns all these fleeting cultural phenomena, that it serves us the fastest, zaniest, frothiest pop cultural morsels.

Stuntman audition tapes that go horribly wrong (*Afro Ninja*) and 'bag-of-snakes mad' vloggers (see: Chris Crocker inconsolably wailing 'Leave Britney alone!') help fill our daily screen-diets. Catchphrases such as 'Don't taze me, bro', and 'I like turtles', and 'Boom goes the dynamite' can come out of nowhere, reach almost everywhere, and they make us smile for the briefest while.

The internet reflects us at our eccentric, absurd and trivial best. It shows us as stoned online game-players and people wearing home-made Tron suits. It reveals that we enjoy watching people blend things like an iPhone, and mix 200 litres of Diet Coke with 500 Mentos mints. Laughing babies and sneezing baby pandas speak to us, despite having nothing to say, and we find all these things hypnotically watchable and briefly hysterical.

And then too there's stuff of genuine human interest and clear talent out in cyberspace. Parody ads for energy drinks that 'contain lightning' and 'harness the power of 400 babies' can get populized by Hollywood comedians. Even if creepily self-obsessed, a time-lapse video of someone who's taken a daily picture of themselves (*Noah K Everyday*) for six whole years can kick-start a successful photography career.

The internet is Society writ small, where we have this burning want to share the small stuff. The more off-the-wall or off-the-chart the better, and it's all for sharing.

LIFE IS FOR SHARING

With *Life's for sharing*, T-Mobile has really embraced this user-generated theme as a strategic platform for their global advertising. First we saw T-Mobile's flash mob at London Liverpool Street Station (15 January 2009). I love the idea that a flash mob – a piece of field marketing, a media stunt no more – can be recorded and turned into a piece of content with global reach. Then on 30 April of the same year, T-Mobile threw a mass singalong in Trafalgar Square, where they also invited Pink to plug her new tune, 'So What'.

I was on the judging panel (2010) that awarded T-Mobile and Saatchi & Saatchi a Silver Effie for their 'Singalong' campaign. There was so much to like about it.

In particular, I liked the idea of turning a TV ad's production budget into a party budget, which is what T-Mobile effectively did. Rope-in a pop star, rig up a giant karaoke machine, rock-up with a film crew, and record people having a good time together. Footage of real people having a really good time is only likely to make anyone later watching smile and feel a little bit good too. Who needs a shooting-script when you can capture 'honest emotion' and a fine slice of authenticity?

I believe that brands like T-Mobile are really getting it, understanding that a clear way of generating human appeal is by doing things that are very human, like throwing a party. It's unlikely that T-Mobile could have evoked the same kind of feeling if they'd optioned the default trip to South Africa, hired a bunch of models and had them frolic on the beach, even if they'd used a director keen on grainy film stock and cinéma vérité to capture it all. Because where's the honest-to-God humanity or genuine sense of fun for everyone in that?

Brand invention should never be so serious a business that it precludes having some fun.

So what I find myself delighting in right now is how you don't have to be a Warhol or a Banksy or an Effie winner to make your mark. You can just, say, document your amazing cake-making skills, and the ripples of influence will simply follow.

When T-Mobile took super-sized Angry Birds to the streets of Barcelona in Spring 2011, the inspiration came from an uploaded home video of a dad making a 'playable angry bird cake' for his son, Ben. From cake-sized to city-sized, T-Mobile just scaled a piece of UGC they'd seen on their travels through YouTube.

Ivan Pollard, a big-brain I've seen in action first-hand, writes with his signature loony-smarts when he says:

> *A person's feeling towards a brand is made up of the aggregation of their experiences... The most powerful force for vicarious experiences now is the connection between ordinary people.*
>
> *This leaves us with two routes for communication – create more stand-alone experiences ourselves and work with the fluid, active, multi-dimensional mediation of the collective.*
>
> *And working with the collective – really working with them – will take us to a new place in our thinking about the way big brands need to behave.*

The *lumpenproletariat* is no longer a 'raggedy' crew of non-achievers. Genius cake-makers and Jedi wannabees the world over are now showing everyone else their moves. They're firing up their Macs, sharing the life they've got, and leaving it in the hands of their fellow Jedis to decide whether or not it's a thumbs-up.

It's a thumbs-up.

THE SECOND FUNDAMENTAL: AVOID LAUNCHING GHOST SHIPS

> **"** Content-*creation* is not enough.
>
> Brands can't *just* be film-makers.
>
> A film-maker is nothing, has no audience, without a film-distributor. **"**

There's a current assumption that traditional advertising formats are being superseded by 'content', where everyone in agencies gets to be journalists and film-makers.

In this exciting new world scenario, entertainment is 'brand-funded', and the 'hidden' persuasion behind the content is consequently *better hidden* and 'all the more persuasive'. 'Better' and 'all the more' because audiences won't see it as *advertising*, because they'll be too busy enjoying it.

In theory, it all sounds rather lovely and very sexy. Viewed through another lens, this is second generation ad-funded programming, which has been knocking around in various guises for a good 15 years, and which BMW 'film' had one of the best early (2001/2) stabs at with their eight ten-minute shorts directed by the likes of Guy Ritchie, Ang Lee, John Woo and Tony Scott. Sometimes 'new news' isn't so new. Sometimes it's the same old tough nut, and few new ways to crack it.

Still, brands that cry, *'Let me entertain you!'* is a wildly more powerful idea than brands that interrupt with, *'Let me sell to you'*.

There is no dispute that 'brands that entertain' is a thriller in the making, but it necessitates the observance of two fundamentals:

First, you have to make something thrilling.
Second, you have to get it into market and create mass interest.

There is an ever-growing body of evidence that brand-builders are capable of the former, of making entertaining, even thrilling content, whether starring Clive Owen in BMW's *The Hire*, or using Justin Timberlake 10 years later to launch Audi A1's *The Next Big Thing*.

There are considerably fewer examples where brand-builders and content-creators nail the second fundamental, namely content distribution, and this can only drive failure rates through the roof, irrespective of the Hollywood star cast in the driving seat.

GHOST SHIPS

A common and cautionary tale of many excited people in many excited meeting rooms just lovin' their new brand film tragically climaxes with: let's get this up on YouTube, sit back and watch the phenomenon unfold!

And upload.

And...

Nothing. Well, pretty much nothing. Some people see it, and it passes the rest of the world by.

Build it and they will come is *not* a distribution strategy. It's a blind, misguided leap of faith. Internet phenomena are the exception, not the norm. Cyberspace is cluttered with duds, with floating content-debris that no one knows about. Former Head of Planning for Aegis, Malcolm Hunter, has a brilliantly evocative descriptor: *ghost ships*.

Imagine an infinite ocean of drifting content ghost ships, launched and lost in a digital mist. On board: a crew of hugely talented entertainers… with no one to perform to.

The trick is to avoid creating a ghost ship. The trick is to be a cyber Columbus.

CONTENT HAS TO BE 'CONTENT + DISTRIBUTION'

We need to observe the film industry, the Jedi masters of content-that-entertains, which entertains so much that people are willing to pay for it.

Content *creation* is not enough. Brands can't just be film-makers. A film-maker is nothing without a film-distributor. 'The internet' is a distribution infrastructure, but its mere existence doesn't provide a distribution strategy. No one can risk simply uploading the content they've got and bank on it being the next *Blair Witch Project* (read: US$250 million worldwide gross; made for $500k).

In this inviting digital age of content creation, we need to practise the film industry's time-honoured conventions. Content and creativity green-lights the project, but distribution and marketing brings in the bucks. We can think of 'the brand' as an executive producer, as 'the money'. And also a creative consultant. But no agency partner has the right to play auteur and indulge in building ghost ships.

It doesn't matter whether it's the brand that needs promoting, or the brand's *content*. The fundamental triggers remain the fundamental triggers. Early buzz. Escalating hype. Reaching an absolute number of eyeballs. Culminating in: mass awareness. It might all sound a bit old school, but the new school still has much to learn.

MOBILE: THE NEW DEPENDENCY

> " It used to be that
> our only daily
> Screen-Fix came from
> the one in the corner
> of our living rooms.
> 3.5 hours a day
> was a very average
> TV diet.
> Today, we screen-
> binge, no longer
> have to leave our
> homes and feel
> screen-bereft.
> Our screens come with
> us; have become our
> crutch, our comfort
> blanket, our
> umbilical cord and
> keyhole on the world. "

We are a screen-avid society.

In an analogue age, *pre-mobile*, before cell phones (BCP), society only gathered around two screens: the one in the corner of the living room, the other in the darkness of the movie theatre. Both hypnotized in their own ways. Both commanded an avid following.

The digital age created 'screen competition' – a *convergence* of content across a *divergence* of screen hardware – and while the term, 'screen-based society' has been doing the rounds for a while, it no longer quite cuts it. *Tempus fugit* and Society & Technology have waltzed hand-in-hand into a whole other dance craze.

Personal screens are becoming 'the new dependency'. Prevalent is giving way to ubiquitous, which will soon give way to universal. Just look around, and look at how many of us are busy looking down at their screens.

Screens. And more screens. They're *everywhere*.

A 'mobile' phone, a phone you carried around with you, was initially a novelty of the few. But it didn't take the late majority long. We all quickly arrived at the party and quickly developed a dependency on a technology we'd never previously needed... because the benefits were so clear. It was hellishly useful to be able to get hold of someone in an instant, whatever they were up to, wherever they were.

All narcotics have to be benefit-based, otherwise they wouldn't be narcotic – and the mobile phone was all about clear benefit.

Today, the mobile phone has progressed to a higher purpose. It has become a more ambitious kind of 'life support' – a label I give quite literally. It genuinely *supports* the way people *live* their daily lives.

How well could the majority function without it? How much would people give up in place of giving up their mobile phone? On the totem pole of daily importance, our mobile phones sit pretty close to the top, maybe even up there above caffeine and chocolate, if push came to shove and something had to go.

And because everyone loves a good infograph:

FIGURE 33.1 Phone wars infograph (2011)

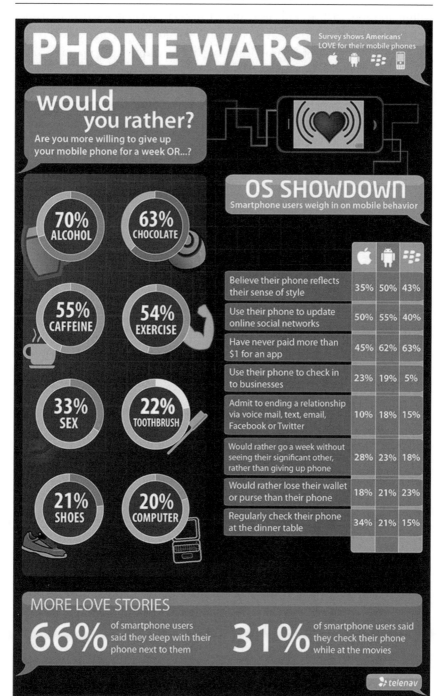

Yes, you read it right. According to a recent US survey of those asked, 70 per cent were more willing to sacrifice alcohol for one week than they were their mobile phones. The thought that 22 per cent of people are more readily willing to forgo their toothbrush, and 21 per cent their shoes, overall paints a picture that is as hilarious as it is slightly bewildering. Perhaps there really are a lot of tough-footed Americans out there, happy to reappraise their once highly held belief in good dental?

Our phones are becoming 'all screen', some have grown into tablets, and few remain 'just phones'. They're hand-held computers that fit in our pockets, and because they connect us to the digital world, they are the world in our pocket.

When Charles Dunstone launched Carphone Warehouse (1989), he was looking no further into a future than where a phone in your home was naturally scale-able to a phone in your car.

The business opportunity kind of got bigger than that.

Today 3.6 billion people own a mobile phone; 91 per cent of Americans use a mobile phone. By the end of 2012, more Americans will have smartphones than feature phones. It's projected that there will be 2.9 billion mobile internet users worldwide by 2016 (Source: PWC).

So, from a primordial analogue soup of car phones and cathode tubes, we now have a screen-dependent society where everyone carries one or more life devices: an iPad; a Kindle; a smartphone for calling, gaming, Googling and Facebooking, and that handily is also a camera that stores your music collection. It sometimes sounds like we're living in a time that comes after *The Jetsons*.

And our wireless, world-wired screens are only going to usurp other 'daily dependables', where one device can meet a greater number of needs. Our car keys, our credit and debit cards, our boarding passes: all replaceable with a single cellular solution, a solution soon loaded with NFC (Near Field Communication) technology. Everyone's getting to feel a little more like James Bond, equipped with the latest gadgets from Q-Branch.

It used to be that our only daily screen-fix came from the one in the corner of our living rooms. Three and a half hours a day was the average Western TV diet (a figure that's now fluttering around four).

But today, we no longer leave our homes and have to feel screen-bereft. Our screens come with us; have become our crutch, our comfort blanket, our umbilical cord and keyhole on the world.

And shortly, as 'augmented reality' starts to find its feet and spread its wings, our screens will *redefine* how we interact with our physical world.

Our screens will provide the looking glass for what we see, how we experience, how we behave with our everyday.

Layer a digital graft over the physical world, and the view fundamentally changes. The synthetic or virtual world is starting to fold back into the physical world, is going to start allowing people to self-define their own 'real', allowing people to create as many *physi-digi* unicorns as they please.

> *One of the most important technology trends over the next 3–5 years will be the effort to embed the dynamics of networked gaming into everyday life.*
>
> EDWARD CASTRONOVA, ECONOMIST

To wonder what's next is indeed to wonder. Prospection is a tricky business... but I'd hazard a guess that the screen business will always be good business.

TEEN ALIENATION IS SO ANALOGUE

> " Twenty years ago, being 'The only Goth in the village' would typically lead to introspective and/or outward cries of, *'No one understands me'*, *'I'm all alone in the world!'* Now, 'The only Goth in the village' can log-on and link to a Global Goth Community of the Like-Minded and Similarly Attired. *'No one understands me'*, replaced with 'check out my blog, *My Life* as a Goth'. "

When Roger Ebert, the film critic, reviewed the teen comedy *Heathers* (1989), he opened with:

> I approach Heathers as a traveller in an unknown country, one who does not speak the language or know the customs and can judge the natives only by taking them at their word.
>
> The movie is a morbid comedy about peer pressure in high school, about teenage suicide and about the deadliness of cliques that not only exclude but also maim and kill. Life was simpler when I was in high school.

Roger Ebert (b. 1942) was 47 at the time of his review, and the only clear thing to him about *Heathers* was that it was a movie that made him feel old. Exposed to one beat of the movie's black heart and he found it impossible to relate.

A client, a West Coast movie studio, once asked me to give a talk on teen audiences and how they've changed over the last 20 years. Let's take 1991, they suggested, and compare it with 2011.

Of course, when you get asked, '*What's changed in the last 20 years?*', you know upfront that the answer is going to be, '*A lot*'. Because a lot *should* have changed, because we are talking *20 years*.

Then... when the last 20 years rewinds us to year zero of the internet revolution, the scope of social change that follows is likely to stretch out towards some crazily far and wide horizons.

Then... within that, air-drop teens, mostly *digital natives*, sometimes labelled *millennials* – both badges meaning folk who arrived into a world where the digital revolution *wasn't* a revolution. Rather, just life. Just their 'every day'.

Long-short, for my presentation to the movie studio, I wasn't struggling for material.

THE TEEN TROPE

In global cinema admissions, teenagers represent a good two-thirds of all tickets sold. The marketing minds coming up with how to sell movies to teens are in their thirties and forties, and their very fair front-of-mind fear is that they're just like Roger Ebert: travellers in an unknown country, out of touch and step with digital teen tribes populated by some born as recently as 1998.

Teens are a fascinating audience. They're trying on identities, toying and trialling personas. Personality-wise, The teen is a work in progress; they're far from fully formed, and by way of compensation, in their 'early-days' search for identity (and belonging), they often affiliate with strongly flavoured cliques.

```
                           RANDY
        You can't win. You know that, don't you?
        It doesn't matter if you whip us, you'll still be
        where you were before, at the bottom. And we'll
        still be the lucky ones at the top with all the
        breaks. It doesn't matter. Greasers will still be
        Greasers and Socs will still be Socs.
        It doesn't matter.
                                        The Outsiders (1983)
```

Greaser, Soc, Mod, Rocker, Punk, Prep: irrespective of specific clique club, there's a groove-worn cliché that runs through all...

The teen: estranged, isolated, alienated, on the outside, even to or beyond the point of social delinquency.

This at least, is the well-trodden 'teen trope'.

THE PAST WAS EASY TO PAINT BLACK

Whether Jimmy Dean depicting American youth in moral freefall, or Billy Idol giving voice to *Rebel Yell* in 1983, 'rebellious' has been a well-flexed prefix to 'youth'.

Teens, almost by definition, used to be at arms-length to, well, pretty much anyone who wasn't a teen. They were at arms-length to parents, society, social mores, conventions and to a grown-up sense of conformity and 'doing things the way things should be done'. The teen was intimately in touch with The Roger Ebert Sensation, of feeling like a stranger in a foreign land, only one where they viewed from the other side of the looking glass, into 'The Land of Adult'.

In consequence, through the decades, pop culture has reflected the teen condition. Take 1990s movies such as *Slacker* and *Pump Up The Volume*, *Clerks* and *Office Space*. These are commentaries that reflect *their* time, where disaffection was close at hand.

MARK HUNTER / HARD HARRY
You see, there's nothing to do anymore.
Everything decent's been done. All the great
themes have been used up. Turned into theme
parks. So I don't really find it exactly cheerful
to be living in the middle of a totally, like,
exhausted decade where there's nothing to look
forward to and no one to look up to.

Pump Up the Volume (1990)

I mean, *really*? Come on? *That* bad? A little hard to say where the hyperbole ends and the legitimacy starts. While today, the counterculture vibe feels really quite retro, it's quite imaginable that there were more than a few Hard Harrys lost in the early 1990s, sincerely struggling to find cheer and originality.

And from the 1990s, it's easy enough to follow the thread further back.

The slacker was, of course, a throw-forward from the 1980s, a slothful, sloping, baggy-shirted archetype born of Generation X parentage.

Where Douglas Coupland populized the phrase in his novel, *Generation X: Tales for an Accelerated Culture* (1991), the Gen X tag had been making the rounds through 60 years prior:

'Generation X' has always signified a group of young people, seemingly without identity, who face an uncertain, ill-defined (and perhaps hostile) future. Subsequent appearances of the term in the mid-1960s and mid-1970s narrowed the referent for 'Generation X' from Capa's global generation to specific sets of primarily white, male, working class British youth sub-cultures, from the spiffy mods and their rivals the rockers, to the more overtly negationist punk subculture.

JOHN ULRICH, AUTHOR

'Without identity... facing an uncertain, ill-defined, hostile future.' Pretty bleak stuff – but not all bad if you happened to be an Ad Guy in the 1980s, sitting on a brief to position a certain computer manufacturer as a challenger brand. Even dystopia can have a silver lining; can make for rich fruity pickings.

Consider Apple's entry into the Best Ad of All Time category, '1984':

On January 24th, Apple Computer will introduce Macintosh. And you'll see why 1984 won't be like '1984.'

FIGURE 34.1 '1984', by Apple Computers. Dir: Ridley Scott. Agency: Chiat/Day (1984)

Back in 1984, Apple struck a chord because on some level, to many people (and not just Teens), 1984 *did* feel as if Orwell's vision had subtly come good, that there was something ever-so-slightly-controlling in the air. To some small degree, perhaps everyone's inner Jimmy or Billy identified with the hot blonde runner hurling a sledgehammer at a bleached blue face of State control?

Time trek back to the here and now and '1984' is still a great ad, but it does feel like it's one from the vaults, a comment on a different time and place, conceived and calling out to a very different set of hearts and minds.

GOTHS DENIED THEIR ISOLATED DYSTOPIA

Courtesy of easy-access social media, I believe the traditional teen trope has had a reboot, is now grooving to a rather different beat. In a digital age of Facebook, Twitter and Tuenti, and a list that rolls on and on, an 'always on' society can reach out, connect, find voice, understanding and even kinship.

Do you like polishing your collection of monkey skulls and storing them in your sock drawer? By conventional tastes, you're really very creepy, but little doubt there's an online chat room out there for you, that may even have suggestions on the different types of polish to use. Park monkey skull-polishers – broaden it out to a more palatable subgroup such as teenagers, or a teen subgroup therein, say Goths – and the same principle applies.

> The Goth subculture remains a visual shortcut through which young persons of a certain damp emotional climate can broadcast to the other members of their tribe who they are. Goth is a look that simultaneously expresses and cures its own sense of alienation.
>
> THE NEW YORK YIMES, 17 SEPTEMBER 2008

Teen alienation is a whole heap easier to sidestep these digital days. Twenty years ago, being 'the only Goth in the village' (or whatever other teen-clique psyche-attire you were trying on for size) would typically lead to introspective and/or outward cries of, 'No one understands me', 'I'm all alone in the world', 'No one can imagine what it's like to be me!'

Bemoaning would be part cure, as would listening to a lot of *The Cure*.

Social media has largely vaccinated against this particular strand of estrangement. Now, 'the only Goth in the village' can log-on and link to a 'global Goth community' of the like-minded and similarly attired. 'No one understands me', replaced with check out my blog, 'My life as a Goth'.

Without getting too carried away, too overly cheerful and utopian, I think we might just be standing on the doorstep of something really rather good.

There's a new idealism in play. Not a movement that is sweepingly political or grandly idealistic. More so, the kind of idealism that is immediately accessible and in limitless supply to all teens: the ideal of self-expression and micro-group identification.

Rather than *raging against the machine*, teenage time is taken up with digital articulation and social outreach.

FROM DISAFFECTED TO AFFECTED

Disaffected has always, to me, sounded a bit too phonetically close to 'disinfected', uncharitably implying a significant number of teenagers need a good wash. Teen hygiene aside, the notion of disaffection is starting to feel rather dated.

Teenagers used to partly define themselves based upon 'what they were *not*' and what they *didn't* want. Now they (like everyone else), can focus instead on a 'positive', on definition of self, based on wants, on 'what they wish to be', and the instantly accessible groups to which they wish to affiliate.

To this end, I'm not convinced that teenagers, in particular Western teenagers, are outsiders any more. They're insiders. They're able to reach out and sound off to the thin-sliced social set of their choosing.

Society has gone multi-micro, meaning there's someone there for everyone, leaving nothing left to feel *on the outside of*. And most crucially, this makes it harder to be 'against' a society or system.

Put another way, this is bigger than just making Goths feel happy.

Teens are 'Avatar-ing' themselves all over the internet, are re-articulating self-reliance as self-invention. 'Being teen' is becoming the pluralization of self, of creating multiple and carefully brushed digital personas, heroic within vivid and highly documented 'life factions'. We're seeing teen affectation in overdrive.

'Teens' was once an optional shorthand for 'anti-establishment', because the Establishment didn't speak for them, wasn't them. Curiously, the Establishment once stood for something long-standing, something *old* and *established*.

'Established' doesn't take so long these days. Potentially, it can be uploaded, made real and gain following over a weekend.

The digital age can instigate change overnight, build new 'virtual' edifices that are as real as any forms made of bricks and mortar. No shopper has ever physically walked through the door of Amazon, but we visit Amazon all the time. Amazon is just as trusted and real as Borders or Bertelsmann or Barnes & Noble, and given square-foot overheads, is likely to be around a lot longer.

No longer in the same way, nor in the same number, do teens still want to tear down the place and rebel yell at the walls of conformity, at the System, as created time in memoriam, inherited and upheld by each generation of 'grown-ups'.

Contrast Pink Floyd's take on institutional learning with *Spinebreakers*, Penguin's endeavour to embrace the digital age, involve teens, and show how publishing can be a future-proofed business.

Launched in September 2007, Spinebreakers.co.uk was the UK's first online book community for teenagers. Its editorial team is run by teens, aged 13 through 18, and it makes an open invitation to teens everywhere to join in, contribute, to say something.

As they put it:

> *Spinebreakers*
>   *Welcome to your site where the world inside a book can*
> *come to life.*
>   *There are author interviews, reviews, alternate endings, illustrations,*
> *short stories, poems and the best part is that you can join in too –*
> *contribute your ideas, and have your say about the books you've read.*
>   *So be creative and click here to send us your stuff!*

The truth is, if you have a voice, you don't find the same compunction to yell (the way Billy Idol once did). If you have the means to channel your anger, you never boil over. Perhaps 'digital media' partly stifles the rebel yell because so many now get to yell so freely, as often as they want, as fast as their fingers can cover a keyboard. Now that there are outlets such as Facebook, perhaps fewer teens feel compelled to feel like Che Guevara?

THE KIDS HAVE TAKEN OVER THE PLACE

To complement our open-access age, these are currently open-minded times. *Gen X...* became *Gen Y...* became *Gen Why Not?* (Maybe I've engineered that one a bit, but I think it holds.)

The prevailing mood today isn't an *exhausted* one. Today, twentysome-things can become billionaires. Teens have role-model proof points that encourage their self-belief.

> MARK ZUCKERBERG
> I think if your clients want to sit on my
> shoulders and call themselves tall, they have
> the right to give it a try — but there's no
> requirement that I enjoy sitting here listening
> to people lie. You have part of my attention —
> you have the minimum amount. The rest of my
> attention is back at the offices of Facebook,
> where my colleagues and I are doing things that
> no one in this room, including and especially
> your clients, are intellectually or creatively
> capable of doing.
>   *The Social Network* (2010)

Forbes pegged Mark Zuckerberg's fortune at £6.7 billion in 2011, placing him 14th in their list of the 400 richest Americans.

THE FINAL WORD FROM JOHN HUGHES

In 1991, the internet was effectively 'switched on', made available for unrestricted commercial use. The number of computers that connected across 'the net' numbered (wait for it) one million.

By 2020, 'mobile internet' is trended to top 10 billion, meaning that the internet is there for *everyone*. The 'PC', the personal computer, has in reality become the phone on our pocket.

Coca-Cola's fabled vision-mission *'to have a Coke within arm's reach of everyone on the planet'*, is likely to always be just that, a fable. For analogue brands, the world's just too damn big. For digital brands, for social media brands, they can fulfil Coca-Cola's vision without breaking sweat. And what this really means is that anyone can 'feel' at arm's reach of everyone else. And where does that then leave teen alienation?

Potentially, obsolete, is where.

So times have changed, but then, they always will. It's what they do.

Have teens changed *that* radically over the last 20 years? Of course not. What we're witnessing is simply new ways of meeting old (read: fundamental) needs. This is all about *change within the frame*.

Being a teen will always be about reconciling inner conflicts born of self-defining and self-discovery. Of wanting to stand out and fit in. Of needing to rebel against something or someone in order to slowly accept who you might be and might become.

In spite of the massive cultural and technological swells that have figured over the last 20 years, a teen's rites of passage remains set to a fixed bearing. Film-maker John Hughes knew well of the journey of self-esteem and belonging that all teens have to sail:

BRIAN JOHNSON

Dear Mr Vernon, we accept the fact that we had to sacrifice a whole Saturday in detention for whatever it was we did wrong... but we think you're crazy to make us write an essay telling you who we think we are. You see us as you want to see us... in the simplest terms and the most convenient definitions. But what we found out is that each one of us is a brain... and an athlete... and a basket case... a princess... and a criminal. Does that answer your question? Sincerely yours, the Breakfast Club.

The Breakfast Club (1985)

Whether you left high school 30 years ago, 20 years ago, or you're still walking through the door, the bottom line remains the bottom line. It is... and always will be... about the air punch.

FIGURE 34.2 The bottom line: it is... and always will be... about the air punch

Only these days, there are more ways to do it.

EFFICIENCY AND EFFECTIVENESS: FISH WITH FEET SIDESTEP MOVING TREES

 If you're sitting on a marketing budget with a bottom line breathing damply down your neck, then practices that are 'efficient and effective' are going to feel pretty top of the agenda.

Efficiency and effectiveness. Heard of 'em? I know you have. I hear them said all the time. They're boiler-plate words in the private sector. And they are *good* words... if only they were always used mindfully and deliberately, rather than reflexively, too often without thought to have real meaning or intent.

Context, the circumstances of the given day, is everything.

If you're sitting on a marketing budget with a bottom line breathing damply down your neck, and other spectral words such as 'accountability' bouncing off the boardroom walls, then practices that are 'efficient and effective' are going to feel pretty top of the agenda.

There was a time in the (what sometimes feels) 'long-and-distant' when shares were high and CFOs cheery. Consider 'a before' when no one had tasted that first dip of recession, where 'effective' remained a primary goal and efficient was preferred, but *not* to the sacrifice of all else. In prosperity, people are more inclined to risk, and are more driven by reward. Hence, they take the odd leap of faith in the name of innovation. But the downside with leaps of faith is that not all of them come good. Some come with a drop. And that drop can never be termed 'efficient'.

In the current and inclement climate too many people have had their faith shaken, making the smallest leap bring on palpitations. *Countries* can file for bankruptcy. Double dips loom large. The thought of doing something 'inefficiently' feels to many like a starched collar drawing a razor-fine line of blood. Before it then goes deeper.

So let's pause for a moment and consider these good words. Efficient and effective.

Efficient is about *practices*, the manner in which something is done. It's an *undertaking*. I take efficient to mean the leanest, most expedient means available for getting between two points.

 EF · FI · CIEN · CY The leanest, most expedient means available.

Effectiveness is an *outcome*. It's the effect of (hopefully the most efficient) actions to arrive at a desired destination.

 EF · FEC · TIVE · NESS The most desirable effect/outcome.

Effectiveness *should* be the consequence of efficiency – but this is an occasionally overlooked point, so let's not go swimming in shark-infested assumptions. Instead, let's state clearly for the record. Efficiency and effectiveness: they come as a package, like shark-proof water wings, one for each arm. You simply can't have one without the other.

For want of a working analogy, if 'efficiency' is the manner and motor in which you drive from A to B, it's pointless driving with great efficiency if 'B' isn't a place you want to end up. Like Tijuana.

And I don't think this is such a 'given', that efficiency and effectiveness are hand in glove and everyone knows it, that it 'stands to reason and goes without saying', because by that thinking no one would ever feel the need to say, to *stress*, that '*this new campaign must be as efficient and effective as possible*'. Because that's surely then 'a given' too, given that I've never been in a room when anyone's ever excitedly pitched an inefficient and ineffective campaign idea.

Peter Drucker put it like this:

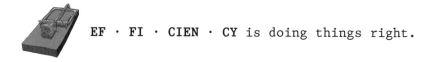

EF · FI · CIEN · CY is doing things right.

EF · FEC · TIVE · NESS is doing the right things.

What, of course, becomes the fun part, is how 'doing things right' and 'doing the right things' requires constant trial and revision. In brand communications, there's no definitive double-helix, where once you've cracked it you can then keep wheeling it out and work everything else around.

Media and technology continue to change; will always continue to change. Technology is *change* by definition, which means that while the game stays the same (encouraging people to love and buy brands), the field of play keeps changing; sometimes with goalposts, suddenly without, an even field, then on a slope, and then where someone takes your ball away. You get the idea...

For marketing success to remain a fixed and desirable destination, brand-builders have to keep taking paths formerly less travelled (to riff on Frost), if they are to make all the difference.

It's a fine line, of course, because trial implies occasional error, and for many marketeers this is a tough pill to take, even with water, as their bonus-eligibility likely entailed that someone from finance had to first burn ROI on their retina. A happy, soothing trail is a well-trodden one in today's uncertain times. And the irony is that sticking to the same trail is broken logic in a wood where the trees keep moving.

Einstein defined insanity as *'doing the same thing over and over again and expecting different results'*. The same principle applies if you flip it.

Against a backdrop of constant change – economic, cultural, techno-logical – you can't afford to keep doing things the same and keep expecting to achieve the same results. That's insane too. Success is a matter of constant adaptation to a changing environment. Y'know, like fish with feet. Some-thing Darwin knew a thing or two about.

THE EFFIES – IT'S IN THE NAME

For the past few years I've been a panel judge for the Euro Effies. It's a one-day affair, fly in early, fly out late, spend the day in Brussels with some very astute industry minds, and debate the hell out of a shortlist of papers that all hope they'll get some recognition.

And we're talking recognition for something deserved. The Effies are no ego-feasting industry love-in, where creativity is self-congratulated, even if the TV ad only aired once and the brand in question has subsequently perished from a cold winter of consumer indifference.

The thing I've always liked about the Effies is that they're all about 'effectiveness'. They pitch themselves as *'the Gold Standard in Marketing Communications Effectiveness'*. Their submission papers run with section headlines that ask: *'Countries in which effectiveness is proven'*.

The words used say everything. Effectiveness. Proven. No need to enter if you can't argue causality. That's the point, the point of the Effies. You have to prove your work made a difference. With the Effies, the aim is for the ad industry to truly prove itself, to hold itself to account and demonstrate a tangible and clear cause and effect.

The classic line from Lord Leverhulme (1851–1925), the founder of Unilever:

> *Half the money I spend on advertising is wasted, and the problem is I do not know which half.*

Advertising and consequence are a good deal less estranged these days, because they *have* to be. 'Advertising' has to be a rationally argued case of *investment*, a judicious speculation to accumulate, rather than a blind gambit that will only (maybe) come 50 per cent good. And the accumulation doesn't have to be a fiscal one. There's more than one kind of bottom line.

Past Effie Golds have been won by the likes of Coca-Cola and Nespresso, Nike and adidas, Audi and Ford. Some big brand names and some great work getting the gongs, but I was a particular fan of the 2011 Euro Effies Gold we awarded for 'Best demonstration of Social Media Effectiveness'. It went to Switzerland's Federal Program for Road Safety – 2007 had been a tough year for traffic-related deaths in Switzerland; the casualty rate rose 4 per cent year-on-year, its first rise in four years.

Targeting 18–30 year olds with a 'drive slow' message is a tough brief. How do you make 'slow' sexy? The agencies answer was to make it groovy, the campaign, 'Slow Down. Take it Easy'.

'Slow Down...' was a theme-song that played across MTV and 33 radio stations and reached Number 1 in the Swiss singles charts. It was a Facebook movement that gained 235,000 fans, 10 times its set target. It was a brand film played in cinema, on national television, and watched more than a million times on YouTube. All in, the campaign hit an awareness level of 88.5 per cent amongst the target group. Free media coverage of 'Slow Down...' was estimated at a further €1.5 million.

I can't think of a better kind of effectiveness than trying to save people from killing themselves.

FIGURE 35.1 'Slow down, take it easy' (2011). Media mix: Cinema, TV, Radio, Social. Agency: Rod Kommunikation. Market: Switzerland

Efficiency and effectiveness. Sometimes brand invention is a long-haired dude with a beard singing to a groovy beat. Go figure the ROI on that.

SHIFTING ICONS

> **"** Our most valued icons
> are becoming the
> ones on our desktop,
> a quick-click by
> which we update our
> personal profiles.
>
> These icons are our
> means, by which we
> chronicle, curate,
> and self-narrate. **"**

W|e all look up to something. Raise our chin, gaze heavenwards, aspire, dream, revere, offer up some kind of worship. Icons force us to check our own worth, make some kind of comparison and, as the calculation was meant to net out, we fall short. In the 'looking up', we naturally feel small. Icons, in their statuesque sense, were meant to demean our self-worth.

I see the equation starting to change for people. I see the weights and measures starting to balance out differently. I see what icons *mean* to people changing, where this worth transaction is no longer inevitably short-changing. It's a digital thing, I think. Let me explain.

Icons exists because we all and always want to worship *something*, pay our respect at one kind of altar or another, whether it's ecclesiastical or secular, spiritual or physical.

Faith, worship, belief: these were the foundations upon which icons were first built. And over time, they have changed. Remove desperation, create empowerment – and society 'evolves', with fewer people turning to the likes of institutional religion.

```
            INT. BOARDROOM — DAY
    A floor-to-ceiling window frames a suited figure
    in part-silhouette, arms folded behind his back.
    Beyond the window, glass towers, citadels of
    commerce and ambition, stand shoulder to
    shoulder, competing to outstretch the other.
    Given the view, we too are clearly very high up,
    perhaps even the tallest poppy on the skyline.


                SUITED SILHOUETTE
    There was a time, it was all fields
    and meadows; everyone working the land
    by day then praying by night, that
    the skies would deliver a bountiful
    harvest, that everything would work
    out okay.
    Everyone chopping wood, scattering
    seeds and what-not, so dependent,
    so desperate for hope, no one able
    to sign their own guarantees,
    everything beyond their control,
    everyone always turning the same
```

```
way, to The Lord. Maybe a
convenient invention to help the
superstitious and needy get their
well-deserved sleep?
The agrarian way, the Arcadian
ideal, all very sweet and innocent.
Well, that was then.
And then a few bright sparks came
out the evolutionary copper wire,
and they thought, Screw this!, and
started taking a little control.
Hello Industrialism, Capitalism,
control, POWER, and with it... we
put aside our childish ways, left
the Almighty, if he was ever up
there in the first place, to spend
more time on his golf swing.
We gave up on The Lord when we
started affording our Gucci loafers
and our branded cashmere sweaters
and our German sports cars.
Money and Greed, that's the New
Religion... where we became our own
Gods and Monsters.
```

The above is from a screenplay I wrote once upon a time. Think, *The Apprentice with a body count*. That was my pitch-opening. And in answer to the fantasy casting question, I saw Jack Nicholson or Christopher Walken delivering those lines, really hitting the beats. The script got a modicum of praise and attention (for a short while), then went the way of most screenplays. Nowhere. It's okay, the world is full of screenplays serving as door wedges and levelling table legs.

The extract does, however, illustrate the point I'm getting at, about how our icons reflect our values, reveal (even betray) what we (really) worship, the particular religions of the day.

Consider the prevailing ideas and images of each decade, say, from the 1950s onwards. Consider the screen icons who set the mood and defined their time. Consider the major archetypes and seminal pop cultural images of each decade... then let it out. There's no science to this, but there's something revealing in the free-association.

THE 1950S

A cathartic salve to post-war austerity. Put another way: glamour and tough guys. Gary Cooper. James Cagney. Cary Grant. Bogart and Baccall. Mansfield and Monroe. Early Elvis and Jack Kerouac. The Rat Pack. The birth of 'cool'. Real men, real women, no fuzzy in-between.

THE 1960S

Social revolution. Baby-boomers with hope and opportunity, having a swinging time. Miniskirts and Mini cars and *'You're only supposed to blow the bloody doors off'*. Hitchcock blondes, Ursula Andress and Raquel Welch. McQueen and Connery. Warhol. *The Graduate*. Twiggy and Shrimpy. James Dean and *Easy Rider*. James Bond and Harry Palmer. Burton and Taylor. The Beatles and The Stones. George Best and Jackie O, JFK and Martin Luther King. Vietnam, Kruschev, Castro and the space race.

THE 1970S

Anti-establishment edge. Grit, authenticity, realism. Eastwood and Hackman. Travolta and *Midnight Cowboy*. Ali McGraw and Dunaway. *Jaws* and *Star Wars*. Woody Allen, Hunter S Thompson and *The Godfather*. Pacino and DeNiro. Redford and Newman. Ali's jungle rumble. Wide lapels, bell-bottoms and big moustaches. Jim Morrison, ABBA and Elton John. The best days of disco.

THE 1980S

Stallone and Schwarzenegger. Rambo and *The Terminator*. Indiana Jones and Gordon Gecko. The Brat Pack and John Hughes. Eddie Murphy and Michael J Fox. *Blade Runner* and *Top Gun* and Hi Concepts. Culture Club and Duran Duran. Freddie Mercury and Bob Geldof. Thatcherism, Reagonomics, self-interest without blush and loadsamoney. Live Aid, AIDS and Tiananmen Square.

THE 1990S

Madonna, postmodernism. Tarantino, Tim Burton and Tom Hanks. Demi Moore and Julia Roberts. *Forrest Gump*, *Jurassic Park* and *Toy Story*. *Jerry Maguire* and Hugh Grant. *Braveheart* and *Barton Fink*. *Titantic* and *The Matrix*. *The Truman Show* and *Good Will Hunting*. Bono, George Michael and supermodels. Blur, Oasis and pub rock. Desert Storm and New Labour.

THE NOUGHTIES

Sexy vampires and *Harry Potter*. *Lost*. *Finding Nemo*. Hobbits and *Avatar* and Slumdogs and gay cowboys. Glam rock and sex comedies and gore-porn. Will Smith and Bill Murray. Johnny Depp and Keira Knightley. *Spiderman* and *X-Men* and Christopher Nolan's Batman. Jack Bauer and Jason Bourne and Bond-Rebooted. Clooney and Branjolina and Bromances. 9/11 and 'The Falling Man'. War in Iraq… and Afghanistan… and Darfur. Lehmann Brothers and sub-prime. Obama and 'Yes, We Can'. Google and Facebook. iPod and *Idol* and *X-Factor*. *High School Musical* and *Glee*. Lady GaGa and post-postmodernism (if you want to argue that such a thing exists).

THE NOW…

And let's all come up for air.

Before we get into the here and now, it's clear from the above that each decade has its own movers and shakers; icons that concisely reflect the prevailing trends and popular appetites. Some icons have longevity, can reinvent and span across decades, others are more fixed and occupy a finite window. Others still are straight replacements, younger for older.

And, of course, the icons of any age are *meant* to change, to shape-shift. Icons and *iconoclasm* really go hand in hand. The dawn of each new generation inclines to dislike the inherited icons as cast in the early light; the wanting for something new, more *relevant*, the rubbishing of something past.

French Dadaist bad-boy Marcel Duchamp is famous for applying a goatee to a copy of Da Vinci's *Mona Lisa* and adding the title 'L.H.O.O.Q.', pronounced in French as '*Elle a chaud au cul*', and broadly translated as

FIGURE 36.1   'Then and Now. The Queen is dead, long live the Queen.' *Vanity Fair* (1991), Madonna, the former queen of reinvention, giving it her iconic best

FIGURE 36.2   *i-D* magazine (2011), 'The Exhibitionist Issue', Lady GaGa: perpetual shape-shifting reinvention

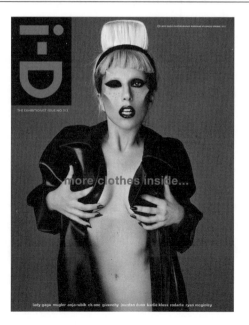

'she has a hot ass'. Certainly cheeky, the art theorists would further suggest that Duchamp's was an anti-establishment gesture born of anger at a world rebuilding from the ashes of the Great War. A horny and hirsute Mona Lisa serves as fair example to illustrate a broader point.

Icons: something old, something borrowed, tending to make each new generation feel blue... and get out a wrecking ball.

> " We must not roughly smash other people's idols because we know, or think we know, that they are of cheap human manufacture.
> OLIVER WENDELL HOLMES, SR,
> THE POET AT THE BREAKFAST TABLE (1872)

Yet we *do* tend to smash other people's idols, if not literally, then through turning our backs and conceiving new idols for worship, more reflective of what we're into and all about. And whether other people's, or our own, the fundamental point I think is that they are all of *human* manufacture. Our icons are a comment on where society finds itself, at any given point in time, and an illustration on where those within that society aspire to be.

Which all leads to the obvious questions.

Where do we find ourselves? Where do we aspire to be?

Who and what are the icons that reflect *our Now*?

THE 'LA WAY' — THE WORSHIP OF EMPTY ICONS

The first time I spent any real time in LA, I was struck by the iconography.

Driving along Sunset, east-west, west-east: it doesn't matter because the view is consistent. It's the billboards. Standing tall, unavoidable, playing back why so many come to LA, those billboards mirror what so many WANT. Fame and celebrity. To make it. To make it BIG. Name in lights. Face on Sunset. Larger than life. Iconic. That's the LA dream, what drives so many who live there.

By consequence, LA is a place of artifice and edifice, a city where everyone arrives with a big dream, bigs-up everything, and inevitably most are lost souls nursing self-doubt and shattered hope in the sunshine. It leaves you wondering if the LA-collective has created a karma debt where every earth tremor could be payback – the Big One, north of 9 on the Richter, the Lord finally calling time on an experiment he's let get out of hand.

I find LA hypnotic. It sucks you in. The only way to thrive is to join the vampires. It can feel like everything that's going on is going on there... and yet, there is almost nothing to the place except for the ambition, which is raw, ravenous, feral, blood-sucking. There's the shallow part of me (where beauty is skin deep and blood runs close to the surface) that enjoys LA.

From seeing it at close quarters, I think the 'LA Way' is a concentrated version of a more widespread cultural trend, a set of wants and ambitions that now stretch far beyond the city limits. I think the *want fame game* has gone global.

CELEBRITY, REALITY, SELF: THE STRETCH EFFECT

The more people that want celebrity, and believe they can have it, the wider the implications for what celebrity means, and its distance from people.

Celebrity 'from a distance' has become 'celebrity within perceived reach', by the examples set and the technological means available. By example, now everyone is shown that they too can be famous... because anyone can be famous for almost anything. Having attitude. Having a haircut with attitude. No substance, depth, dimension, or inherent talent is necessarily necessary. Famous for being famous makes 'modern day sense' by today's pop-cultural standards.

Celebrity has, in part, gone the way of food and furniture. Fast food with no nutritional value. Flat-pack furniture with a shelf life similar to the time it takes to build a shelf unit. And today we have fast-celebrity that's equally cheap and throwaway.

American Idol at least presupposes talent, but it's an open-casting talent show giving everyone their shot. *Big Brother* presupposes a blend of ego, extroversion, eccentricity and idiocy. For the TV show's producers, finding ready and willing 'housemates' is not an issue. By consequence, celebrity has *stretched*, has had no choice, has had to, in order to survive. To retain balance.

At the fast and disposable end, where celebrity has truly devalued itself, everyone gets to gorge on their 15 minutes. The craving: public attention at any cost, for any reason. While at the premium end, the A-lister's exude the qualities of luxury brands. And yet, even the A-lister is a very different breed of icon to yesteryear.

The A-lister has become more humble, human and accessible, tweeting their failings, keenly revealing themselves as being husbands and wives and parents... as well as globally recognized movie stars.

On the flip, the unknown majority is starting to betray signs of LA ambition and egotism – and like celebrity, 'reality' and 'self-concept' are also undergoing stretch.

FIGURE 36.3 The stretch effect

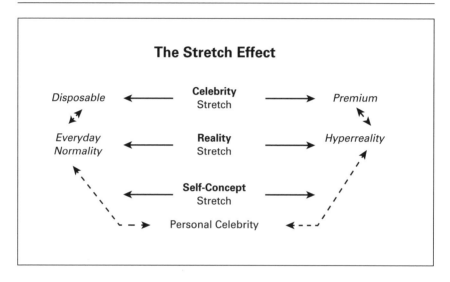

Reality is becoming exaggerated, 'everyday' at one end of the continuum, 'hyper-reality' at the other.

The kind of folk who once kept private journals and captured cherished photo album memories are now likely to go public with these past privacies. Social media is doing away with many people's former discretions and natural reserve. Self-definition, self-documentation: 'ME' front and centre. Cyberspace allows everyone to feel like they have an audience; invites everyone to take a bow and continue their personal PR-ing crusade.

To the earlier question, *who and what are the icons that reflect our Now?*

This is the moment when we look in the mirror, and the occasion where we turn to our computer screens. While there are icons who continue to smile back at us from the glossy magazine covers, there's a second set of equally important and vital icons, icons that live on our desktop, a click away.

GODS AND MONSTERS

The movie stars are still up on the billboards, blue-steeling down at us, but they're also micro-blogging to our smart phones. Celebrities 'tweet': their followers know it's not one-to-one, but it doesn't *feel* like it's one-to-many, either. There's a pseudo intimacy in play. And a real-time sense of accessibility. 'Celebrity' feels like it's graspable. Stalking is no longer a black-and-white act. There are shades of grey, where grey-stalking has become openly invited, digitally enabled, text-based, where the *stalkee* has approved the T&Cs. Invasion of privacy is part-replaced with, I *want* to tell you what I'm doing and I'd be delighted if you're interested enough to care... because my agent says it'll be good for me, to up my followers, to show my human side.

FIGURE 36.4 Supermodels: then and now. Left: the 1990s supermodel – fresh-faced archetypal beauty; right: Audrina Patridge toasts (and later tweets about) her new Bongo swimsuit billboard on Sunset Boulevard (7 April 2011)

And now, more than ever before, we worship too at our own altars, plumping our own egos and sense of worth, quite possibly fuelling our own delusions. Our icons are now our *means*; the means by which we chronicle and curate and self-narrate. Anyone can be a *self-idol*, anyone can craft, expand and share their own mythology, create their own personal celebrity. Our icons have become a quick click by which we update our personal profiles.

For me, the script-line still chimes. We've become our own gods and monsters.

ED BURNS, TRIBECA AND THE FILM-MAKING REVOLUTION

 Of all the speakers who addressed the 2011 congregation of *Adweek*, it was a guy who worked outside the ad industry who, to me, showed he best understood the daunting 300lb digital goliath in his opposing corner. 　"

FADE IN:
Simple white text appears on black:

> "Great small films don't
> always find their audience."
> Ed Burns, Film-maker,
> *Advertising Week*, NYC, 3 October 2011

CUT TO:

EXT. STREET SCENE, SPECIFICALLY, 242 W 41st ST,
NEW YORK — DAY

A professionally dressed line of diverse ages
queue outside a glass-fronted building. There's
buzz and Blackberry-busyness, but it merely
blends into the autumnal fabric of a typically
New York street scene.

CUT TO:

INT. Auditorium — DAY

An 80+ audience sits expectantly in tiered rows,
the view looking down on to a stage of 3 chairs,
a white screen behind wears the projected logo of
a 'flip-top head' in side-profile. Above the logo,
a title:

THE FUTURE OF FILM, *Advertising Week* 2011.

The following sequence progresses in fast-
forward, as if someone has taken hold of the
remote. Three men walk on to the stage, take
their seats, mike-up. Words are spoken by a fourth
man at a podium, some kind of compère. Applause
from the audience follows. Frame freezes in a
wide angle on the three seated men. They are:

Ed Burns, Film director
Rich Lehrfeld, VP Global Sponsorship, American
  Express
Jon Patricot, COO, Tribeca Enterprises

CUT TO:

A DEATH TO SYMBOLS AND SYMBOLIC RENEWAL

> ISAAC DAVIS
> Chapter One. He adored New York City. He idolized
> it all out of proportion. Eh uh, no, make that
> he, he romanticized it all out of proportion.
> Better. To him, no matter what the season was,
> this was still a town that existed in black and
> white and pulsated to the great tunes of George
> Gershwin. Uh, no, let me start this over.
>
> *Manhattan* (1979)

Movies and New York City have always been inextricably intertwined. Each has added their mystique and mojo to the other. Woody Allen's *Manhattan* is arguably the sweetest, most sincere love letter to any city ever committed to celluloid.

Then consider the grotesque-genius of *9/11*, the cinematic-style destruction of the very global icons that spelt American capitalism; a numbing, sickeningly symbolic gesture, the death to towering symbols that only an unimaginable horror could make kneel.

In the wake of a city left reeling, the Tribeca Film Festival was one small post 9/11 step on the road to comeback. Founded in 2002 by Jane Rosenthal, Robert De Niro and Craig Hatkoff, it was a shot-in-the-arm for TriBeCa, a Lower Manhattan neighbourhood that felt like it was waking up from being shot in the head.

Flash forward a full decade, and the Tribeca Film Festival is now into its 11th year, going strong, continually looking to innovate, stay fresh, be relevant. There's an estimated 40,000 movies made around the world every year. Of these, Tribeca receives 5,000 movie submissions per year. The chosen few are then showcased at the two-week festival. But it doesn't end there. Tribeca runs as an online film festival during the two-week window, and has also gone the way of Kerouac, has left the island and now surfaces in major US cities such as Houston, Chicago and San Francisco, part of a 40-State roll-out.

> *Tribeca Film and American Express® invite you to experience Tribeca Film Festival On The Road, an exclusive Cardmember-only event coming to select cities across the country. Enjoy exclusive screenings of some of the year's best independent films followed by a Q&A session with the filmmakers after each showing.*

SOURCE: WWW.TRIBECAFILM.COM/AMEX/

CUT TO:

ED BURNS

Of all the speakers who took the mike and addressed the October 2011 congregation of *Adweek*, it was a guy who worked outside the ad industry who, to me, showed he understood all the moving parts, understood the daunting, exhilarating, 300 lb digital machine that the ad industry is trying to stare down.

Film-maker Ed Burns knows the score because he's there on the front line, already eyeballing the digital goliath in his opposing corner. Competing with the big movies backed by the big studios, Burns is awake at night with the question, 'How the hell can I get people to see my latest 90-minute "walk-and-talk" movie?'

As Burns puts it with knowing emphasis, '*Good* big movies *find their audience.*' But the same isn't necessarily true of the good small ones, and that's what's going to give him the night sweats. Unless you're the guy making the next *Transformers* movie, or something with Johnny Depp as a pirate, then there are few guarantees.

Burns rightly observes that people have 50 inch HD flat screens at home, work long hours, don't necessarily want to schlep an hour into the city to an art house, schlep another hour home, then peel off notes for the babysitter. Who says movie people aren't grounded?

What's really impressive, though, is that film-makers like Burns are dealing with it, working new angles in the new digital order, in order to get their movies made and to market.

Purple Violets marked Ed Burns breaking new ground in movie marketing and distribution. It was the first feature film to premier... on iTunes, at a cost of US$14.99. Apple had a one month exclusive. The Weinstein Company then distributed the DVD.

'I'm okay with my films playing in your living room', claims Burns. 'The old rules don't have to apply.'

'Straight-to-video' used to be a dirty word, the giveaway tell of a poor product that wasn't movie-theatre worthy. Not so these digital days. Now it's about new routes to market, about video-on-demand 'impulse buys' off the back of seeing a clip or trailer, and working from the end point to the start point; it's about brands stepping up and bankrolling production, inventive funding arrangements in the cause of mutual benefit.

This is where brands such as American Express and guys like Rich Lehrfeld come in.

CUT TO:

SPONSORSHIP IS ALL IN THE FIT

The challenge with any sponsorship association is that it doesn't feel cheap, manipulative and clunky. A sponsorship property typically sells itself on having an emotional appeal, a set of values and a built-in audience that makes it attractive to any brand that wants all those qualities; all those qualities it doesn't naturally possess.

Piggy-back, slip stream, benefit from the halo of association: the obvious benefit is that there will be a rub-off. You hang out with the cool kids, you're cooler by proximity. That's the hope. And the thinking plays both ways. A new sponsorship property wants to attract the big brands, wear the logos like medals of honour, show they're keeping tall company in the majors.

With any brand sponsorship, the key is 'fit'. Logical, intuitive, either is good. Contrived or forced, both are bad. The catalogue of examples in both columns is numerous. AmEx and Tribeca sit in the right column.

American Express is, and always has been, the Tribeca festival's headline 'Founding Sponsor'. *Founding*, I think, is crucial. American Express and Tribeca *feels* right, and the proof lies in the fact that they continue together on their long walk towards building something they can be forever proud of.

American Express is a credit card provider, but that provision is an *enabler* for people. For people to buy what they like and enjoy, so satisfying their wants.

What actually makes the world go round is not money *per se*, but people's drive to spend it on the things they feel they need and know they enjoy. All meaning that American Express 'the business' is not the same as American Express 'the brand'. The business is about making money through providing plastic that allows people to spend money. Flipping utility into a consumer benefit, American Express 'the brand' wants to be about passion, about being synonymous with people's passions.

And Rich Lehrfeld, VP of Global Sponsorship at American Express, wants AmEx to be all about what people love, helping *provide* that which they long for. Film, fashion, sport, your prototypical passion points and forever-fun preoccupations: these are the worlds American Express is working hard to become intimate with.

It reminds me of the line from the poet and novelist, Anatole France: '*Our passions are ourselves.*'

I believe this wholly. Without passion, we're pretty dead-eyed, empty vessels. Passion for life, for our families. Our love of music, art, books, design, travel, food, wine, sex: most people groove to a certain something, and it's those passionate *somethings* that define and explain us. That which we love and hate is who we are.

Brands such as AmEx appreciate that looking to *be what people like* is the ticket to consumer loyalty. (See also 'The Age of the Accelerated Consumer', page 97)

Lehrfeld talks also of the 'Memory Realm', maybe a little grandiose as descriptors go, but revealing enough of smart brand intent. Working the 'membership has its privileges' angle, AmEx wants to be the brand that makes it happen for their cardholders, manufacturing moments worthy of becoming cherished memories.

CUT TO:

A THREE MUSKETEERS ARRANGEMENT

The Tribeca Film Festival is a Three-Musketeer-style collaboration. The talent, the platform, the money. Athos, Porthos and Aramis. Tact and diplomacy aside, there's a lot of collaboration and respect in the mix, born of understood mutual benefit. Burns, Tribeca, AmEx: they're all bringing it to the party, and all getting something from the deal.

It's hard chasing down a buck. 'The dollars are always tough to come by', Burns comfortably admits. 'It comes down to the sensibilities of the marketers and filmmakers and how they can make it work.'

Acknowledge the role you play, and the role you don't. American Express are shrewdly light-touch where they need to be, giving talent such as Burns the space to do their thing.

'We're in it for as long as we may continue to innovate', is the simple line that American Express takes. To which the guy from Tribeca Enterprises just smiles, a shrewd Ari Gold-type who knows he's got the right people in the room.

Within this musketeer dynamic, there's also a D'Artagnan. D'Artagnan is the audience, the consumer, film-lovers, who are increasingly invited to do a lot more than just buy a ticket to the two-week festival.

'My Movie Pitch' is the latest innovation, an invitation to all to pitch an idea for a short, with Ed Burns donating the creative expertise necessary to turn the winning pitch idea into silver-screen reality.

> Hosting a one-of-a-kind contest in the spirit of great storytelling and independent cinema, film enthusiasts everywhere can visit www.amexfilm.com today to upload their 60-second, dream movie pitch in hopes of seeing their idea brought to life on the big screen.
> SOURCE: WWW.TRIBECAFILM.COM/AMEX/

As memory realms go, it's a pretty nice one. And it's also clearly reflective of what the Tribeca Film Festival is becoming. The Festival was always meant to be and remains a platform for good, a cultural gift to New Yorkers – small annual payback maybe in the absence of residuals to a city whose screen-idol looks have been exported via celluloid more than any other.

But over the last decade, the Festival has judiciously extended its wings; it is appreciating that it can be a brand, can follow in the footsteps of Sundance, can be its own kind of Cannes. Indeed, its ambitions, I suspect, have further-reaching horizons, not just as an event but as a broadcaster. And with help from the right friends, friends like Burns and AmEx, Tribeca is becoming more than just a gift to New Yorkers, but a passion provider to cinephiles everywhere.

CUT TO:

```
INT. AUDITORIUM — DAY
The clock on the wall reads 2.40 pm. The
45-minute session is drawing to
a close. Fingers are twitching, some grab for
their Blackberrys like jittery gunslingers.
Post-prandial is a distant memory. Many are
considering whether another free coffee in the
break will be a wise or unwise way to manage the
aging afternoon.

                                    CUT TO:
```

LONGEVITY: IT'S A DARWIN THING

Ed Burns isn't alone. He's part of a newer breed, Darwin-trained, happy to adapt. Doesn't matter whether you're an auteur or A-lister, adaptation is key.

When Tom Cruise walks into a marketing summit at 20th Century Fox, he doesn't talk about how the movie he just made was 'so much fun', he bigs-up how his latest completed project is a four-quadrant event movie, with mass appeal for the young, the old, the guys and the girls. All because Tom Cruise knows the business of movie-*selling*. Tom's not about being discrete and going niche. When it comes to his movies, he doesn't do cult. His joint-venture film production company *Cruise/Wagner Productions* has grossed north of $2.9 billion in box office returns since launching in September 1993.

Career longevity is all about adaptation and constant reinvention. It's about building those better mousetraps.

Burns tweets requests for script details, like the names and professions of characters he's developing. He's toying with the idea of a staggered four-module movie format, shooting and releasing acts one at a time, inviting feedback, inculcating public opinion into the creation of the subsequent module.

Crowd-sourcing as part of the creative process, 'The Movie' an organic, participatory form. Burns is one open-minded film-maker, a guy pioneering his craft, comfortable venturing into unfamiliar places.

And some of those places are in Tribeca.

FADE TO BLACK

THE FABRIC OF THINGS

> " 'The Inventor' wants to change the world, sees the potential to build better mousetraps everywhere.
>
> Better Mousetraps are the inspired creations of frustrated minds, mavericks, who will always believe the fabric of our world is there for the unpicking. "

The inventor's mind is not a happy one. It's a frustrated one, compelled to question and change and improve the world it observes.

I've always been fascinated by this urgent imperative, as felt by this frustrated few, *to create* out of discontentment, to fill a widely unseen vacuum of absence with something new. A light bulb, a light sabre, an ironing board, a motherboard, a better mousetrap of some kind or other.

It's an inversion of British mountaineer George Mallory's reason for climbing Everest. 'Because it's there', he said. The inventor invents... because in the beginning, it isn't there.

Of course, most pass over the fabric of their everyday, seeing the warp and weft, and simply getting on with it, getting on with the job as it asks of them. They accept how things are, the inherent frustrations behind every corner, irking but tolerated in every second or third stitch.

An angry and mercurial minority, however, *rebels* is really the word – look otherwise upon the fabric of our lives. They ask *'why not?'* and *'what if?'* and they believe with conviction (and yes, some conceit) that they can do a better job. The warp and weft is not a given to them. It can be improved; they want to take a look at the loom, then dismantle it.

The inventor wants to change the world, to make it better; sees the potential to build improved looms and better mousetraps everywhere. I have a crazy admiration for these people and their way of thinking, and I have the greatest enthusiasm for the brands and innovators who attempt to restitch the tapestry of everyone's everyday.

Invention is a disruptive force, an upheaval to the status quo, and brand invention is very much part of this.

RE-STITCHING THE EVERYDAY FABRIC

At a very literal level, here are three sterling examples of brands that manipulate the everyday fabric, to get their 'better message' across: a German camera manufacturer, a German employment agency, and a British supermarket chain operating in South Korea. In each case, our outdoor world is ingeniously adapted for purpose.

Leica

And who doesn't love Leica? Leica cameras have always been objects of such simple beauty, and this poster execution dramatizing a 12x zoom capability is simply smart, making me love Leica just that little bit more.

FIGURE 38.1 Leica 12x zoom. Agency: Young & Rubicam. Market: Switzerland

This image is a photograph of the actual poster in situation.

Jobs in Town

For German employment agency Jobs in Town, why buy pre-existing poster panels when it's possible to do your own thing your own way, and make your point so much better? Turning coffee vending machines, petrol pumps and ATMs into media spaces and ingenious *message carriers* is inspired. Dull, functional, everyday machines become irreverent statements, and underline Jobs in Town's belief that people shouldn't feel like wage slave automatons, that they can be so much more. Clever stuff.

While static 2-D posters can still cut through and make brands heard loud and clear, 'flat passive print' is now being usurped, replaced with outdoor media you can play with. A movie poster on a bus shelter is no longer always a straight movie poster on a bus shelter. It can now be an invitation to use your NFC-equipped smartphone to stream the movie's trailer. Leica and Jobs in Town prompt us to think, maybe smile, but digital outdoor now invites us to *do* and download.

FIGURE 38.2 Jobs in Town. Inner workings: ATM, vending machine, gas pump. 'Life's too short for the wrong job!'

Tesco Homeplus

Arguably the most sophisticated invitation 'to do' piloted recently in South Korea, where Tesco Homeplus was able to expand its store footprint using subway station media. Tesco Homeplus turned poster locations into 'virtual shopping aisles' where QR-coded products could be bought directly off the virtual shelf and paid for with a smartphone. The products were then delivered straight to the shopper's front door.

Tesco Homeplus reported that 10,287 people shopped while waiting for their subway train, with a corresponding sales uplift of 130 per cent. This concept has since been taken into Prague (by P&G) and London (by Ocado).

Today's digital technology makes buying groceries off the virtual shelves of a tube station possible, but I'd argue that the damnable genius lies in the idea, not the execution. The 'idea of it' is the true invention, not the technology *per se*. By this thinking I'd like to introduce you to four guys I know. I suspect they've never considered themselves *inventors*, but I'd suggest that's exactly what they are. In their own ways, each is picking and playing with the fabric of our world, pioneering their craft and building their own mousetraps. Each is bringing new, damnably good ideas to life, where previously there had been a void. I have masses of time and no end of admiration for what they're about. Meet Craig, Douglas, Chris and Ashley.

FIGURE 38.3 Tesco Homeplus, virtually. (Seoul, 2011)

The Farm Collective (farmcollective.com)

A dear friend of mine, Craig, set up his own company a few years back.

I've known Craig over 10 years and my belief is that he simply tired of being very clever on behalf of other people's brands. Rather than being impressive from inside Saatchi and McCann Erickson in order to earn a crust, and then popping out to Prêt in his lunch hour, Craig chose to get into his own crust business.

Craig launched a sandwich shop, The Farm Collective, meaning he no longer had to work for The Man, or eat sandwiches made by him.

Now, 'a sandwich shop business' is a rather meek and off-the-mark descriptor for what continues to prosper as an ambitious brand invention, born of a very shrewd and genuine ideological view of the world.

The Farm Collective is more a mini food empire, with hopes of world domination. This ambition is where Craig's similarity to Bond villainy ends, though he does sport a fantastically impressive mountaineer's beard, affording him a certain quirkish eccentricity.

And in truth, 'world domination' is off the mark and missing the point, because The Farm Collective is all about local farmers providing foods in season, locally produced and locally sourced: the polar opposite of all things globalizing, mass and homogenous.

> We are the Farm and we serve up great food and tasty treats at fair prices served by kind and smiley staff. You can sleep easy that our food is sourced with all the right credentials from Red Tractor accreditation to the Marine Stewardship Council Mark to bring you 'responsible' food.
>
> SOURCE: WWW.FARMCOLLECTIVE.COM

'Eat well and sleep easy' is a benefit double-whammy of the tastiest kind, and for a good decade now, and in ever-growing numbers, people are waking up to what *their* brands are truly about. People are increasingly conscious and curious as to the types of businesses and kinds of practices that lead to products getting on shelves and into their homes. They're not just interested in the brands on display, but how they got to market. Many consumers are keen to follow the production chain right the way back to source. Provenance and authenticity, these are not mere words but potentially determining factors in the personality and appeal of a brand. Very simply, brands from businesses that operate within companionable distance of a noble cause are brands that many folk are going to feel a whole lot happier buying into.

I think The Farm Collective could be to sandwich-and-salad what Innocent is to smoothies; a small agribusiness as opposed to a big evil business, operating with charm and a whole lot of ethics in mind.

The 'why?' may seem obvious, but I still wanted to ask Craig the question: 'Why The Farm Collective?'

> Why is good food the reserve of the few? Organic, provenance, traceability, transparency were rapidly becoming financial levers for brands to raise their prices and create food snobbery. And I hated that, that the idea of mud and 'from a farm' equated to a financial equation, when it could instead be equated to a well understood value equation – making people value the food, not driving them away by premium pricing. So our challenge was to serve-up honest British food, with all the credentials that we all deserve as a right and not a privilege. Out of this, The Farm Collective was born, and collective not to bandwagon a naming trend but to genuinely work with our suppliers and where possible help them scale their

business, aid them with marketing, or maybe just have very open conversations about products.

CRAIG WILLS, FOUNDER, THE FARM COLLECTIVE

If you ever find yourself over in London's Farringdon and you're feeling peckish, go check-out The Farm Collective on Cowcross Street. You won't be disappointed.

The Merchant Fox (themerchantfox.co.uk)

My brother-in-law Douglas Cordeaux has been a clothes designer for something close to 30 years. Douglas knows a thing or two about fabrics. He's one of those guys who's graced with seemingly effortless good taste. Some people are just made that way, as if style is DNA-encoded. Maybe it is?

Douglas recently co-bought a cloth mill in Somerset. Fox Brothers Mill has been going since 1772, employed 5,000 people in its heyday, but by 2009 was on the verge of fully stopping and folding – flannels and worsted cloths feeling rather out of step with the times. And there is no question such a passing would have been a horrid shame, the sad demise of artisan excellence being the kind of thing you hear happening all too often. Fortunately, this isn't one of those times.

> *In its illustrious history 'Fox Flannel' has been worn by all manner of folk and famous faces, adorning amongst many others, the Duke of Windsor, Sir Winston Churchill and Hollywood legend, Cary Grant.*
>
> *At The Merchant Fox, we combine gorgeous cloth made by Fox Brothers with the equally exquisite goods we've discovered on our travels. Everything you see on The Merchant Fox is the very best of British.*

SOURCE: WWW.THEMERCHANTFOX.CO.UK

The global rag trade has had better reps. Sweatshops, child labour, the First World exploiting the Third: these are evil themes and the inconvenient truths of certain brands and the global businesses lurking omnipresent in the shadows. The Merchant Fox is one of those counterpunches to all the bad stuff you read about and suspect is going on in dark corners despite the protests and lobbying.

The Merchant Fox is all about preservation and revival, preventing the extinction of local craftsmanship by repurposing it, creating a new luxury goods brand for people who like the best, and who rather like the idea of possessing beautiful things that few others have. (See also, 'Irrational reasoning, magpie desire and the watch from outer space' on page 156).

The 'why?' may seem obvious, but I still wanted to ask Douglas the question: 'Why The Merchant Fox?'

> It felt like the right time, with discerning consumers of high-end goods seeking more than a luxury brand name attached to a mass produced product. Our customers are interested in the provenance, they like to know about the materials used, the often traditional techniques applied by the artisan producers we've discovered on our travels around Great Britain. The Merchant Fox is about creating exquisite investment pieces, heirlooms of the future.
> DOUGLAS CORDEAUX, MANAGING DIRECTOR, FOX BROTHERS

Douglas has launched a luxury British label that's actually British-owned and made in Britain. This is not about flag-waving jingoism. It's about keeping heritage and regional expertise alive. It's all about authenticity and truth. No spin. No bullshit. Just a brand that stands for something very genuine.

Spotify (spotify.com)

Standing an easy 6 ft 7 in socks, Chris Maple's stature is eclipsed only by the size of his personality and generosity. Chris is a recent friend and an absolute force of nature, arguably existing on a scale suitable for a bigger planet, but he seems to get by ably enough.

Chris is also Spotify's UK MD, who joined the business in 2011 with a remit to build it, make it all it can be, take it global, and in terms of 'all things music', one day be bigger and better than Apple. It's a helluva remit.

Spotify streams music, connects cyberspace to your ear via any internet-connected device. You can either pay a subscription, and circumvent the ads, or you can register for free, and accept some ads as fair trade for the freebie.

It's a really smart idea; a grown-up digital business; a *charismatic* digital brand; a music-business reply to a music industry that has in so many quarters refused to adapt, or even acknowledge that the world is radically changing.

Of course, this radical change doesn't mean people have stopped loving music. Music is a fundamental human need. People always will love music. As Friedrich Nietzsche put it, 'Without music life would be a mistake.' It doesn't get much more fundamental than that.

But what people have less love and no fundamental craving for is going down the high street, into a music store and buying a handful of CDs. Not when there are easier and cheaper means. Regardless, so much of the music industry is in what can only be termed denial. Arguably, it's harder smelling the coffee if you've got your head in the sand and your arse in the air. But the record labels have had theirs respectively submerged and skyward for more than a decade now, and with little indication of coming up for air. As a consequence, record labels continue to operate to an analogue business model, begrudging the digital world that's come to pass.

But here's the thing. Napster wasn't the beginning of the end, it was just a new chapter heading, and Spotify is fast becoming the most adaptive and pioneering expression of a brand solution.

The 'why?' may seem obvious, but I still wanted to ask Chris the question: 'Why Spotify?'

> Spotify was launched out of a desire for a better, more convenient and legal alternative to music piracy for consumers, whilst making sure that artists get a fair deal. We knew that having a true, free element would always remain core to Spotify's DNA – drawing people away from piracy, ensuring maximum engagement from our users and maximum benefit for the music industry as a result.
>
> With Spotify, music can be a truly digital experience for people; personalized, shared, without limits, and wholly in step with our lifestyles; still loved in all the old ways but now also enjoyed in so many new ones.
>
> CHRIS MAPLES, UK MANAGING DIRECTOR AND
> EUROPEAN SALES DIRECTOR, SPOTIFY

It's all too easy to come a cropper with predictions but I say Spotify is a brand to seriously watch, as well as listen to.

Base 79 (base79.com)

I first met Ashley Mackenzie on a cricket field in the mid 1990s, a good half-a-decade before anyone was listening to music on their iPod, back when people with e-mail addresses were considered early adopters.

I suspect Ashley wasn't thinking too hard about digital rights management on the sunny day he smashed a century against the team I was playing in. Many years later, digital rights is a big part of his world, and I try and ensure that we only ever play cricket on the same side.

Ashley launched Base 79 in 2007. Operating out of London and New York, Base 79 is a commercially astute parry to the internet's open-source origins. They're a 'new world order' video rights company, endeavouring to monetize web-based content. Imagine an income sniffer-dog hard at work across a digital landscape, where free-for-all still reigns.

The 'why?' may seem obvious, but I still wanted to ask Ashley the question: 'Why Base 79?'

> Why? Because no one else was doing it, and someone really needed
> to. We guessed that the world would change very fast and the
> incumbent players couldn't change their businesses fast enough, nor
> really afford to do what needed to be done to make the most of
> what they had created. We passionately believe that without us,
> the geniuses that have the spark to make compelling content won't
> do it any more – they will become bankers 'cause that's the only
> way to put food on the table. Today, we have two and a half million
> videos from over 100 leading rights-holders, generating more than
> 15 million daily views globally. We're about creating new value.
> I want Base 79 to be the leading creators of content-driven value
> across PC, Tablet and Connected TV. Doesn't matter whether
> people are buying iPods, subscribing to Netflix or searching on
> YouTube, all that consumers really want is relevant content.
> And content that people want should be worth its weight in gold.
> Oh, and we'll probably keep doing a lot of guessing!
>
> ASHLEY MACKENZIE, FOUNDER AND CEO, BASE 79

I'm with Ashley. Even if, as they say, 'content is king', where's the treasury?

THE HAPPY RESHAPING OF THINGS

Neil LaBute's play *The Shape of Things* (2001), and subsequent movie of 2003, is a bitter-pill comment on influence, love and manipulation. It's a mean affair, but a provocative one, about how a female art student's thesis on how to change the world becomes a task in how to change 'someone's world', an unknowing English major who thinks his relationship with her is for real.

The Shape of Things is a dark tale, but in a parallel universe where the sun shines, the play's themes, of how we can shape and sculpt and change the world is an invitation I look upon with hope. Life's fabric is there to be influenced, stitched, re-stitched. It can be improved. It's a betterment thing. Changing the fabric could mean more ethical sandwich options when you step on to the street in your lunch break. It could mean quality fabrics and furnishings made by people who really have been making the stuff for 240 years. It could mean being able to bring a lifetime of listening into any room in your home, instantly, or actually making a buck or two from that last piece of video footage you uploaded to YouTube.

Sandwich bars and Spotify, luxury wools and digital sniffer dogs, better mousetraps come in many shapes and guises. They are the inspired creations of frustrated minds, mavericks who will always believe the fabric of our world is there for the unpicking. They need little encouragement but, by bold example, may we all dare to take up the needle and once in a while attempt a better stitch.

EPILOGUE — TAKE COMFORT, 'NOBODY KNOWS NOTHING'

> " It's time to start
> feeling reassured.
>
> Most folk, in
> whatever they
> do, are simply
> blagging.
>
> Be 'The Exception'.
>
> Be Exceptional. "

The screenwriter and Hollywood insider William Goldman is credited with the line, *'Nobody knows nothing'*. It takes a guy as smart as Goldman to so accurately nail it, and while he was talking pointedly of the movie industry, the line applies pretty much across the board.

Of course, the more strict observers of to-the-letter English will note the double negative and suggest Goldman therefore infers that *everyone* knows at least *something*.

No, that's not what Bill means; maybe further underlining his point.

Goldman means that no one knows *anything* for sure, that foresight is a hunch, that everyone is making it up as best they can, and that life's winners are those who smile at the truth of it and can cut a wake through a Sargasso of ego, guesswork, bullshit and chance.

Short a bear market, go long in a bull market, either play, you do it on a hunch, harbour a whole lot of hope, then sit back and try not to bite your nails. As City analysts occasionally say, 'It's a Spec's Paradise'. And it really is *all speculation*. Confidence, loss of confidence, 'More Cristal!' peaks and 'Sell the Aston!' troughs, all making for a white-knuckle paradise in as much as if you can ride the trends and pre-empt the twists and turns then you're liable to do very nicely indeed.

So it's time to start feeling reassured.

Yes, really.

While Goldman made few friends in Tinseltown by suggesting everyone's hustling and bluffing, I'd say that tremendous opportunity derives from the reality that most folk, in whatever they do, are simply blagging and just aren't that great at whatever it is they do.

The majority, in all things, are 'mediocre'. This is a fact; I'm not being mean, it's nothing more than statistical truth, albeit a little brutal. Most people are 'average', populating by greater and lesser degree, the big hillock that is the Bell Curve – meaning quite 'major opportunity' lies in positioning yourself the 'right side' of the curve. Because aside from the likes of building jet engines, decommissioning atom bombs, and conducting cardiothoracic surgery, there's huge scope for honing your given expertise above a pretty large safety net that declares that no one knows anything categorically, and if you do get it wrong, no one's going to die.

The line holds and it always will; *'It's not life and death, it's just advertising.'*

Common sense, clarity of thought, single-mindedness, force of personality, non-delusional self-belief, conviction, concision of purpose – all hugely powerful tools that allow almost anyone's performance to soar above the mainstream and the mediocre. If you're packing even half of the aforementioned, you're 90 per cent there already.

I say this. *Never* be the norm, because 'The Norm' is unacceptably average. Be 'The Exception'. Be Exceptional. And in case you haven't already started, then by exception to Goldman's rule *know* this, it can start now.

SP
London, 2012

ACKNOWLEDGEMENTS

Matthew Smith at Kogan Page. Without whom, no book. I am indebted. Helen Kogan, Madeleine Voke, Heather Langridge, Fiona Dempsey, because the debt extends. Truly, thank you.

Faris Yakob and Tom Himpe, gentlemen scholars and 'Brilliant Misfits'. You guys set the example. I just followed.

Andy Day, buddy, you were right, it's only ever just words and pictures.

Spotify and LoveFilm, because it's not just words and pictures, but also playlists and movie collections.

CJ and HW, fellow Jedis and ever-indulging sounding-boards. Yes CJ, *everything* is interesting.

TP and GP. Without whom, no me.

Alison. How can you be so sure? Thank you for being so sure.

THE LISTS

THE BRAND LIST

Brands referenced in *The Better Mousetrap*:

1	Abercrombie & Fitch	30	Citröen
2	Accenture	31	Club 18–30
3	adidas	32	Coca-Cola
4	Alka-Seltzer	33	Converse
5	Amazon	34	Credit Suisse
6	American Apparel	35	Deutsche Bank
7	American Express	36	DFS
8	Apple	37	Diet Coke
9	Aruba Tourism Authority	38	Diners Club
10	at&t	39	DKNY
11	Audi	40	Dolce & Gabbana
12	Barclays Capital	41	Dove
13	Barnes & Noble	42	Dunhill
14	Base 79	43	Durex
15	BBC iPlayer	44	Dyson
16	BBC World	45	Emanuel Ungaro
17	Ben & Jerrys	46	Ernst & Young
18	Bertelsmann	47	Facebook
19	Bing	48	Fairy Liquid
20	Bisto	49	Federal Program for Road Safety
21	Bling H_2O		(Switzerland)
22	BMW	50	Ford
23	Boden	51	Foursquare
24	Borders	52	Fred Perry
25	Boss Orange	53	Gillette
26	Burger King	54	Google
27	Cadbury	55	Guinness
28	Calvin Klein	56	Häagen-Dazs
29	Carphone Warehouse	57	Halda

58	Heinz	97	Patek Philippe
59	Honda	98	Penguin
60	Hoover	99	Pepsi
61	Hotmail	100	Post-it
62	Hovis	101	Prada
63	HSBC	102	Primark
64	IBM	103	Reebok
65	Innocent	104	Rolex
66	Jaguar	105	Ronseal
67	Jobs In Town	106	Ryanair
68	Julius Bär	107	Samsonite
69	Kaupthing	108	Sega
70	Kelloggs	109	Seiko
71	L'Oreal	110	7-Up
72	Labour	111	Shulips
73	Lego	112	Silk Cut
74	Leica	113	Sisley
75	Louis Vuitton	114	Skype
76	Lynx	115	Smart
77	M&S	116	Snickers
78	Mattel	117	Sony
79	McCann-Erikson	118	Spotify
80	McDonald's	119	Starbucks
81	Mercedes	120	Stella Artois
82	Microsoft	121	Sunny Delight
83	Milky Bar	122	Swatch
84	Moet & Chandon	123	Tesco Homeplus
85	Molten & Brown	124	The Economist
86	Mont Blanc	125	The Farm Collective
87	Morgan Stanley	126	The Kooples
88	National Airlines	127	The Merchant Fox
89	Nespresso	128	Tipalet
90	Nike	129	Tipp-Ex
91	Nikon	130	T-Mobile
92	Nintendo	131	Tom Ford
93	Nivea	132	Tribeca Film Festival
94	Ocado	133	Trust Investment Bank
95	ooVoo	134	Tuenti
96	Panerai	135	Twitter

THE YOUTUBE BRAND CHANNEL

Go to **www.youtube.com/simonpont,** or scan the QR code with your smartphone for supporting video content as referenced in *The Better Mousetrap*.

THE BETTER MOUSETRAP BLOG

If you'd like to contact Simon, ask a question or just say hello, then please do so at **thebettermousetrap.typepad.com/blog**, or at **www.simonpont.com**.

You can also follow Simon on **twitter.com/#!/SimonPont**.

THE LOVEFILM MOVIE COLLECTION

As referenced in *The Better Mousetrap*:

1	Back to the Future	16	Pump Up the Volume
2	Blade Runner	17	Purple Violets
3	Clerks	18	Rebel Without a Cause
4	Cowboys & Aliens	19	Reservoir Dogs
5	Glengarry Glen Ross	20	Slacker
6	Heathers	21	The Bourne Identity
7	Indecent Proposal	22	The Breakfast Club
8	Jerry Maguire	23	The Dark Knight
9	Kick Ass	24	The Matrix
10	Kill Bill	25	The Outsiders
11	Limitless	26	The Shape of Things
12	Manhattan	27	The Social Network
13	Minority Report	28	The Tempest
14	Mission Impossible II	29	To Die For
15	Office Space	30	Unbreakable

Go to **www.lovefilm.com/simonpont**, or scan the QR Code with your smartphone, to automatically access *The Better Mousetrap's* Movie Collection.

And if you're not currently a LOVEFiLM member, the following code: AMAP1 entitles you to a 30-day free trial and a £15 Amazon voucher (redeemable after the first payment). Enjoy.

THE SPOTIFY PLAYLIST

As referenced in and inspired by *The Better Mousetrap*.

1 Opening – Paul Leonard-Morgan
2 POWER – Kanye West
3 Ball And Biscuit – The White Stripes
4 Boys Don't Cry – The Cure
5 Stuck In The Middle With You – Stealers Wheel
6 Dreadlock Holiday – 10cc
7 Man Fi Cool – Roots Manuva
8 West Coast Poplock – Ronnie Hudson
9 Que Sera, Sera (Whatever Will Be, Will Be) – Sly and The Family Stone
10 Little Green Bag – George Baker Selection
11 Rebel Yell – Billy Idol
12 World On A String – Neil Young
13 Shelter From The Storm – Bob Dylan
14 Midnight Rider – Gregg Allman
15 Sweet Home Alabama – Lynyrd Skynyrd
16 Mystery Train – Elvis Presley
17 Lover's Walk – Elvis Costello & The Attractions
18 Do You Remember – PT Walkley
19 Bleed Forever – Super Furry Animals
20 Wave Of Mutilation – Pixies
21 Titanium Expose – Sonic Youth
22 Omen – Prodigy
23 I Gotcha – Joe Tex
24 The Power Of Love – Huey Lewis & The News
25 Mystify – INXS
26 Don't You (Forget About Me) – Simple Minds
27 Rockstar – Nickelback
28 All By Myself – Eric Carmen
29 Street Of Dreams – Little Jimmy Scott
30 Rhapsody In Blue – George Gershwin
31 Creep – Scala
32 Hand Covers Bruise – Trent Reznor and Atticus Ross
33 The Bourne Identity – John Powell
34 Harvey Two-Face – Hans Zimmer and James Newton Howard
35 A New Beginning – John Williams (Minority Report/Soundtrack Version)
36 Clubbed to Death (The Matrix) – Robert D

Go to **http://spoti.fi/simonpont**, or scan the QR Code with your smartphone, for *The Better Mousetrap* Playlist to automatically open in your Spotify player.

And if you don't yet have Spotify, go visit **www.spotify.com**.

LIST OF FIGURES

© Simon Pont. Photograph: Hermione Hodgson (2012)

Simon Pont is a writer, commentator and brand-builder.

His agency career includes being part of Saatchi & Saatchi and Naked Communications, the pioneers of Communications Planning. Hollywood movie studios, Icelandic investment banks, British chocolate bars and Middle Eastern airlines figure amongst his time on the inside of Adland. He is Chief Strategy Officer at agency network Vizeum, and an EACA Effies judge. 'The Better Mousetrap: Brand Invention in a Media Democracy' is his first work of non-fiction.

Say hello at: **www.simonpont.com**

Simon is currently at work on his next book, '**Digital State: How the Internet is Changing Everything**', scheduled for worldwide release April 2013, through Kogan Page. Simon and a global panel of experts examine and assess the digital impact on our world and consider its future implications. From new realities to transparency, the digital world is open source and instant access; a world with no more secrets. What will be the likely impact on each and every one of us?